REPRINTS OF ECONOMIC CLASSICS

# A HISTORY OF THE SCOTCH POOR LAW

*Also Published In*

REPRINTS OF ECONOMIC CLASSICS

*By* Sir George Nicholls

A HISTORY OF THE ENGLISH POOR LAW
3 VOLS., [1898]

A HISTORY OF THE IRISH POOR LAW [1856]

# A HISTORY

### OF THE

# SCOTCH POOR LAW

BY

SIR GEORGE NICHOLLS

[1856]

REPRINTS OF ECONOMIC CLASSICS

AUGUSTUS M. KELLEY · PUBLISHERS
NEW YORK · 1967

First Edition 1856

(London: John Murray, *Albemarle Street;*
Knight & Co., *90 Fleet Street*, 1856)

Reprinted 1967 by
AUGUSTUS M. KELLEY · PUBLISHERS

Library of Congress Catalogue Card Number

67 - 28455

PRINTED IN THE UNITED STATES OF AMERICA
*by* SENTRY PRESS, NEW YORK, N. Y. 10019

# A HISTORY

OF THE

# SCOTCH POOR LAW,

IN CONNEXION WITH

## THE CONDITION OF THE PEOPLE.

BY SIR GEORGE NICHOLLS, K.C.B.,

LATE POOR LAW COMMISSIONER, AND SECRETARY TO THE POOR LAW BOARD.

LONDON:

JOHN MURRAY, ALBEMARLE STREET.

KNIGHT & Co., 90, FLEET STREET.

1856.

"Time is the great innovator, and if time alters for the worse, and wisdom and counsel do not labour to alter for the better, what will be the end?—A stiff and froward retention of custom is as turbulent as an innovation, and they that reverence ancient usages too superstitiously are the scorn of the present age. It were prudent therefore, if men in their innovations would follow the example of time itself; for time innovates more than anything, but does it quietly, and by degrees scarcely to be perceived."—BACON.

# DEDICATION.

To the members of the several Parochial Boards, in the hope that the account given in the following pages of the rise and progress of the Scotch Poor Law, may be found useful to them in its administration, this Work is dedicated

By their faithful servant,

THE AUTHOR.

*September* 1856.

# INTRODUCTION

It was originally intended that the History of the Scotch Poor Law, should form an appendage to the Author's account of the Poor Law of England;[a] but he found, as he proceeded, that the materials which it was necessary to collect and arrange in order to afford a complete view of the subject, increased so much in bulk, and assumed a character of so much importance, as to warrant their publication as a separate work, and hence the appearance of the present volume.

Although now published separately, both the English and Scottish Histories may however for the present purpose be regarded as one; for the Poor Laws of the two countries were so nearly identical in their origin, and for a time were likewise so similar in spirit and operation, that a certain knowledge of both is necessary to a right understanding of the character, and a full appreciation of the advantages and disadvantages of either. They are in fact, or rather in their progress they became, the opposite extremes of the same system; and they should both be kept in view when seeking to arrive at a sound conclusion as to the nature and extent of the assistance that may with safety, and at the same time with advantage, be administered at the public charge in relief of destitution. The Irish Poor Law, it may be remarked, is a compound of the English and Scottish systems, deriving nearly as much from the

[a] See Introduction to the 'History of the English Poor Law,' p. 8.

one as from the other, and aiming at embodying the excellences, and avoiding the defects of each.

The Author was required to take a prominent part in the framing and introduction of the Irish Poor Law, and this made it especially necessary that he should make himself acquainted with the Poor Law of Scotland. He mentions this as one reason for his venturing to undertake the present work, and it may be stated as a further reason, that during many of the best years of a now somewhat protracted life, it has been his fortune to be connected with the Poor Law question—not speculatively only, but practically, and on the most extensive scale—in England as well as in Ireland; and his attention could not therefore fail of being much directed to what had been done, and to what was doing in Scotland.

The Author's inquiries in this direction were necessarily extended, when he commenced the preparation of his 'History of the English Poor Law,' with which the Scottish law is so nearly allied. Both systems had grown up together, and although they afterwards diverged, that of Scotland assuming in a great degree the nature of an ecclesiastical institution, whilst the English system retained its purely civil character; we now again find the two systems approximating, and promising to become one, or as nearly one as the circumstances of the two countries permit or render expedient.

Notwithstanding therefore, that the Author has not had the advantage of being practically engaged in administering the law in Scotland, he trusts that his long connexion with the general subject will exempt him from the charge of presumption, in thus undertaking a History of the Scotch Poor Law, in preparing which he has endeavoured to apply the practice and the experience of one country, in elucidation of the events in the other.

It is right however to observe, that he has not relied upon secondary researches entirely, but in order the better to qualify himself for the task, he has twice visited Scotland with the view of obtaining information on the spot, as to the condition of the poor, and the present working of the law; on all which points he received the most frank and cordial assistance from the Board of Supervision in Edinburgh, and likewise at the several local institutions that he visited.

The interest which the Author felt in the question as it applied to Scotland, was certainly not lessened by what came under his observation on these occasions. On the contrary, all that he then saw of the people and the country, greatly increased the interest he had taken in their well-being, and made him if possible more desirous of contributing to promote it. If the present work shall help in any way to that end, be it in ever so slight a degree, he will feel amply rewarded for whatever pains he may have taken in its preparation.

# CONTENTS.

## CHAPTER IV.



## CHAPTER V.

# HISTORY

OF

# THE SCOTCH POOR LAW,

IN CONNEXION WITH

THE CONDITION OF THE PEOPLE.

## CHAPTER I.

Condition of Scotland in the middle ages — Desire of English sovereigns for a union — Clanship and feudalism — Legislation on the subjects of mendicancy and vagrancy down to the abdication of Mary — Laws of James VI.: Act of 1579, the basis of the Scottish poor-law — First notice of gipsies or Egyptians — Parochial chargeability — Acts for promoting Bible-reading and psalmody — Acts against beggars and vagrants — Divergence of English and Scotch laws — Powers of kirk sessions and presbytery — Acts of 1617, 'anent the Justices' and 'anent the Poor'—Acts against 'Egyptians' — Highland clans — State of clanship — Population.

THE relative position of England and Scotland as parts of the same Island, the identity of origin language and character of at least a large portion of the people, and the general similarity of their habits and religion, would seem to lead to the establishment of a single government as naturally, and almost as necessarily, as in the case of the Heptarchy in the Saxon period. If not thus combined, feuds jealousies and strifes would be certain to prevail between the two countries, impoverishing each, retarding improvement, and giving an undue ascendancy to the military element, and to the influence of daring adventurers and ambitious chieftains. The Border Wars which so long prevailed, and with such injury to both countries, were the natural fruits of the want of such an union, as were likewise the struggles for ascendancy in the direction of Scottish affairs between the French and the English parties—each mindful of its own particular interests, and little regarding the welfare of Scotland. The portion of the British Island thus named, was not sufficiently powerful to take an independent part in the contests perpetually occurring between the greater kingdoms of France and England, but its alliance was courted by each. If it sided with France, the action of the English was embarrassed by the existence of an adversary in their rear, prepared to take advantage of every failure, and to carry havoc and devastation across the Border whenever the English crossed the Channel. If on the contrary Scotland sided with its neighbour, or became pledged to take no part against it, the English embarked on their foreign wars with confidence, feeling that their home was secure from invasion.

We accordingly find that all the more politic rulers of England, evinced the greatest solicitude for a close and entire union with Scotland. Our first and third Edwards laboured throughout their reigns to accomplish this object by force, but their efforts were frustrated by the energetic resistance of the Scottish people. The two last Henrys and Elizabeth aimed at effecting the same object by a less violent and more circuitous policy; but whether by force or by political combinations, the results sought to be attained were the same, that is—to establish a unity of action for England and Scotland, to bring the whole of the Island under one system, and by thus consolidating to increase the power and influence of the entire people. The greater part of Scottish history consists of incidents and events referable to these struggles—on the one side for establishing a unity, and on the other for maintaining a separate and independent action.

It is not necessary for our present purpose to trace the progress of these struggles, or to attempt to describe the incidents appertaining to the troubled period of Bruce, Baliol, and Wallace, or of the time which intervened between that and the reign of James the First, whose superior education and training during his long residence in England, joined to his high natural qualifications, peculiarly fitted him for introducing order and a desire for improvement into his distracted country, and constituted him perhaps the most eminent of Scottish sovereigns. He was however unhappily assassinated in 1437, from which time, throughout the reigns of his five successors, James the Second, Third, Fourth, and Fifth, and Queen Mary,[a] and down to the assumption of the government in 1577-8 by James the Sixth (then only in his thirteenth year), Scotland exhibited a nearly unbroken series of violence and confusion, of perpetual strifes and party contentions, in which law was nearly powerless, right was little regarded, and the country was subjected to the rude and selfish dictation of rival factions.

The general condition of the Scottish people was, on the whole, very similar to what prevailed in England at the same periods, excepting that Scotland was more backward, the impediments to improvement being there greater, and its progress consequently more slow. The state of England during the Wars of the Roses, may perhaps be taken as nearly representing the condition of Scotland during a great part of the period prior to the accession of James the Sixth to the English crown in 1603. Rapine and murder prevailed to a fearful extent, and to apprehend and punish a criminal sometimes required the united efforts of half the kingdom.[b]

---

[a] All these monarchs suffered violent deaths, with the exception of James the Fifth, and he can hardly be said to have died naturally, having sunk under the accumulated disasters and disgrace brought about through the disaffection and treachery of the nobility, and the defection of his troops.

[b] An instance of this occurred so late as 1561. Mary having appointed a court of justice to be held on the Borders, the inhabitants of no less than eleven counties were summoned to guard the person who was to act as judge, and to enable him to enforce his decisions.—Robertson's History, vol. i. p. 20.

The nobles rose to be independent of the law, as the sovereign failed in the power to enforce it; and in Scotland the proper balance between the power of the nobility and that of the Crown was almost entirely destroyed. The great halls of the barons were often more crowded than the court of the Sovereign, and the strong castles in which they resided were the retreats of rebellion and the harbours of crime, their revenues being spent upon a multitude of retainers, who followed them in peace and defended them in war. The usual retinue of one of the Earls of Douglas consisted of two thousand horse, and other nobles were similarly attended in proportion to their means.

The want of towns contributed to increase the power of the nobility, and to depress the mass of the people. Where numbers are assembled, as in towns and cities, their power is concentrated and forms an equipoise to that of the nobles — order can be more readily established, the laws enforced, and individual liberty maintained; but in Scotland there were at that period few towns.

The division of the people into clans, likewise tended to increase the power of the superior class; for the members of the clan regarded its chief in a kind of patriarchal light, as the head of their family or tribe, in all whose alliances and quarrels they were necessarily included, and whom they were ever ready to follow and defend. Feudalism, in its simple state, and distinct from clanship, likewise existed in Scotland as absolutely as it had done in England or in any part of Europe; and it continued to prevail there in full vigour after it had disappeared or been greatly modified in other countries. The feudal serf, villein, or slave, was there, as elsewhere, an article of property, as completely as the land on which he was bred, and to which he was bound, and with which he might be transferred at the will of the owner. He had no rights, individual or social. Himself, his children, and his children's children for ever, were the property of another, who might sell and dispose of them when, where, and as he thought fit. But there was one means of emancipation from this feudal thraldom in Scotland, as well as in England; for a vassal or slave who escaped from his master, and resided a year and a day in a town, could not be reclaimed, and was afterwards a free man.

The state of Scotland, and the general conformation of society there, being thus so nearly similar to what prevailed in England, added to the proximity of the two countries, and the constant intercourse between them, would naturally lead us to expect a similarity in their laws and institutions; and making allowance for the less advanced state of civilisation in Scotland, there can be no doubt that such similarity did exist in a remarkable degree. We may therefore, without further introduction, proceed at once to consider the enactments having reference to the poor in Scotland, whether as vagrants or mendicants, or as infirm and impotent persons suffering from destitution; and for illustration of the general circumstances and state of society at the period of the several enactments, the reader may refer to what existed in England at a like or somewhat earlier period, as shown in the 'History of the English Poor Law,' which may for this purpose be regarded as forming a portion of the present work.

In the preface to the volume of Acts of the early Scotch Parliaments, printed by command of her Majesty in 1844, it is said that the constitutional history of Scotland commenced with the disputed succession and war of independence at the close of the thirteenth century,[c] and extended to the return of James the First

[c] The disputed succession between Bruce and Baliol, and the war of independence against Edward the Third.

from England in 1424. In the same preface it is likewise stated, that in the year 1507 the art of printing was introduced into Scotland under the auspices of James the Fourth, for the purpose of "imprenting within our Realme the Bukis of our Lawes, &c.," and exclusive privileges were conferred on the first printers for their encouragement and support in the execution of these national works; but it was not until the year 1541 that any of the statutes were actually printed. Previous to the publication of the above-mentioned volume of the early statutes however, 'The Acts of the Parliament of Scotland' had been published between the years 1814 and 1844, under direction of Commissioners appointed for the purpose, in ten volumes folio, commencing with the reign of James the First, and ending at the Union in 1707; and from these volumes such of the Acts as bear upon our subject are hereafter quoted.[d]

1424. James I., cap. 7. May 26, No. 7.

The seventh enactment of the 'Statute of Perth,' in the first year of James the First, directs that companies of people shall not be permitted to traverse the country begging and harbouring on kirkmen or husbandmen, and if any complaint be made of such trespassers to the sheriff, he is to arrest such folk, and challenge them as breakers of the king's peace; and if they be convicted of such trespass, they are to be punished, and find security to the satisfaction of the king and the party complaining; and if such trespassers suffer any harm in the arresting of them, it

[d] This collection of the statutes differs in some respects from the collection made by Sir Thomas Murray, of Glendock, clerk to the council, and printed at Edinburgh in 1682, in 3 vols. 12mo., by Joshua Solingen, for D. Lindsay and his co-partners, under the title of 'The Laws and Acts of Parliament made by King James the First and his Royal Successors, Kings and Queens of Scotland.' In the folio edition, the Acts are not chaptered consecutively. In the smaller edition they are so, and this collection is in consequence generally used by the Scotch Bar. I have therefore in most cases given the date and the marginal number of the statute from the folio edition, together with the number of the chapter from the smaller edition, so that reference may be made to either at the option of the reader.

is to be imputed to themselves. In case no complaint be made to the sheriff, he is nevertheless to inquire at every head court that he holds, whether any faltours be within his sheriffdom, and if any be found they are to be punished as is before written. It was also in the same year ordained, that no thiggar (beggar) be thoiled to beg, either in town or country, between the ages of 14 and 70, nor unless they may not win their living otherways, in which case they are to be furnished with a certain token or badge, by the sheriff in landward places, and by the aldermen and bailies in boroughs; and persons having no such token are to be charged by open proclamation to labour for winning their own living, under pain of burning on the cheek, and being banished the country. In the year following it was further ordained by the king, with consent of parliament, that the sheriffs within their respective jurisdictions shall diligently inquire after idle men that have no visible means of living, and shall arrest and confine all such idle men, that the country may be unscaithed of them, until it be ascertained where they reside or belong to; whereupon the sheriff shall assign forty days to such idle men to get them masters, or to betake themselves to some lawful craft; and after such forty days, if they be found idle, the sheriff shall arrest them again and commit them to prison, there to abide and be punished at the king's will; and this is to be done in boroughs, as well as in landward places throughout the realm. And two years afterwards it was ordained by the king, "with the consent of his whole parliament," in addition to the statute of beggars previously made, that the chamberlain in boroughs shall inquire whether the aldermen and burgesses have kept the said statute; and if they have failed in so doing, they are subjected to a fine of forty shillings to the king,

1425. James I., cap. 66. March 11, No. 20.

1427. James I., cap. 103. March 1, No. 4.

as are likewise the sheriffs for a like failure on their part.

These enactments respecting the poor, having been passed so immediately after the return of James the First from his protracted residence of twenty years in England, warrants the supposition that they were of English origin. This accords with the view taken by Tytler, who, in adverting to these and certain other statutes enacted about the same time, observes that "they are with a few changes to be found amongst the statutes of Richard the Second, and the Fourth and Fifth Henries, and prove that the king during his long detention in England, had made himself intimately acquainted with the legislative policy of that kingdom."[e] The species of semi-captivity in which James from the age of fourteen was held in England, did not prevent his receiving all the instruction which the English Court could then impart; and he is represented as profiting largely by the opportunities thus afforded him of gaining knowledge, and as being highly esteemed for his qualifications both natural and acquired; so that on his return to Scotland he would most likely be far in advance of the generality of his countrymen in point of intelligence, as well as fully informed on all matters of English policy general and social. England then stood high, perhaps the highest, among the powers of Europe, and James would naturally be desirous of introducing into his own country such of the English institutions as his observation of their working showed to be beneficial; and hence arose, we may presume, the enactment of the above statutes regarding the poor, with others on various matters fiscal, commercial, and ecclesiastical, which followed immediately after his return and taking upon himself the government.

---

[e] See Tytler's 'History of Scotland,' vol. iii. p. 216.

These laws of James the First did not however prove sufficient, and as was the case in England, further coercive measures were found to be necessary for putting down mendicancy and vagabondage in Scotland. A quarter of a century afterwards, and in the following reign, by a parliament held at Edinburgh in 1449, it was ordained "for the away putting of sornares,[f] overlyars, and masterful beggars," that all sheriffs, barons, aldermen, and bailies, as well within burgh as without, shall take inquisitions of such persons at each court that they hold, and if any such be found, that they shall be imprisoned at the king's will, and their horses hounds and other goods be escheated. And also, that the sheriffs and other officers inquire at each court if there be any that follow the profession of "fools, that are not bardis, or sick like rinners about." And if any such be found, they are to be imprisoned or put in irons for their trespass, "as long as they have any goods of their own to live upon." And if they have nothing to live upon, "their ears are to be nailed to the trone, or to any other tree, and then cut off, and themselves banished the country." And if they return again, they are to be hanged.

1449. James II., cap. 22. January 1, No. 9.

If severity would deter people from pursuing a vagrant course of life, or prevent the increase of beggars, the above statute might be expected to prove sufficient for the purpose; but it did not prove sufficient, and further legislation was still found to be necessary. Another Act was therefore passed in 1455, directing that wherever Sornares are overtaken in time to come, they shall be delivered to the sheriff, and that forthwith the king's justice shall

1455. James II., cap. 45. August 4, No. 8.

[f] Sornares are described as stout armed vagrants, who insist on taking up their abode for an indefinite period at the houses they visit.—See Tytler's 'History of Scotland,' vol. iv. p. 136.

"do law upon them as upon a thief or a reffar"—(i. e.
1457. James II., cap. 79. March 6, No. 17. robber). Two years afterwards (1457) the statute of the first year of James the First, directing that no beggar should be thoiled to beg between the ages of 14 and 70, unless unable to win his living by other ways, and that transgressors of the statute in this respect should be burnt on the check and banished the country, was re-enacted in
March 6, No. 26. nearly the same words. In the same session it was declared "speedful," that at the holding of justice ayres the king's justice shall take inquisition of all sornares, masterful beggars, or feigned fools, and banish them the country, or send them to the king's prison. These enactments were intended, we must presume, to enforce and give additional impulse to the execution of the previous statutes against this description of persons, whose number apparently continued to increase, and had become oppressive and a public nuisance.

Twenty years afterwards another effort was made
1473. James III., cap. 77. June 1, No. 10. "for the staincheing of masterful beggars and sornares, that daily oppress and heryis the king's puir lieges;" and it was ordained that the statutes of James the First should be put into sharp execution, and the Act passed in the last reign, directing that where any common sornares are overtaken in time to come they shall be arrested and delivered to the sheriff, and that the king's justice shall execute the law upon them as upon a common thief or reffar, was re-enacted, as was also the provision directing that such offenders should be inquired after and punished at all justice ayres.

The next statute "anent beggars" was enacted in
1503. James IV. cap. 70. March 20, No. 14. 1503, when it was directed, in a somewhat milder tone than had been manifested in the later Acts, that the statute of King James the First made upon "stark beggars" be observed and kept, and that the sheriffs, provosts, and bailies see to the

same, and thoil none to beg within their boroughs "except cruiked folk, blind folk, impotent folk, and weak folk," under pain of paying one mark for every other beggar that shall be found therein. This statute is in some respects similar to that of the 11*th Henry* 7*th* passed a few years previously.[g] It subjects the borough authorities to a penalty for permitting other than infirm persons to beg, and the Act of Henry the Seventh subjects persons to penalty for relieving disorderly beggars when they are set in the stocks. There is nothing revolting in either of these statutes, as regards the punishment of the beggar class; and the declaration in the English Act, that the king desireth above all things the prosperity and rest of the land, and for his subjects to live quietly and surefully, and that he is always willing and intending to reduce them thereunto by softer means than are provided in the earlier statutes, might be applied to James the Fourth and this statute of the Scottish parliament. The similarity of the two statutes in this respect, shows that the two countries were influenced by similar circumstances; and that they were acting and reacting upon each other, and moving onward concurrently in the race of improvement. The amity between them had been cemented, and their intercourse increased, by the marriage of James in the year preceding the present Act with the Princess Margaret, daughter of Henry the Seventh—an event fraught with most important consequences to both countries at a subsequent period, and which at the time secured their friendly alliance for several years, until it was put an end to by the events which led to the fatal battle of Flodden, in 1513, in which James the Fourth lost his life.

In 1535, a little more than thirty years after the Act last quoted, another statute "for the stanch-

---

[g] See 'History of the English Poor Law,' vol. i. p. 97.

ing of maisterful beggares, with additions," was passed. It approves and ratifies the Acts of James the First, and other of the king's predecessors, "for the refreyning of the multitude of maisterful and strang beggaris," and ordains that they be observed and kept, and put to sharp execution in all punctuality, with this addition—that no beggars be thoiled to beg in any parish who are not born therein, and that the head men of each parish make takings (collections) and give to the beggars thereof, and that they be sustained within the bounds of that parish, and that none others be permitted to receive alms therein; and the justice-clerk is directed to make inquisition, and take dittay hereupon at every justice ayre. It is also ordained, that letters be directed to command and charge the provost and bailies of Edinburgh, and all other provosts bailies sheriffs and other king's officers, to put this Act in execution in all punctuality, and that the same be published at all places needful, "so that none shall pretend ignorance, or allege they know not the same in time to come."

1535. James V., cap. 22. June 12, No. 29.

The distinction between the aged and the adult or able-bodied poor, was recognised by the statute of James the First in 1424, and a further distinction in favour of the blind weak and impotent poor, was made by the statute of James the Fourth in 1503. We now find that these classes, namely the aged and the infirm poor, are to be sustained by collections made in the parishes in which they were severally born, to which they are considered to belong, and beyond the limits of which they are no longer permitted to wander for the purpose of gathering alms. Every parish is now, therefore, made liable for the support of its own aged and infirm poor, who alone are permitted to beg within it, and the head men of the parish are likewise required to make collections for the purpose. This was a great advance towards an organised system of relief;

and as regards the description of persons permitted to beg, and the fixing a limit within which they might so do, it is very similar to the *22nd Henry 8th, cap.* 12,[h] passed four years previously; but the English Act does not authorise or require collections to be made. This was delayed until 1535, the year in which the present Scottish Act was passed, when the deficiency was supplied by the *27th Henry 8th, cap.* 25,[i] which directs the head officers and others of every parish to take such convenient order by gathering voluntary alms, as that the poor impotent sick and diseased people may be provided holpen and relieved. The alms are however to be voluntary. The collectors are indicated, but there is no power given to enforce contribution, although the latter Act does direct that every parson vicar and curate, shall from time to time exhort the people to make charitable contributions for this object, with which, moreover, it couples the setting to work all such as are able to labour, "whereby every one of them may get their living with their own hands," a principle that was, whether wisely or unwisely, continually kept in view throughout the whole range of legislation for the relief of the poor in England.

The next enactment immediately bearing upon our subject took place in the reign of Queen Mary, who, when an infant of eight days old, succeeded to the crown in 1542, on the death of her father James the Fifth.

1551. Mary. February 1, No. 16.

In 1551 an Act was passed commencing thus: "Forasmuch as there has been divers Acts made before, and especially by King James the Fifth, for staunching of beggars, yet notwithstanding, in default of due execution of the said Act, beggars daily and continually multiply and resort in all places

[h] See 'History of the English Poor Law,' vol. i. p. 114.
[i] Ibid., vol. i. p. 121.

where my Lord Governor[k] and other nobility are convened, so that none of them may pass through the streitis for raming and crying upon them, contrary to the tenour of the said Acts"—for preventing which, it is ordained that the said Act be put in due execution in all respects, and that open proclamation be made at the market-cross, charging all officers named therein to do the same, under the penalties named in the Act—after which the statute of James the Fifth is recited at length, and re-enacted. We must presume that this re-enactment, and the admonition set forth in the preamble, failed in putting an end to the "raming and crying" complained of; for four years afterwards another statute was passed, ordaining "that the Act of Parliament made by King James the First, and afterwards enlarged by King James the Fifth, for stanching of maisterful beggars, be observed and kept in all time coming; and that they be of new published at the market-cross of every shire within the realm. And that every sheriff, steward, bailie, as well of regalitie as rialte, and their deputies, and the provosts, aldermen, and bailies of boroughs, shall each one of them put the same to due execution within the bounds of their offices, under the pains contained in the said Acts."

1555. Mary. June 20, No. 38.

The Reformation in Scotland may be said to have been coeval with Mary's reign. Several executions for what the Romish Church deemed heresy had previously taken place, but it was in 1545 that the pious reformer Wishart was burnt, and in revenge for whose death Cardinal Beaton was assassinated, from which time the reformed doctrines spread more rapidly than before. The first Covenant, binding the Reformers in one great association, was framed in 1557; and in 1560 "The Confession of Faith professed by the Protestants within

[k] The Earl of Arran, then Regent of the kingdom.

the realm of Scotland, was published approved and ratified in parliament, as wholesome and sound, and grounded upon the infallible truth of God's word" — immediately after which, three Acts were passed, abolishing the authority of the Bishop of Rome, declaring all Acts made in times past contrary to "The Confession of Faith" to be of no force, and prohibiting idolatry and the service of the mass. The Reformation may therefore be considered as then complete. This great religious revolution was not only similar, but it was also nearly simultaneous in England and in Scotland—awakening the people to a higher sense of their own duties and responsibilities, individually and socially, and leading them to take an active part in whatever concerned their own or the public interest. There was however this difference in the circumstances of the two countries—in England the sovereigns Henry the Eighth, Edward the Sixth, and Elizabeth, supported and helped forward the Reformation, but in Scotland the sovereign was opposed to it; and hence perhaps chiefly the Reformation there assumed a more stern unbending character, its professors having more opposition and greater difficulties to overcome than was the case in England. Mary's reign terminated with her enforced resignation, and the transference of the crown to her infant son, James the Sixth, in 1567, followed by her flight into England the year following.

1560. The Reformation.

The first enactment connected with our subject after Mary's abdication, took place in 1574, when an Act was passed commencing with this preamble: "Forasmuch as sundry loveable Acts have been made for the stanching of maisterful idle beggars, away putting of sornares, and provision of the poor"—the several Acts noticed in the preceding pages are then recited at length—which Acts are declared not to have been put in due execution through the iniquity of the

1574. James VI. April 30.

times by-past, and also by reason that there was not heretofore any order of punishment so specially devised as need required. Therefore, for avoiding the confusion of sundry laws, and that some certain execution and good order may follow thereanent, to the pleasure of God, and common weal of the realm—it was ordained, as well for the utter suppression of the said strong and idle beggars, as for the charitable relieving of the aged and impotent poor people, that the order and form following be observed until the next Parliament or Convention General of the Estates. The Act then proceeds at great length to prescribe regulations for effecting these objects. But as the subject came again under consideration at the end of five years, and was then more fully dealt with, although in the same spirit and for the most part in the express terms of the present Act, it would involve much useless repetition to give its several provisions here, as they will all be found, with many additions, in the following Act of 1579.

1579. James VI., cap. 74. October 26, No. 12.

The statute passed in 1579, to which reference has just been made, and on which the Scottish system of Poor Laws mainly rests, is headed 'For punishment of the strong and idle beggars, and relief of the poore and impotent.' The preamble is the same as in the preceding Act of 1574, except that an additional reason is assigned for its being passed, namely, "that the said beggars, besides the other inconveniences which they daily produce to the common wealth, procure the wrath and displeasure of God for the wicked and ungodlie form of living used among them, without marriage or the baptising of their children;"[m] wherefore, for avoiding these and other in-

[m] This addition may be attributed to the more strict principles of religion and morality inculcated at the Reformation, which had now become firmly established.

conveniences, and for the charitable relief of aged and impotent poor people, it is ordained—

1st. That all strong and idle beggars above the age of fourteen, and under the age of seventy, found wandering and misordering themselves, shall be apprehended and brought before the provost and bailies within burghs, and justices in landward parishes, and by the same be committed to prison the stocks or irons, there to be kept until adjudged, which shall be done within six days thereafter; and if they be convicted, they are to be scourged and burnt through the ear with a hot iron, unless some honest and responsible man will of his charity take and keep the offender in his service for one whole year next following; and if the offender leave such service within the year, on being again apprehended he is to be scourged and burnt through the ear as is before directed; after which he is not to be again punished in like manner for the space of sixty days. But if at the end of sixty days he be found again in his idle and vagabond trade of life, then being apprehended anew, "he shall be adjudged to suffer death as a thief." And that it may be known what persons are meant to be idle beggars and vagabonds, and worthy of the punishment here specified, it is declared that—all idle persons going about, using subtle crafts and unlawful plays, as juglerie, fast and loose, and such others; the idle people calling themselves Egyptians, or any feigning themselves to have knowledge of prophecy, charming, or other abused sciences, by which they persuade people that they can tell their fortunes, and such other fantastical imaginations; all persons being whole and stark in body, and able to work, alleging themselves to have been herryit or burnt in some far part of the realm, or alleging themselves to be banished on account of other's wicked deeds; and others having neither land nor master, nor using any lawful merchandise craft or occupation whereby they may win their livings, and can give no account how they live; and all minstrels, songsters, and tale-tellers, not in the special service of some lord of parliament or great baron; all common labourers, being persons able in body, living idly, and fleeing labour; all counterfeiters of licences to beg, or using the same knowing them to be counterfeit; all vagabond scholars of the universities of St. Andrews, Glasgow, and Aberdeen, not licensed by the rector and dean of faculty to ask alms; all shipmen and mariners alleging themselves to be shipbroken, without they have sufficient testimonials—shall be taken adjudged and punished as strong beggars and vagabonds.

2nd. It is further enacted, that any person who shall after the 1st day of January next coming, give money, harbour, or lodging, or any other relief to any vagabond or strong beggar, "marked or unmarked, wanting a licence of the provost and bailies within burgh, or judge within that parish," the same being duly proved, shall pay for the use of the poor of the parish such sum (not exceeding 5*l.* Scotch) as the judge shall decide. And if any person or persons shall disturb or prevent the execution of this Act, or make impediment against the judge or ordinary officers, or other persons travelling for the due execution thereof, "they shall incur the same penalty which the vagabond would have incurred in case he had been convicted"—provided that shipmen and soldiers landing in this realm, having licence of the provost or bailie of the town, or judge in the parish where they were shipbroken or first entered the realm, shall pass according to the tenure of their licences to that place where they intend to remain, so that, if the person have further journey, he procure the like licence of the judge of the next parish or town through which he must pass, and so from parish to parish until he be at his resting-place.

3rd. It is also ordered that certain persons, one or

more, be nominated in every parish and burgh to be officers and judge thereof, for searching after receiving and conveying the vagabonds to the common prison, irons, or stocks, at the common charge of the parish; which persons so elected, shall be bound to do their duty diligently, as they will answer thereupon.

4th. "And since charity would, that the poor aged and impotent persons should be as necessarilie provided for, as the vagabonds and strong beggars repressed, and that the aged and impotent poor people should have lodging and abyding places throughout the realm to settle themselves into"—it is therefore ordained that the lord chancellor, according to the direction of sundry good Acts of Parliament heretofore made, shall call for the "erections" of all hospitals to be produced before him, and inquire into and consider the present state thereof, restoring them as far as possible to their first institution, as may best serve for the help and relief of the said aged impotent and poor people. And also that the provost and bailies in each burgh and town, and the justice constituted by the king's commission in every landward parish, shall take inquisition of all aged poor impotent and decayed persons born within the parish, or dwelling or having their most common resort therein the last *seven years*, and who of necessity must live by alms; and upon the said inquisition shall make a register-book containing their names and surnames, to remain with the provost and bailies in burghs, and with the justice in every landward parish.

5th. And in order that the number of the poor people in every parish may be known, it is further ordered—that within eleven days after the proclamation of this Act at the Market Cross of Edinburgh, all poor people do repair to the parish where they were born, or had their most common resort or residence the last *seven years*, and there settle themselves, under pain of being punished as vagabonds and contraveners of this Act. And the said space of eleven days being passed, that then the provost and bailies within burghs, and the judges constituted by the king's commission (*i. e.* justices) in each landward parish, make a catalogue of the names of the said poor people, inquire of the men and the women where they were born, whether married or unmarried, when and by whom they were married, what children they have, and whether their children were baptised, and to what trade or form of life they and their children address themselves, and if they be diseased or whole and able in body, and what they get commonly on the day by begging; and such as must necessarily be sustained by alms, to see what they may be made content of their own consent to accept daily to live on without begging, and to provide for their being lodged in a house by themselves, or with others of the parishioners, so that the said poor people may best abyde; and thereupon, according to their number, to consider what their needful sustentation will amount to, and then, according to the good discretion of the said provosts bailies and judges, and such as they shall call to assist them in that respect, "to tax and stent the whole inhabitants within the parish according to the estimation of their substance, without exception of persons, to such weekly charge and contribution as shall be thought expedient and sufficient to sustain the said poor people," the names of the inhabitants so stented, together with their taxation, to be duly registered.

Power to tax and stent the whole inhabitants.

6th. The said provosts bailies and judges, are moreover directed to appoint *overseers* and *collectors* in every burgh, town, and parish, for collecting the said weekly portions, who are to receive the same, and deliver so much thereof to the said poor people, and in such manner, as the said provost, bailies, and judges respectively shall ordain and command. And the overseers of the said poor people,

Overseers and collectors to be appointed.

being so appointed, are to continue for a year, and at the end of the year the taxation and stent-roll is to be always made anew, on account of the alterations which may have taken place through death, or by the increase or diminution of men's goods and substance.

7th. The provost and bailies in towns, and the judges in landward parishes, are required to give a testimonial to such poor folk as they find not born in their own parish, or residing therein the last seven years, directing them to the next parish, and so from parish to parish until they be at the place where they were born, or had their most common resort and residence for the *seven years* preceding, there to be put in certain abyding places, and sustained upon common alms and weekly contributions, as is before ordained—except leprous people and bedridden people, who may not be removed. But it is provided that the poor people so sent to their own abyding places with testimonials, may ask alms in their passage, so as they pass the direct way, not resting two nights in any one place, without occasion of sickness or storm impeding them. And if any of the poor people refuse to pass and abyde in the places appointed, or after the appointment be found begging, they are then to be punished by scourging, imprisonment, or burning through the ear, as vagabonds and strong beggars; and for the second offence they are to be punished as thieves, "as is before appointed."

8th. If the persons chosen as collectors refuse the office, or having accepted the same be found negligent therein, or refuse to make their account every half-year at the least to the provost and bailies in burghs, and the judges in landward parishes, and to deliver the surplus of that which remains in their hands at the end of the year, or half-year, to such as shall be chosen collectors anew—then each one of the collectors so offending shall be imprisoned during the king's pleasure, and be subject to a fine of 20*l.* Scotch, to the use of the poor of that parish, for which penalty the said provost, bailies, and judges are empowered to distrain.

9th. If any person, being able to further this charitable work, shall obstinately refuse to contribute to the relief of the poor, or discourage others from so doing, such obstinate and wilful person, being called before the provost and bailies within burgh, or the judges in landward parishes, and convicted thereof by testimony of two honest witnesses his neighbours, shall upon application of the provost and bailies, or the judge, as the case may be, be imprisoned in such place as the king and council shall appoint, and there remain until he be content to obey the order of his said parish.

10th. If the aged and impotent poor persons, not being so diseased, lame, or impotent but that they may work in some manner of work, shall by the overseers in any burgh or parish be appointed to work, and yet refuse the same—" then first the refuser is to be scourged and put in the stocks, and for a second fault is to be punished as a vagabond."

11th. If any beggar's bairns (male or female), being above the age of five years and under fourteen, shall be liked of by any subject of the realm of honest estate—such person may have the bairn by direction of the provost and bailies within burgh, or the judge in landward parishes, if he be a man-child to the age of 24 years, and if a woman-child to the age of 28 years. And if they depart or be taken or enticed from their master's or mistress's service, the master or mistress shall have the like action and remedy as for their "feit" servant or apprentice, as well against the bairn as against the taker or enticer thereof.

12th. In cases where the collecting of money cannot be had, and that it would be overgreat a burthen to the collectors to gather victuals, meat and drink, or other things for relief of the poor, the provost and bailies in burghs, and the judges in landward parishes, by advice of certain of the most honest parishioners, may give licence under their hands to so many of the said poor people, or such others as they shall think good, to ask and gather the charitable alms of the parishioners at their own houses, "so as always it be specially appointed and agreed how the poor of that parish shall be sustained within the same, and not to be chargeable to others nor troublesome to strangers."

The poor may be licensed to beg.

13th. And seeing that by reason of the present Act, the prisons irons and stocks of every head burgh of the shire and other towns, are like to be filled with a greater number of prisoners than before has been accustomed, in so far as the said vagabonds and other offenders are to be committed to the common prison of the shire or town where they are taken, the same prisons being in towns where there is great number of poor people, more than they are well able to sustain and relieve, and so the prisoners are like to perish in default of sustenance,—It is therefore directed that the expenses of the prisoners shall be paid out of, and be a part of, the common distribution and weekly alms of the parish where he or she was apprehended, allowing to each person daily one pound of oat-bread and water to drink, for payment whereof the committer of him or her to prison shall give security or make present payment.

14th. And finally, the sheriffs stewards and bailies, and the lords of regalities and their bailies throughout the realm, are charged and enjoined to see the present Act put into due execution in all points within their jurisdictions, as they will answer to God and the king.

This comprehensive Act seems to have been prepared with all the care and precision which the subject demanded, and when contrasted with the previous legislation, enables us to judge of the large use which was made of the 14*th Elizabeth, cap.* 5,* in the framing of it, and it may be added, also of the previous Act of 1574. The Acts prior to these are brief and general in their provisions, but these two are full and precise, and in their spirit and general import are indeed almost identical with the English Act, allowance being made for certain shades of difference in the circumstances of the two countries, and for the fact that the progress of legislation, including that having reference to the poor, was in England considerably in advance of that which existed in Scotland. The present Act however brought the legislation of the two countries nearly on a par with respect to our immediate subject, and may be taken as a proof of the intercourse and sympathy subsisting between them, as well as of the readiness with which the Scottish parliament availed itself of the example and experience of its southern neighbour. In this Act the Gipsies, or Egyptians, are first mentioned. They had been long known in England, and severe enactments were passed against them in the reigns of Henry the Eighth, Mary, and Elizabeth, but this is the first notice taken of them by the Scottish legislature.

The general approximation of this Act of 1579 to the English statutes, and its close similarity to *The* 14*th Elizabeth*, (which Act has been commented on in the 'History of the English Poor Law,'[n]) renders lengthened comment upon it here unnecessary, notwithstanding the interest attached to it as constituting the basis of the Scottish Poor Law. Its importance with reference to our present object consists in the comprehensiveness of its provisions, which go so much beyond anything that had been enacted before. It directs inquiry to be made into the number and circumstances of the poor, both in towns and rural parishes, and it

---

[n] See 'History of the English Poor Law,' vol. i. pp. 161–166.

empowers the magistrates to "tax and stent the inhabitants" for their support. It fixes seven years as the term of residence for establishing parochial or burghal chargeability. It provides for the appointment of overseers and collectors, and for punishing poor persons who, being able, refuse to work—thereby implying that they are to be set at work. It also imposes a penalty on persons for relieving unlicensed beggars, and it provides for the putting out of pauper children to service. These are all important provisions, going far towards the formation of a practical system of relief. They are indeed, as is before observed, nearly identical with the 14*th Elizabeth*; but there is one material distinction between the two Acts—that of Elizabeth more distinctly inculcates the policy of as far as possible coupling employment with relief, and this not for the infirm and partially disabled poor alone, but it directs if any surplus money should remain after the impotent poor are provided for, "that the justices shall place and settle to work the rogues and vagabonds that shall be able (that is, the idle and able-bodied poor), there to be holden to work by the oversight of the overseers, to get their livings and to live and be sustained only upon their labour and travail." [o]

If the "labour and travail" thus to be provided were of a repulsive or penal nature, and if it were enforced upon convicted rogues and vagabonds only, there could be no objection in principle to such a provision. So likewise with regard to the employment of the infirm poor directed by Elizabeth's Act, if these were so far disabled by age, disease, or other infirmity, as to be unable to support themselves, but were still able to do work of some kind, there could be no objection to their being employed in such a way as they are fitted for in easement of the charge for their maintenance. The

---

[o] See 'History of the English Poor Law,' vol. i. p. 165.

real danger in both cases, whether as regards the able-bodied or the partially disabled is, lest the employment conjoined with maintenance which is thus provided, should induce an unhealthy feeling of dependence in the persons occupied in the one and partaking of the other, and that the repulsiveness of the labour would not counteract the attractiveness of the subsistence. There is obviously less of such danger to be apprehended in the case of the infirm poor, although there is some even with them. But with the able-bodied the danger is imminent, as has been shown by the whole tenour of our English experience. The results in England have proved beyond a possibility of doubt, that eleemosynary aid of any kind or in any form, if unaccompanied by some sufficient test for establishing the fact of necessity, invariably leads to an increase of the evil it was intended to remedy. Against this danger however, the Scottish legislators appear to have been always sufficiently on their guard.

About the same time with the preceding Act, two others were passed closely connected with the feelings and habits of the people, and therefore requiring to be noticed. The reading of the Bible in a Scotch or English translation had been authoritatively permitted in 1543, in despite of the opposition of the Romish clergy.[p] But now an Act was passed, directing "that all gentlemen householders and others worth 300 marks of yearly rent, and all substantial yeomen or burgesses being householders, and esteemed worth 500*l.* in lands or goods, shall have a Bible and a Psalm-book in the vulgar language in their houses, for the better instruction of themselves and their families in the knowledge of God, under a penalty of 10*l.*" And the provost and bailies in boroughs, and persons holding the king's commission in landward

1579. James VI., cap. 72. October 26, No. 10.

[p] See Tytler's 'History of Scotland,' vol. i. p. 326.

parishes, are required to search for and try whosoever have failed in this respect, and on their conviction to enforce the penalty, one-third of which is "to go to themselves for their pains, and the other two-thirds to the help and relief of the poor of the parish." Shortly afterwards another Act was passed (No. 50), 'For the Instruction of the Youth in the Art of Music and Singing,' which is declared to be almost decayed, and will soon be altogether lost, unless timely remedy be provided. Wherefore the king, with advice of his three estates of parliament, requests the provosts bailies council and community of the chief boroughs of the realm, and the patrons and provosts of the colleges, "to erect and set up one song-school, with a master sufficient and able for instruction of the youth in the said science of music, as they will answer to his Highness upon the peril of their foundations." Both these Acts were evidently fruits of the Reformation, which may now be said to be established, although Episcopacy was not yet abolished. John Knox, the great Reformer, had died in 1572, but not before the form of worship he loved, and which he had laboured so strenuously to establish, had been generally adopted by his countrymen; and the reading of the scriptures and psalmody constituted so important a part of this primitive and simple ritual, that in the then state of Scotland, legislative interference was found to be necessary for compelling the people to furnish themselves with the one, and for providing them with the means of acquiring the other.

Another Act 'for Punishment of Masterful Beggars, and Relief of the Poor,' was passed in 1592. It expresses approbation of the Act of 1579, and ordains that it shall be put in execution in all parts of the realm, as it has been in Edinburgh. But "because some of the sheriffdoms are of wide and long boundaries, throughout which it will be difficult to convey vagabonds and persons offending to the prisons

1592. James VI., cap. 149. No. 69.

of the head boroughs of the shires"—it is further ordained that all sheriffs, stewards, bailies, lords, bailies of regalities and their deputies, and provosts and bailies within boroughs, shall provide prisons stocks and irons, not only at the head boroughs, but also at the principal thoroughfare towns and parish kirks within the bounds of the shire, as well to burgh as to landward; and they are also to constitute one or two persons of good repute to be sheriff deputies for putting the Act in execution. If the sheriffs or other ordinary judges be found remiss or negligent, authority is given to the ministers elders and deacons of a parish, or of so many parishes as shall concur together for the purpose, to nominate and elect one, two, three, or more persons of the best ability zeal and discretion within the same, "whom his Highness makes and constitutes justices and commissioners in that part, and gives them jointly and severally full power and authority to execute the said Act concerning the punishment of strong and idle beggars and vagabonds, and provision for relief of the poor and impotent;" and for that purpose to hold courts, appoint officers, summon an assize, levy fines, and if need be to impound distrain and apply the same to the uses of the Act. In case the ordinary judges or their deputies, or the persons nominated and elected as above said, should refuse or delay to accept and use the said commission, or having accepted should be found remiss or negligent in execution thereof, they will incur the penalties appointed by the Act against judges and magistrates so acting. And for the better trial of common sornares, vagabonds, and masterful beggars, feigned fools, and counterfeit Egyptians, and that they may be pursued until they be compelled to settle at some certain dwelling, "or be expelled forth the country," the sheriffs, ordinary judges, and their deputies, and the other justices and commissioners above specified, are directed to take

Justices and commissioners appointed.

inquisition at the head courts yearly of the names and "takynis" (tokens) of them, and make denunciation of them to the neighbouring judges and parishes, and also to the king and his council.

This Act was evidently intended to facilitate and enforce the carrying out of that of 1579, especially in the suppression of vagrancy, for which purpose it makes provision for increasing the number of prisons, stocks, and irons, creates a new description of officer in the deputy or assistant sheriff; and in case of negligence on the part of the constituted authorities, it empowers the kirk session to elect one or more persons of zeal and discretion, who are thereupon to be created justices and commissioners, and are to hold courts and do all that is necessary for carrying the Act into execution, as well in punishing strong beggars as in relieving the poor and impotent. And further, in order to ensure the due fulfilment of the law, the judges and other officers, both ordinary and those newly created, are subjected to heavy penalties for remissness or negligence in performance of the duties required of them. These provisions manifest an earnestness of purpose in the framers of the statute admitting no doubt of their sincerity, and likewise indicating the magnitude of the evil against which it was directed.

In the following year another Act was passed 'anent Beggars.' It recites that the king and his estates remembering the many good and loveable Acts made for the punishment of strong and idle beggars, and relief of the poor and impotent, and how through the negligent execution of these Acts by some of the judges, and also by sundry of the sheriffdoms being of wide extent, whereby it was difficult to convey persons offending to the common prisons, for which cause, it is said, the Acts of 1579 and 1592 were passed (the Acts are then recited), which, containing as large commission as necessarily can be required, have notwithstanding

1593. James VI., Sept. 12.

proved ineffectual, it being testified by noblemen and others of the estates, that lymmers and sornares are so multiplied, and grown to such boldness, that they spare not to pass and wander over all parts of the realm singly and in companies, armed with swords hacquebuts pistols and other weapons, sometimes alleging themselves to be banished for slaughter or burnt or herried in the Borders and Highlands, sometimes disguised with false beards, or in linen clothes, or in fool's garments, hagging and extorting not only meat drink and victuals, but money, and in case of refusal awaiting privately until they may steal and rob the same in the night, compelling both gentlemen and yeomen after their daily labours to stand on their feet all night for safety of their own gear. In which kind of trade are sundry feigning themselves passing in pilgrimage to chapels and wells, and the counterfeit idle lymmers and harlots falsely calling themselves Egyptians, being nothing else but thieves, witches, and abusers of the people. For remedy whereof it is ordained, that letters be directed charging all judges as well to burgh as in landward, and in case of their negligence the justices or commissioners nominated or to be nominated in the parishes and presbyteries, to put the said Acts into due execution in all points. And that inquisition be taken of the names of all common sornares, vagabonds, masterless beggars, feigned fools, and counterfeit Egyptians, within twelve days after the charge, under the pain of rebellion in case they fail. Power is then given to the judges justices and commissioners, to proceed against the said strong idle beggars vagabonds thieves and sornares, or the partakers in their "thiefteous" and wicked deeds, and on conviction to punish them to the death, or otherwise as they shall find cause. All wandering beggars are likewise charged to resort to the parish where they were born, or where they dwelt the last *seven years*, and in no wise to remove therefrom in begging, nor to visit convents[q] or markets, under penalty of being punished as vagabonds and thieves as by law is appointed.

These Acts of 1592 and 1593, especially the latter, are full and explanatory as to the nature and extent of the evils against which they were directed, and which are very similar to those existing in England sixty years previously, as described in the *22nd Henry 8th, cap.* 12.[r] The punishment of the offenders likewise is not very dissimilar. But there is this striking difference between the legislation of the two counties, that whilst in the English Act vagabonds and other offenders are directed to be punished with a severity or rather a cruelty nearly equal to that directed by the Act of James, there is not in this latter Act the same degree of care manifested for the really poor which appears in the Act of Henry; indeed they are never mentioned, and seem hardly to come within the purview of the statute. Another difference appears in the time required for conferring a right of residence in a parish. The English Act names three years, the Scotch Act seven; but both concur in naming birth as conferring a right of residence.

1597. James VI., cap. 272. November 3, No. 39.

At the end of four years legislation was again resorted to, in order, as the title of the Act expresses it, "that strong beggars, vagabonds, and Egyptians should be punished." The Act commences by declaring that the king and estates of parliament ratify and approve the statute of 1579, against strong and idle beggars, vagabonds, and Egyptians, with this addition—"that strong beggars and their bairns be employed in common work during their life times; and in place of the several commissions in land-

The powers of justices and commissioners granted to the kirk sessions.

q Conventions or meetings.

r See 'History of the English Poor Law,' vol. i. p. 115.

ward places to be granted by the king for the execution of that statute, the power thereof is now granted to the particular session of the kirk." This is the whole of the Act. It is very short, but also very important. It directs that strong beggars and their bairns (that is, the able-bodied poor of every class, sex, and age) shall be employed at common labour, and therefore of course be prevented from begging; and it likewise transfers to the kirk session itself, the execution of the duties which we have seen by the Act of 1592 they were empowered to nominate certain commissioners to perform. Thenceforward therefore the kirk session[r] became the sole administrators of the law for relief of the aged and infirm poor, and in great measure also the administrators of the law affecting the idle and vagabond classes. This was a great change, and it led to important results, not as respects the employment of "strong beggars and their bairns," for it does not appear that this provision was ever acted upon to any material extent, if acted upon at all, but as respects the poor generally, and the disabled and necessitous poor in particular—each and all of whom were now subjected to the supervision of the kirk session, to which the needy would look for relief, and which the idle and dissolute would view with apprehension.

This Act of 1597 was cotemporaneous with the 39*th Elizabeth*, *caps* 3 *and* 4, and it is worthy of remark how exceedingly different were the proceedings of the English and Scottish legislatures in their attempts to remedy evils precisely similar, and which were common alike to both countries. The parliament of England framed two carefully devised Acts, embodying and systematising the previous legislation — one providing for the effectual relief of the destitute poor, the other for the punishment of vagabonds and sturdy beggars; and each with a minuteness and precision manifesting the fullest information on the subjects treated of. The Scottish parliament, on the contrary, wearied it would seem by the ill success and disappointments attending their previous efforts, enter into no details, prescribe no conditions, give no particular directions, but briefly and without limitation or exception commit the administration of the existing law to the kirk sessions, to be interpreted and applied according to their discretion. There can hardly be a greater contrast than was exhibited on this occasion, and henceforward the proceedings of the two countries in reference to the relief of the poor, assumed a character distinct and divergent—in one sternly repelling the indigent, in the other ministering to poverty with perhaps an unwise profusion.

Henceforward the English and Scotch laws become distinct and divergent.

The kirk sessions seem however to have succeeded little better than preceding authorities, for three years after the above Act, another was passed 'Anent strong and idle Beggars,' which, after ratifying the last Act, recites that the king and lords of secret council, remembering how there have been divers good and loveable Acts made heretofore for punishment of strong and idle beggars, and relief of the poor and impotent, and how the said Acts have produced little or no effect, by reason of the oversight and negligence of the persons who were nominated justices and commissioners for putting them into execution, and that there was not some special penalty appointed to those who should be remiss or negligent therein, so that the said strong and idle beggars, being for the most part "thieves, bairdis, and counterfeit lymmers,[8] living most insolently and ungodly, without marriage or baptism of a great number of their bairns," are suffered

1600. James VI., cap. 19. No. 28.

---

[8] Thieves, contumacious persons, and scoundrels.

to vaig[t] and wander throughout the whole country, and the poor and impotent persons are neglected, and no care had nor provision made for their entertainment and sustentation. For remedy of this state of things, and in furtherance of the said loveable Acts, and especially of the Act of 1597, whereby the execution of the said Acts is committed to the particular sessions of the kirk—It is now ordained that the kirk sessions, whenever need is, shall be assisted by one or two of the presbyters, and that they shall put the said Acts into full and due execution in all points within their respective bounds, under the penalty of twenty pounds to be exacted of them so often as they shall be found to be remiss or negligent herein. And in order that the king may be the better assured of the care and diligence of the kirk sessions in due execution of the said Acts, the whole of the presbyteries in the whole land are commanded to take diligent tryal of the obedience of the said sessions hereanent, and to report their certificate and testimonial thereupon to his Majesty's ministers, so that proceedings may be taken accordingly against such as shall be negligent. Letters thereanent are moreover to be directed to every kirk session that they may not pretend ignorance, commanding them to put the said Acts against strong and idle beggars, whereof the execution is committed to them by the said Act of 1597, to due and full execution in all points, "under the said penalty of 20*l.* to be exacted of them as often as they shall be found remiss, after the said certifying them that the said penalty will be uplifted of them with all rigour; and in like manner to command and charge the said presbyteries to take tryal of the said sessions hereanent, and to report their testimonial thereupon, as they will answer to his Majesty upon their obedience."

---

[t] To stroll or wander.

We here see that the entire execution of the law, as regards the infirm poor and the vagabond classes, is in the first place consigned to the kirk session, and secondarily to the presbyteries. On the ability of these bodies for performing the duties assigned them, the administration of the law, and its efficiency for the objects intended, must therefore in great measure depend. Both the kirk session and the presbytery are ecclesiastical institutions, specially created for the government of the Scottish church. The former is composed of the minister of the parish and certain lay elders chosen by the session, and who may therefore be considered as self-elected, although a right of objecting in any particular case rests with the parishioners at large. The presbytery consists of all the ministers of the parishes comprised within its limits, and of a lay elder from each. There is no prescribed number of parishes for constituting a presbytery, and they vary in amount from five or six to thirty and upwards, according to circumstances. The kirk session is in its constitution not very dissimilar to the English parish vestry, and seems well suited for dealing with the aged infirm and impotent poor; but notwithstanding that it was armed with all the powers of control and punishment conferred by the Act of 1579, it does not appear well adapted for dealing with the strong rogues and masterful idle beggars complained of in all the preceding Acts, and against whom their most stringent provisions were directed.

Powers of the kirk sessions and presbytery.

The supervision of the proceedings of the kirk session conferred upon the presbytery by the present statute, constituted as both the bodies were, could hardly have been effective, and the right of interference vested in the latter would we may presume be rarely used. It seems intended that the presbytery should interfere somewhat in the way that justices of peace interfered with the parish authorities in England; but there is so little analogy between the presbytery of the kirk and the English magistracy, that it is difficult to believe there could be any real similarity in the action of the two. The presbytery would naturally have a fellow-feeling with the inferior body, each of its members being likewise a member of some one of the kirk sessions within its boundaries, and all necessarily acting under similar influences.

We have seen that by the Act of 1592 justices and commissioners were appointed, with authority "for the punishment of strong and idle beggars and vagabonds, and for relief of the poor and impotent." We have also just seen, that by the Acts of 1597 and 1600 like powers were conferred upon the kirk session and the presbytery.[u] It may be presumed that these powers did not in either case prove sufficient for the purpose intended, as in 1617 another statute was passed under the title of an 'Act anent the Justices for keeping the King's Peace and their Constables,' conferring large powers upon these functionaries, and minutely defining their several duties. James had then been seated on the English throne upwards of thirteen years, and must therefore have been acquainted with the state of social organisation in England, of which the justice of peace and the parish constable had long formed important portions, binding and cementing the various and sometimes discordant materials into one harmonious whole; and these authorities he would naturally be desirous of establishing in Scotland, then in a less forward and orderly state. The elaborate Act of 1617, the title of which is given above, was accordingly framed for this purpose, apparently with great care, and keeping the example of England closely in view; and to this Act we will now direct our attention.

The Act begins by declaring that the king, with advice and consent of parliament, having considered

---

[u] Ante, pp. 28, 31, 33.

the articles and instructions before given by his Majesty to the justices and commissioners appointed for keeping the peace, and the said justices and commissioners being desirous that the same should be authorised by decree of parliament, they were accordingly confirmed in every point to the purport following:—The commissioners and justices at their first admission to the bench, are to be sworn to do equal right to rich and poor, according to their knowledge wit and power, and to conform to the laws and customs of the land. Their powers are then minutely defined, and their duties pointed out. They are directed to put the law into "due and full execution against wilful beggars and vagabonds, solitary and idle men and women without calling or trade, lurking in alehouses, tied to no certain service, reputed and holden as vagabonds, and against those persons who are commonly called Egyptians." And they are to punish and fine their receivers, and the setters of houses to them, "by such competent paines as is proper to them to enjoine." They are to hold a session quarterly, for attending at which they are to be allowed forty shillings Scots[v] daily, not exceeding three days; and any justice having the benefit of that allowance, who shall be absent from the ordinary session or otherways when required, "not being lawfully excused, and the excuse allowed by the rest of the justices there assembled," will incur the penalty of forty pounds Scotch. But earls, bishops, and privy councillors are not to be allowed anything for their attendance.

1617. James VI., cap. 8. June 28, No. 8.

Duties of justices and commissioners defined.

The commissioners and justices are at their quarter sessions to appoint constables to every parish, two or more according to its greatness; but in boroughs and royal free cities the constables are to be appointed by the magistrates. Any one appointed a constable who shall refuse to accept the charge, and

Parish constables to be appointed.

[v] A shilling Scots is equal to a penny English.

give his oath for due execution thereof, is to be "imprisoned and fined at the discretion of the justices at their next sitting." The constables are to "arrest all vagabonds, sturdy beggars, and Egyptians, and carry them before the next commissioners of peace, who shall take order for their commitment or punishment." The constables are also directed to arrest "all idle persons whom they know to have no means to live upon, and will not take themselves to any labour trade or occupation, and carry them before the commissioner of peace, who after examination shall either commit them, or take surety of them for their appearance at the next session." A constable may apprehend any suspected person "who for the most part sleepeth all day and walketh at night," and carry him to the next justice of peace to find surety for his good behaviour, or otherwise to be committed to prison—"and if he be a man of quality, the justice shall go with the constable and do it."[x] Upon the appearance of a fray, the constable is authorised to require the aid of his neighbours for sundering the parties, and he may also require the assistance of all persons in apprehending a thief, murderer, or other capital offender, and conveying him to the next commissioner for examination and commitment; "and any of his Majesty's subjects who shall refuse or delay to aid the constable in the execution of his office, shall be imprisoned and punished by the commissioners and justices."

Their duties and powers.

The commissioners and justices are armed with large powers for preserving the peace and enforcing their decisions. Their duties in regard to beggars and vagabonds, &c., are already described, but many others are required from them. They are to give order "as they shall think most convenient,

Powers of the commissioners and justices.

[x] This last is a remarkable provision, showing that the law did not run indifferently to all. The constable might alone arrest an inferior person, but for "a man of quality" the presence of the justice was likewise necessary.

and with least grief to the subjects," for mending all highways, which are to be twenty feet wide at the least. They are to put the law in execution against destroyers of plantings orchards and gardens, and against the stealers of bees and beehives, users of unlawful games, &c. &c. They are not to permit hostlers to receive any masterless men, rebels, vagabonds, or other persons guilty of known crimes. They are to make order for the governance of the country in time of plague, and are to punish severely the disobeyers of such order, according to the quality of the offence. At their quarter sessions in August and February, they are to appoint the ordinary hire and wages of labourers, workmen, and servants; "and whoever shall refuse to serve upon the prices fixed by them, shall be imprisoned and further punished at their discretion." And that servants may be the more willing to obey the ordinance, the justices are likewise empowered to compel masters to make the payments appointed.

The commissioners and justices are also empowered to rate every parish for a weekly portion, not exceeding the sum of five shillings Scots, for the maintenance of poor prisoners, who might "otherwise famish and starve before they can come to their trial." They are, on being lawfully required, to command their constables to apprehend any person who has contemptuously disobeyed the censure of the church. They are "to set down Acts against notorious and common drunkards, and to impose fines upon contraveners according to the quality of their deserts." And they are moreover "to cause sufficient single and double ale to be brewed in every shire, and appoint visitors[y] to that effect, with consent of the baron and over lord of the ground." This last provision seems out of keeping with the rest

[y] The ale-taster was an officer appointed in most of the old corporate towns in England.

of the Act, but it was probably introduced with the view of checking the excessive use of ardent spirits then common in Scotland, and leading the people to adopt the less exciting and more wholesome beverage of beer.

The establishment of such a combination of authorities as is created by the present Act for the preservation of the peace, the repression of disorder, and the punishment of crime, extending into every shire and parish throughout the country, could hardly fail of producing important benefits; even if, as was not unlikely at first to have been the case, the justices and constables should prove inefficient through ignorance, apathy, or unwillingness to act, or should be over meddling and oppressive through misapprehension of their duties and position. Such drawbacks would however gradually be overcome, and the authority thus intrusted to certain of the people, to be exercised for the general security and benefit of all, could hardly fail of becoming both popular and effective in Scotland, as a similarly organised authority had long proved to be in England. Its popularity and its efficiency would doubtless be impeded by the prevalence of clanship, and by the species of feudalism still existing in Scotland; but these counteracting influences would become less and less, as the law acquired force and got to be more certainly and universally applied, which would be the case as soon as the justices attained to a right apprehension of their duties, and when the constables could feel assured of being supported in the fulfilment of theirs.

1617. James VI., cap. 10. June 28, No. 10.

The kirk sessions and the presbyteries had failed in putting down mendicancy and vagabondage. The creation of justices of peace and constables, and the duties assigned to them by the preceding Act, would no doubt materially assist in effecting this object: but these were not solely relied upon, for immediately afterwards another Act was passed "anent the poor," commencing with the usual preamble, that notwithstanding divers worthy laws have been made for restraining idle and masterful beggars, their number hath daily increased more and more; and then declaring that his Majesty and estates consider the cause of the multiplying of the said beggars to proceed from the circumstance "that no order hath been taken in by-gone time with the children and orphans born of poor and indigent parents, who being tolerated or neglected at their first entry to begging, doth contract such a custom and habit that hardly they can be drawn thereafter to any other calling; whereas, if the said poor children were in their tender years put to any work, and employed and trained up in any commendable labour, they might thereafter not only relieve the country of their charge, but also prove profitable to the common wealth; which might be easily performed if the children were taken off the hands of their parents by some well-affected persons, or by any of the incorporations and burghs within the kingdom, and employed in some calling or vocation that might tend to the good of the realm." Wherefore the king, with the advice and consent of the states, "doth in the most earnest manner recommend to all his loving subjects, requesting them as they tender the good and honour of the realm, to receive within their houses and families, and to take upon them the care, entertainment, and education of some of the said poor and indigent children, one or more to every person according to his power and faculty." And it is declared to be lawful for the said persons, to take such poor children to be educated and brought up either in their own houses, or to put them out to such crafts callings or vocations as they please.

Poor children to be trained to labour.

After this apparently judicious and benevolent exordium, the description of the poor children, and the conditions on which they are to be so received or put out, are set forth and prescribed as follows:—

The children are to be such as shall by the declaration

of the provost and bailies or the kirk session within burghs, or by the kirk session in landward parishes, be certified to be poor and indigent, and to have no means of living. When the said children are under the age of fourteen, they are with the consent of their parents if they have any, and if above the age of fourteen with their own consent, and by advice of the said magistrates or kirk sessions, to be delivered to their masters, with a testimonial in writing of such delivery, and of the condition of the said poor children—which testimonial is declared a sufficient warrant for receiving the children, and for the receivers partaking of the benefits of the statute. The Act then proceeds—"And to the effect that his Majesty's subjects may be moved hereto by the expectation of commoditie and advantage which they may reap by the labours and service of the said poor children," it is ordained that the children received upon testimonial as above specified "shall be bound and restricted to their masters, their heirs and assignes, in all kind of service which shall be enjoined them, until they are past the age of *thirty*; and that they shall be under discipline to their said masters, and subject to their corrections and chastisements according to the merits of their offences, in all manner and sort of punishments, life and torture excepted." It is likewise declared, that whatsoever the said servants may gain shall belong to their masters, and if they absent themselves without the master's licence they shall refund to him the whole damage and loss which he may declare to be sustained through their absence, and suffer such bodily punishment as in his discretion he may inflict. And if any other person shall receive any of the said servants, he is to restore them again within twelve hours after being required, failing in which he is to pay ten shillings after every requisition daily, until they be restored.

Poor children appointed to service till past the age of thirty.

We find a considerable change in this Act, as compared with the Act of 1579,[z] in regard to poor children. A strong desire is now expressed for the education and training of the children, which did not appear in the previous Act, and greater care is shown in providing for the putting out of the children; but the length of their servitude, or modified slavery as it may not unaptly be called, was extended from twenty-four for a man-child and twenty-eight for a woman-child, to the age of thirty without any distinction as to sex. By the intermediate statute of 1597,[a] "strong beggars and their bairns" are required to be employed at common work during their lifetimes, but by whom and for whose benefit they are to be so employed does not appear; and we may therefore infer that the employment was intended to be of the ordinary kind, and that it was to be paid for in the way of remuneration to the individuals themselves, either in money or in articles of subsistence in lieu of money, by which the necessity for eleemosynary relief would be obviated. But according to the present Act, and that of 1579, the children are to be taken separately and treated as apprentices, and are to be deprived of their freedom for a specified time, in order to their being taught, trained, and fitted for earning their own living afterwards. We cannot fail to recognise in these Acts the spirit of the *43rd of Elizabeth*,[b] somewhat more harsh and severe in their provisions, it is true, but still aiming at the same result, that is, to rescue poor children from a state of idleness and mendicancy, and to place them in situations where they will be cared for and trained in some useful occupation.

Such enforced apprenticeships, have doubtless led to evils of no inconsiderable magnitude; but in the then condition of England and Scotland, it may be questioned whether it was not the best as well as the readiest course

---

[z] Ante, pp. 16, 22. Ante, p. 31.
[b] See 'History of the English Poor Law,' vol. i. p. 194.

that could be adopted. It checked the growth of vagrancy by arresting one main source of supply, and it at the same time promoted the increase of industrial power; and these were operations assuredly tending to the general weal. As wealth and civilization extended however, and when the principle of supply and demand came into general operation, such enforced apprenticeships would not only be no longer necessary, but would be a positive evil, by interfering with the free appropriation of labour and the natural development of industry. In this we may perceive another instance, added to the many which observation and experience are continually presenting to us, of a particular act or course of procedure being suitable and beneficial at one time, and injurious at another, according to the circumstances or the state of society under which it is applied.

The above Act has been noticed something out of its regular order for the purpose of keeping the general subject of the poor as much together as possible; but there is a previous Act, "anent the Egyptians," requiring attention, and to this we will now return. In the Act of 1579 we find the gipsies designated as "idle people calling themselves Egyptians," and in the Acts of 1592 and 1593 they are named as "counterfeit Egyptians;"[c] but in all the Acts they are classed with idle vagabonds, masterful beggars, and such like offenders, and are to be dealt with and punished accordingly. At length however the gipsies, whether simulated or real, became so numerous, and were moreover so burthensome to the community, that they were placed in a distinct class of offenders, and had a separate law specially directed against them.

The Egyptians.

In 1609 an Act was passed, which after referring to a proclamation by the secret council in 1603, "commanding the vagabonds, sornares, and

1609. James VI., cap. 13. No. 20.

[c] See ante, pp. 16, 27, 29.

common thiefs, commonly called Egyptians, to pass forth the kingdom, and remain perpetually forth thereof, and never to return within the same under pain of death"—ordains that the same shall have force and execution, and that after the 1st of August next coming, if any of the said vagabonds called Egyptians shall be found within the kingdom, it shall be lawful for all or any of his Majesty's good subjects "to cause take, apprehend, imprison, and execute to death the said Egyptians, either men or women, as common notorious and condemned thieves," who, it is further ordained, are to be tried only as to their being "called known reputed and holden for Egyptians." And at such trial whosoever shall "clenge" (exculpate) any of the said Egyptians, panelled as aforesaid, shall be pursued handled and censured as committers of wilful errour, and whoever shall thereafter receive supply or entertain any of the said Egyptians, either men or women, shall forfeit their escheat, and be awarded at the judge's will. Sheriffs and magistrates within whose bounds Egyptians shall resort and remain, are to be called before the lords of the secret council, and severely censured and punished for their negligence in execution of this Act. All letters of protection or warrants for their remaining within the realm or for entertaining or doing any manner of favour to the said Egyptians, which may have been or which shall be purchased by any of them, or by any other person of whatsoever rank, from the lords of the secret council, are declared to be annulled, as having been surreptitiously and deceitfully obtained.

There was a close similarity in the legislation of the Scotch and the English parliaments with respect to the gipsies, or Egyptians, as they were indifferently called. The first Act respecting them in England was the 22*nd Henry VIII.*[d] in 1530, which describes them as

[d] See 'History of the English Poor Law,' vol. i. pp. 114, 176.

"divers outlandish people, calling themselves Egyptians," and orders them to quit the country under penalty of imprisonment. The last notice of them is in the *5th Elizabeth* in 1562, by which they were not only adjudged to suffer death whenever found, but every person convicted of associating with them for a month was subjected to a like punishment. The first notice of them in Scotland was, as is above stated, in the Act of 1579, and the last in the present Act of 1609; the Scottish Acts being thus in each case, it will be observed, about half a century behind the English; but the enactments are identical in spirit and intention, and nearly so in the punishments which they inflict.[e]

John Faw, lord of the gipsies.

The gipsies seem however to have enjoyed a degree of consideration in Scotland, much beyond what they ever attained in England; for one of them, named *John Faw*, who is styled Lord and Earl of Little Egypt, was by writ of Privy Seal in 1594, supported in the execution of justice on his company and folk "conformably to the laws of Egypt;" and for the punishment of certain persons therein named who had rebelled against him, robbed him, and absconded, James's good subjects are commanded to assist and to apprehend the fugitives. There had been a writ previously granted in Faw's favour by Mary in 1553, and he obtained a pardon for a murder in 1554, so that he must have been a person of importance and notoriety. From him this kind of strolling people received the name of "The Faw gang," which they still commonly retain.[f] It was against such writs, warrants, and letters of protection,

---

[e] Sir Samuel Romilly, in his 'Observations on the Criminal Law of England,' published in 1810, says that the sanguinary Act (5th Elizabeth, c. 20), which made it a capital offence for any person above the age of fourteen to associate for a month with gipsies, was executed in the reign of Charles the First; and Lord Hale mentions thirteen persons having suffered death under it, at one assize, in his time.—See 'Edinburgh Review' for February 1812, p. 391.

[f] This account of John Faw is abstracted from the 'Encyclopædia Britannica,' 7th edition, under the head 'Gipsies.'

that the latter portion of the above Act seems to have been directed. That they were obtained surreptitiously is highly probable, considering the character of the times, and the contributions levied throughout the country by these wandering gangs, which would enable them to pay handsomely for the protection of persons in power. The gipsies seem to have gathered into their company or gang, all the riotous and disorderly spirits of the day, and they must have proved (as we are indeed assured that they were) a great evil and source of oppression to the country wheresoever they appeared, and hence the severity of the laws against them.

Fletcher of Saltoun.

The gipsies, or the vagabond and mendicant class generally, with whom the gipsies were identified, and of whom they formed no inconsiderable part, continued notwithstanding to maintain their ground in Scotland; for Fletcher, of Saltoun, in his second Discourse, written in 1698, says, "There are at this day in Scotland (besides a great many poor families very meanly provided for by the church boxes, with others who by living upon bad food fall into various diseases) two hundred thousand people begging from door to door—and though the number of them be perhaps double to what it was formerly, by reason of the present great distress, yet in all times there have been about one hundred thousand of those vagabonds, who have lived without any regard or subjection either to the laws of the land, or even those of God and nature; fathers incestuously accompanying with their own daughters, the son with the mother, and the brother with the sister. No magistrate could ever discover or be informed which way one in a hundred of these wretches died, or that ever they were baptised. Many murders have been discovered among them, and they are not only a most unspeakable oppression to the poor tenants (who if they give not bread or some kind of provision to perhaps forty such villains in one day are sure to be insulted by them), but they rob many poor people who live in houses distant from any neighbourhood. In years of plenty many thousands of them meet together in the mountains, where they feast and riot for many days; and at country weddings, markets, burials, and other the like public occasions, they are to be seen both men and women perpetually drunk, cursing blaspheming and fighting together." [g]

There may be some exaggeration in this statement, for it is difficult to believe that there could have been so many as two hundred thousand vagrants and beggars in 1698, when the entire population of Scotland was probably under a million. But the writer was an highly honourable, as well as able man: he would not intentionally misrepresent a fact; and we may I think safely conclude that at the time Fletcher wrote there were, as he says, many poor families very meanly provided for by the church boxes, and also that a very large number of vagabonds and beggars were continually preying upon and oppressing the poor tenants —a state of things calculated to endanger property, prevent improvement, and depress the general condition of the country. If such was the state of things in 1698, the date of Fletcher's Discourse, we can hardly doubt that it was no better, or perhaps even worse, at the passing of the 'Act anent the Egyptians' in 1609. Unmistakable proofs of the disorganisation which prevailed previous to and throughout the reign of James VI. are to be found in the legislation of the period; and one instance of this disorganisation, although not

---

[g] See 'The Political Works of Andrew Fletcher of Saltoun,' printed at Glasgow in 1749, p. 100. The reader can hardly fail of being here reminded of Meg Merrilies, and Scott's description of the gipsies in '*Guy Mannering*.' The great novelist, like our own Shakspeare, drew from the life; and the pictures of each may be taken as true representations of the manners, customs, and state of society at the periods to which they refer. Scott likewise quotes the paragraph above extracted from Fletcher's work; but we could not dispense with its insertion here, it being so well calculated to throw light upon the circumstances of the country at that time.

immediately appertaining to our subject, it may not be altogether irrelevant to adduce.

An Act was passed in 1594, the preamble of which declares, that notwithstanding the sundry Acts made for punishment of the authors of thefts, reif, oppression, and sorning,[h] and the masters and sustainers of thieves—yet such has been and presently is the barbarous cruelties and daily heirschippis devastations of the wicked thieves and lymmers of the clans inhabiting the Highlands and Isles (that is to say, Clangregor, Clanfarlane, and seventeen others specially named; also many broken men of the surnames of Stewart in Athol, Lorne, and Balquhidder; Campbells and Grahams in Monteith; Buchanans, M'Cawles, and eleven others named, inhabiting the sheriffdoms of Argyle, Bute, Dumbarton, Stirling, Perth, &c., and the stewartries of Stuthern and Menteith; and likewise a great number of wicked thieves, oppressors, peacebreakers, and receivers ("resettaris)" of theft, of the surnames of Armstrong, Elliot, Graham, and thirteen others specially mentioned, "inhabiting the Borders foreanent England"), that all these clans are therefore declared guilty of the murder, heirschip, and daily oppression of the peaceable and good subjects in the whole country adjacent to the Highlands and Borders, to the displeasure of God, contempt and dishonour of the king, and to the wasting and desolation of a good part of the plentiful ground of the country. The king and parliament understanding moreover that this mischief and shameful disorder increases, and is nourished by the encouraging, receiving, maintenance, and nonpunishment[i] of the thieves limmers and vagabonds, partly by the landlords masters and bailies of the lands where they dwell and

1594. James VI., cap. 231. June 8, No. 37.

The Highland clans.

---

[h] Sorning, or sornaring, *i. e.* obtruding on another for bed and board.

[i] "Oursicht, hounding out, ressett, mantinence, and not punischement."

resort, and partly through the counsel direction receiving and partaking of the chieftains, principals of the branches and householders of the said surnames and clans, who bear quarrel and seek revenge for the least hurting or slaughter of any one of their unhappy race, although it were by order of justice, or in rescue and following of true men's gear stolen or reft; so that the said chieftains, principals of the branches and householders, worthily may be esteemed the very authors fosterers and maintainers of the wicked deeds of the vagabonds of their clans and surnames—for remedy whereof, and that there may be a perfect distinction by names and surnames betwixt them that are desirous to be esteemed honest and true men, and them that are not ashamed to be esteemed thieves, reifers, sornares, and receivers and sustainers of theft and thieves in their wicked and odious crimes and deeds, it is ordained that a roll or catalogue shall be made of all persons of the surnames aforesaid, suspected of slaughter, theft, reif, ressett of theft or thieves, or sornings, within the said sheriffdoms and stewartries, in what towns and parishes, and under what landlords, masters, or bailies they dwell, &c. The landlords, masters, and bailies are then respectively made answerable for the acts of all such persons, and others living under them; and it is further declared that "the Act shall extend not only against the inhabitants of the said sheriffdoms and stewartries, but against the landlords, masters, and bailies of all persons that are or shall be suspected of theft, reif, oppression, and sorning, over all parts of the realm." And finally, "that as thieves and sornares concur assist and maintain others in wicked deeds against true men, without fear of God the king or the laws, so it shall be lawful for true and honest men to concur and join in counsel and action for defence of the lives and goods of themselves and their tenants against

Landlords, masters, and bailies answerable for their clans.

thieves and sornares, and to follow and pursue them and all their races clans and names, and to take and apprehend their persons and goods, and keep them in prison or execute them to death." And in case any of the said thieves and sornares or their assistants happen to be hurt, slayne, or mutilated, their goods to be taken, their houses burnt or destroyed, it is further declared "that the same shall not be imputed as any crime or offence in the true men the authors or executors thereof."

Although this Act applies specially to the Highland and Border districts, its provisions are not limited to them, but extend to the whole kingdom. The preamble is sufficiently indicative of the disorganised state of the country at that period, and it shows how strong a hold clanship still maintained in parts of Scotland, although it had been for a century extinct in England. Clanship as it existed in the Highlands, although differing from feudalism in principle and origin, may practically be said to have amounted to a species of feudalism in its most effective form, governing the wills and affections, as well as exacting the obedience of its vassals. The clansmen were in all things dependent on their chief. They received their lands from him, were of the same tribe or family, bore the same name, used the same arms. The safety and almost the very existence of the clan at times depended on its union and entire subserviency to its chief, and men willingly followed a leader whom they regarded as their natural protector and the head of their race, and served him with more than the fidelity of vassals. With such a variety of separate allegiances existing in the country, it can hardly excite surprise that justice should be imperfectly administered, and that individual will often superseded the general law of the land. The government was in fact too feeble to enforce the law or establish its own supremacy, and was continually

Clanship.

driven to resort to intrigue, partisanship, and compromise for even the partial accomplishment of its objects. After James's accession to the crown of England on the death of Queen Elizabeth in 1603, the Scottish executive partook of the increased influence he thereby acquired; but the country still continued in a backward and disordered state, its general condition being perhaps nearly a century behind that of England, down to the period of the Union in 1707; after which, its progress in all that tends to improve and elevate the condition of a people was remarkably rapid, and has ever since continued fully to equal if it has not surpassed that which has taken place in England.

1603. Population.

The amount of population in Scotland, like its amount in England, was extremely uncertain in the earlier periods, and was subject to great fluctuations through the effects of war, insurrection, famine and pestilence. At the time of the Union in 1707, the population of Scotland was estimated at 1,050,000.[k] There had been great dearths in 1635 and 1688, and from 1693 to 1700, emphatically termed "the seven ill years," the distress was so great and so general that many parishes were nearly depopulated, and farms remained unoccupied for several years afterwards; so that we shall perhaps not be far wrong in reckoning the population to have been about a million at the time of James's accession to the English throne in 1603, as the frequent recurrence of famine, and the other circumstances above adverted to, would necessarily tend to keep it at about the same level by preventing any material increase.

[k] See M'Culloch's 'Account of the British Empire,' vol. i. p. 427. The population of England at that time was about 5,750,000. See 'History of the English Poor Law,' vol. i. p. 374.

## CHAPTER II.

Laws of Charles II.: Establishment of manufacturing incorporations — Dearth of capital and lack of employment — Duties of justices — Overseers of the poor — Regular and casual poor — Ability and disability — Over-facility of relief — Compulsory labour — Privileges of employers — Chargeability by residence — Correction-houses — Treatment of poor — Apprenticeship — Punishment of vagabonds. — Laws of William III.: Proclamations for maintaining the poor and repressing beggars. — Summary of enactments. — Other Acts — Against drunkenness and swearing, profanation of the Lord's day, theft and depredation — Act for encouragement of manufactures — Bank of Scotland — 'Act anent murdering of Children' — Parish schools — The Union — Assessments — Amount of relief — Numbers relieved — Pauperism of Scotland and England.

It was not until after an interval of nearly half a century from the passing of the Act of James the Sixth (the First of England), in 1617,[a] and in the year following the restoration of his grandson Charles the Second, that any further legislation took place with regard to the relief of the Scottish poor. The intermediate period of what has been emphatically called the Great Rebellion, as well as that of the Commonwealth and the Protectorate which succeeded it, although most highly important in their political and social consequences, were too much occupied with the exciting occurrences of the day, to admit of any matters so purely domestic as the relief of the poor being entered upon or considered. The events of these periods, and of the Restoration in which they may be said to have terminated, are so well known that it is not necessary to describe or more particularly refer to them, and we may therefore proceed at once to review the legislation connected with our subject after the return of Charles the Second in 1660.

The first Act of this description requiring to be noticed, was passed in 1661. It is numbered *275* in

---

[a] Ante, p. 40.

the margin, and is entitled 'An Act establishing Companies for making Linen Cloth, Stuffs, &c.' The preamble recites that the king, considering that all the laudable statutes made for enriching his ancient kingdom, and for putting poor children, idle persons, and vagabonds to work for their maintenance, and for relief of the country from the burthen of such unprofitable persons, have been hitherto rendered ineffectual; "and that many good spirits having aimed at the public good have, for want of sufficient stocks counsel and assistance been crushed by such undertakings—doth conceive it necessary to create and erect companies and societies for manufactories, that what was above the capacity of single persons may be carried on by the joint assistance counsel and means of many." And therefore, with the advice and consent of parliament, societies and companies are permitted to be incorporated in the persons of such as shall enter them, and after their decease in the persons of their successors, or any other who shall enter themselves therein, for making linen cloth, worsted stockings, searges, baizes, sayes, cottons, sempeternums, Castilians, perpetuanes, and all other woollen stuffs and cloths. And, for their encouragement, such companies are permitted to export their manufactures and to import whatever articles they may require for the same, free of duty.

1661. Charles II., cap. 42. June 12, No. 275.

Manufacturing incorporations established.

These incorporations are also empowered to make laws "for the better regulating and ordering the company and manufacture, and things belonging thereto." And that this pious, charitable, and profitable design may be no longer frustrated, nor poor children, vagabonds, or idle persons continue to be burthensome to the country, "it is further ordained that in each parish one or more persons be appointed at the charge of the heritors, for instructing the poor children vagabonds and other idlers, to fine and

Poor children and others to be instructed in spinning, &c.

mix wool, spin worsted, and knit stockings." And for the more speedy perfecting of this laudable design and policy, "now prosecuted by his Majesty in his prudence and condescending care for the meanest of his subjects," it is also ordained that the heritors of shires convened for the purpose, shall elect some of their body in each parish to see this present Act made effectual, and persons appointed for instructing the children and others. "And that manufactures may be promoted, and for the encouragement of skilful artisans to come from abroad for training up the persons aforesaid, and working for the use of the said companies," it is further declared, "that all such as shall be brought home and employed for the said companies shall be free to set up and work in burgh and landward where the companies shall think fit, without paying anything whatsoever, and shall be free of taxes, public burthens, or exactions during their life-time."

Dearth of capital and lack of employment.

Scotland was at this time suffering from a dearth of capital and lack of employment, and its manufacturing resources were of the lowest order. To promote the formation of companies, with the view of securing wiser counsels and larger capitals for manufacturing purposes, and thus to extend the means of profitable occupation, was therefore highly judicious, as was likewise the encouraging of foreign artisans to settle. With respect to the provisions for the instruction and putting to work of poor children and idle persons, these are seemingly free from material objection, and were perhaps on the whole the best which could then be devised. They certainly bear evidence of a desire for improving the condition of the people, by substituting employment for idleness and vagabondism. Instruction was the first step in this substitution, and the agency of the commercial incorporations the second—both in a certain degree forced and artificial, but under the circumstances both may have been useful, or even necessary for effecting the proposed object. There is one provision however of which the same cannot be said—that namely, which restrains all other persons from exporting any of the articles enumerated, "except they be free and of one of the companies aforesaid;" but this prohibition was in accordance with the spirit and limited intelligence of the age.

1661. Charles II., cap. 38. July 9, No. 338.

In the same year, and shortly after the preceding Act, another was passed, numbered *338* in the margin, and having more immediate reference to the relief of the poor. It bears the title of 'Commission and Instructions to the Justices and Constables,' and is in fact little more than an extension and a more complete and elaborate exposition of what was intended by the Act of James the Sixth in 1617.[b] It commences by declaring that the king, "taking into his royal consideration how much the appointing of justices and constables within all the shires of the kingdom, did contribute to the peace quiet and good government thereof, and to the speedy and impartial execution of law and justice to all persons subjected to their jurisdiction,"—therefore for the furtherance of these ends in future, and with the advice and consent of parliament, it is ordained that in all time coming there shall be justices of peace appointed within each several shire, to be nominated from time to time by his Majesty and his successors, with power to administer justice and put the laws in execution, according to the instructions contained in the present Act.

Justices of peace to be appointed.

The oaths of allegiance and fidelity to be taken are then prescribed. The justices are directed to meet and convene together quarterly, and to administer justice to the people in all matters within

The duties of justices of peace.

---

[b] Ante, p. 37.

their jurisdiction. They are to elect or continue constables and other officers, with powers and duties as prescribed by the Act of James the Sixth,[c] and to dispose of the fines or mulcts in payment of their salaries —the remainder to be employed as they shall find expedient. They are empowered to proceed upon all rioters and breakers of the peace, "under the degree of noblemen, prelates, counsellors, and senators of the college of justice," concerning whom they are to "use all their power for preventing and staying the riots," commanding the parties to cease and to find caution for keeping the peace, and for appearing before his Majesty's council. They are to give order for mending highways, to put the laws in force against destroyers of plantations, &c., to inform the council of forestallers and regraters of markets, and also of the contraveners of the law anent maltmakers, that proceedings may be taken with them; and "they are to cause sufficient single and double ale to be brewed in every shire." They are to prescribe order in the country for its governance in time of plague, and to punish the disobeyers of such order. They are to rate every parish for a weekly proportion, not exceeding five shillings Scots, nor less than one shilling, for the maintenance of poor prisoners. The presence of three justices is necessary to constitute a quorum, and they are to be paid for attendance and fined for non-attendance, as is provided in the Act of James the Sixth.[c] At their quarter-sessions in August and February, they are "to appoint the ordinary hire and wages of labourers workmen and servants, and whoever shall refuse to serve upon the price set down by them, shall be imprisoned and further punished at their discretion." They may also compel the master to pay the wages appointed. They are to put the law in execution against persons

---

[c] Ante, p. 37.

guilty of the sin of drunkenness, or who shall profane the Lord's Day, or curse and profanely swear, "or who shall be mockers or reproachers of piety or the exercise thereof."

The foregoing are the duties required to be performed by the justices of peace in discharge of their ordinary functions. Their duties with respect to the poor require more particular notice, and to these we will now advert.

After directing the laws to be put into full and due execution against wilful beggars, idle vagabonds, &c., in the precise terms of the Act of James the Sixth,[d] it is now ordered that the justices shall yearly, on the 1st of December and the 1st of June, "make up a list of the poor in every parish within burgh or land, into which number there shall no persons be received who are in any way able to gain their own living. And to the end that these poor may be no longer necessitated to seek their living with such hardship and difficulties by scandalous vaging (wandering), as hitherto they have been in use of," the justices are to appoint two or more persons of good fame and quality in every parish, to be overseers for the poor, "and shall authorise the said overseers to make due trial and examination of the condition and number of such poor aged, sick, lame, and impotent inhabitants of the said parish, who (of themselves) have not to maintain them, nor are able to work for their living, as also orphans and other poor children within the said parish who are left destitute of all help." And the said overseers are to "list and enrol all such persons, and to provide them such a convenient house for their dwelling, either apart or together, as they shall judge requisite; and upon consideration had of what the necessary maintenance will extend to weekly, the over-

Overseers of the poor to be appointed in every parish.

---

[d] Ante, p. 37.

seers are to call for the collections of the said parish, or other sums appointed for the maintenance of the poor thereof, which they are to dispense proportionably to the several poor people as they shall find their necessities to require." The overseers are moreover "to take due trial of the good behaviour and carriage of the poor persons so listed and enrolled; and if any of them being so provided shall go abroad to beg, or otherwise miscarry themselves, or shall refuse, being able to work, any manner of work that they are able to perform"—in all such cases the overseers are to acquaint the justices therewith, "who shall appoint such punishments for the first fault as in their judgments they shall find requisite; and if any shall continue in such miscarriages, they are to be holden and reputed as vagabonds, and so to be proceeded against according to law in that case provided."

And to the end that there may be an exact performance of these regulations, the justices are to call the overseers before them once in every six months, or oftener if they deem it expedient, to give an account upon oath of the moneys received and expended by them, and to produce the rolls of the said poor; "and after due consideration of the charge, together with the discharge thereof, to approve, allow, or disallow the same, as they shall find to be just;" and they are likewise to examine how the overseers have discharged their trust.

The overseers to account half-yearly.

In case any of the overseers nominated as aforesaid shall refuse to accept the office, or having accepted shall be found negligent therein, or shall refuse or delay to account when required, or to deliver the money resting in their hands at the end of the year to such new overseers as shall be appointed—"in all such cases the offenders shall incur the penalty of twenty pounds Scots to the use of the poor, and suffer such further censure as the justices at quarter sessions, upon consideration of their fault, shall see meet to impose."

Neither the presbytery nor the kirk session are noticed in this Act, whence it would seem that the powers conferred on these bodies in regard to the poor by the Acts of James VI. in 1597 and 1600 [d] had in the period of civil strife which intervened fallen into disuse; and we find that the duties which were required of them are now to be exercised under the supervision of the justices of peace, by overseers whom the justices are to appoint in every parish throughout the country, and who are to be accountable to the justices for the manner in which the duty is performed. The appointment of overseers directed by the present Act is nearly the same as is prescribed by the Act of 1579, and is moreover very similar to the provisions in this respect of the 14*th and* 39*th of Elizabeth.*[e] The duties are likewise the same, and the general scope and bearing of the Acts are so nearly identical, that it seems impossible to doubt that the English Acts were the model on which the Scottish Acts were framed—a natural consequence of the approximation of the two countries, not in government only but in social organisation, and the habits of the people.

It has been questioned, and that by a high authority,[f] whether the powers conferred upon justices of peace under this Act, were ever exercised by them in appointing overseers, and in regard to making up lists of the poor, and gathering and distributing collections. The Act itself is however declared to be "very important, as pointing out more clearly than perhaps any other the understanding of the legislature as to the class of persons who, under the statute of 1579, were entitled to parochial relief," and who are said to be the

---

[d] Ante, pp. 31 and 33.

[e] See 'History of the English Poor Law,' vol. i. pp. 162 and 183.

[f] See Dunlop's 'Law of Scotland regarding the Poor,' 1854, p. 16.

aged sick infirm and impotent poor alone, excluding all persons "who are in any way able to gain their own living." Hence it has always been inferred that these provisions were intended only for the ordinary or regular poor, and that there is no provision whatever for the temporary or casual poor, who when not suffering from sickness or infirmity, are regarded as being able to gain their own living in some way. The poor are thus separated into two classes, the "regular" or disabled, and the "casual" or able-bodied; and this distinction has been upheld in the courts of law, and maintained in practice throughout the country. The first are relieved at the public charge, according to their necessities; the last are not so relieved, whatever their necessities may be. They are in fact subjected to punishment on the ground of their being idle and "vaiging," although their efforts to find employment may have been earnest and unceasing.

Distinction between regular and casual poor.

The distinction between ability and disability, is necessarily one of circumstance and degree. A man may be able to do some things, and not able to do others—he may be able one day or one week, and be unable in the next—he may be able in the morning, but if left without sustenance through the day, he may be disabled in the evening. The question of ability must therefore be in many instances one of extreme difficulty to determine, yet on its prompt determination would depend an indigent person's being relieved or not, under the provisions of the Scottish Poor Law. It may likewise be remarked, that the interpretation which has been put upon the present Act, and that of 1579, as to the limiting of relief to the aged infirm and impotent, that is to the "regular" poor, seems somewhat at variance with the provision we find in both the Acts for punishing such of this class of poor as "being able to work, shall refuse any

Difficulty of judging of ability and disability.

manner of work that they are able to perform." It is clear that these could only have been partially disabled, and in strictness might not have been entitled to any relief; and this again raises the question as to the amount of disablement required for entitling an individual of whose actual distress there can be no question, to admission into the list of "regular poor," or in other words, to relief of any kind.

In a popular sense, and under ordinary circumstances, it may in the majority of cases be pretty confidently predicated who are disabled, and who are not; but instances of doubt and uncertainty on this point will often occur, even to the most practised observer, and this independently of the nicer question as to the precise extent or degree of disability. To make the affording of relief to depend solely upon this in many cases extremely doubtful point, must therefore have been the cause of great hardship to many persons, and very probably have driven them to the commission of crime for relief of their necessities—evils which a timely and temporary assistance might have obviated. At the same time however, it cannot be denied that an over readiness to afford relief, and too great a facility in obtaining it, whether by the able or the partially disabled, are productive of very serious evils, by leading persons to depend on the sources of such relief, instead of relying upon their own exertions and forethought in struggling with the various contingencies of life. Between these poles, the healthy and temperate zone of statutory relief seems to lie, care being taken that its administration shall be so regulated as not to invite applicants except in cases of actual necessity, and then as far as possible squaring the aid afforded with the extent of such necessity; and on the other hand taking care that relief shall not be so far restricted as indirectly to cause, or be regarded in any way as an excuse for, the commission of crime. Within these limits, statutory

Over-facility of relief an evil.

relief is not only a benefit and a blessing to the poor, but it is also a safeguard to the opulent, neither life nor property being secure amid the pressure of extreme and unmitigated want. The laws enacted by the Scottish legislature did not conform to this principle. They were chiefly directed against vagrancy, the relief of the necessitous poor being an incidental rather than a primary object; and in this consists the difference between them and the laws of England.

Two years after the preceding statute another was passed, entitled 'An Act concerning Beggars and Vagabonds,' and commencing with the usual declaration, that "our sovereign lord, considering the many laudable Acts made for relief of the poor, and for constraining of beggars vagabonds and idle persons to take themselves to lawful callings, that they might not be burthensome and disgraceful to the kingdom"—(the Acts of 1579, 1597, and 1617[g] are then recited)—"and his Majesty considering that the chief cause whereby the aforesaid Acts have proven ineffectual, and that vagabonds and idle persons do yet so much abound, hath been that there were few or no common works then erected in the kingdom, which might take and employ the said idle persons in their service; and that now, by his Majesty's princely care, common works for manufactures of divers sorts are setting up"—therefore, with the advice and consent of parliament, the aforesaid Acts are confirmed, with the following additions—

1663. Charles II., cap. 16. Sept. 25, No. 52.

It is declared to be lawful for all persons or societies who have or who shall set up any manufactories within the kingdom, "to seize upon and apprehend the persons of any vagabonds who shall be found begging, or who being masterless and out of service have not wherewith to maintain them-

Beggars and vagabonds may be seized and compelled to work.

---

[g] Ante, pp. 16, 31, and 37.

selves by their own means or work, and to employ them for their service as they shall see fit, the same being done with the advice of the magistrates of the place where they are so seized upon." It is further ordained that the parishes where such vagabonds or idle persons were born, or where they have resided haunted or most resorted to "for the space of *three years* immediately preceding their being so apprehended, and who thereby are relieved of the burthen of them," shall pay to the persons or societies which employ them two shillings Scots per diem [h] for the first year, and one shilling Scots per diem for the next three years; and the heritors of each parish assembled upon public notice at the parish kirk on a Sunday, "at the dissolving of the church from the first sermon, are to make up a stent-roll of the poor so employed, and at the rates aforesaid, one half of which is to be paid by the heritors, and the other half by the tenants and possessors, according to their means and substance;" and on failure of such payment, the persons or societies so employing the poor are empowered to make up such stent-roll, and charge the heritors accordingly, and enforce payment by letters of horning. The poor so employed are to continue in the service of the employers, "and under their direction and correction," not only during the space the parishes are to pay for their maintenance, but are also to serve for seven years thereafter for their meat and clothing—that is for eleven years altogether; and all sheriffs stewards bailies magistrates of boroughs and justices of peace and their constables, are charged to be assisting in apprehending the said vagabonds, and in bringing them back to their service.

The employer to be paid by the parish.

This Act seems to have been framed with the view of giving increased facilities to the Act of 1661,[i] by enabling the commercial companies and associations

---

[h] That is, twopence sterling per day.

[i] Ante, p. 54.

which that Act authorises, to seize and compel to labour for their benefit, all beggars vagabonds and masterless persons; and this not only without paying for their labour, but being paid during three years for employing them by the parishes to which they belong. Encouragement could hardly be carried further. The companies were exempted from all duties of import and export, and protected from native competitors by the previous Act; and by the present Act they are empowered to compel the service of all persons out of employment and without means or work, and are to be paid for so doing during the first four years, and are to pay nothing during another seven beyond supplying food and clothing—in short, holding the persons so employed in a state of actual slavery.

The encouragement given to manufacturing industry by the Act of 1661 was, with one exception, of a legitimate character, and was on the whole calculated to produce beneficial results. The same cannot be said of the present Act, although it was no doubt intended to aid the former; for setting aside the objection to forcibly depriving a man of his liberty, and compelling him to labour in a state of bondage for eleven years, how could it be expected that labour performed under such circumstances would ever be effective? Improvement would be out of the question, and the result would inevitably be inferiority of production, enhancement of price, the waste of capital, and in the end general insolvency. Whether this Act was ever carried into effect, and if so to what extent, we have no means of knowing with certainty; but it most probably terminated in a few vain and futile attempts by projectors, disappointing to them, and inflicting a certain amount of hardship and injury upon the poor persons whom it subjected to their control.

The desire for establishing public manufactories and enforcing employment which appears in the present

Act, and also in that of 1661, may not unlikely have originated in, or been strengthened by, Sir Matthew Hale's 'Discourse touching provision for the Poor;' [k] and the enactment compelling parishes to pay manufacturers for employing poor persons, on the ground that the parishes were thereby relieved from the charge of otherwise supporting them, may possibly have arisen from the English Act of Settlement passed in the preceding year,[m] by which parochial chargeability in its widest acceptation is recognised and established.

Residence reduced from seven to three years.

The term of residence, or "most resort," necessary for constituting a claim on any parish, is now reduced from *seven* years, as named in the Act of 1579, to *three* years—a more readily ascertained period no doubt, but still leaving the question of liability open to dispute and litigation, which would assuredly have arisen in Scotland, as a somewhat similar enactment soon occasioned in England, if the provisions of the present statute requiring parishes to pay for the employment of their poor had been extensively acted upon. I say of their poor, for it can hardly have escaped observation that the persons to be employed and paid for, are in some parts of the Act described as "beggars, vagabonds, and masterless persons," and in others as "the poor," whence it might fairly be inferred that the terms were meant to apply indifferently to either one or the other. But it has been held by the courts of law that the stent-roll prescribed and the assessment sanctioned by the present Act, apply only to the case of "vagabonds and idle persons employed by manufacturers," and have no reference to the "regular poor." [n] The Act of 1579 directs the charge for the relief of the poor to be assessed upon the whole of

---

[k] See 'History of the English Poor Law,' vol. i. p. 302.
[m] See ibid., p. 293.
[n] See Dunlop's 'Poor Law of Scotland,' p. 18, edition of 1854.

the inhabitants, according to the estimation of their substance. The present Act directs it to be divided equally between the heritors[o] and the tenants, and this has continued to be the law in Scotland ever since. Three years' residence or sojourn in a parish, likewise continued to be the term for establishing a right of settlement and chargeability until a recent period; so that in these respects this Act of 1663 remained in force, although in all others it soon ceased to be operative, if indeed it was ever in operation at all.

An interval of nine years elapsed before legislation with regard to the poor was again resorted to, and then, all former provisions having apparently failed, an 'Act for establishing Correction Houses for idle Beggars and Vagabonds' was passed, commencing with the declaration that, "the king's Majesty, considering the many good laws made by himself and his royal predecessors for suppressing vagabonds beggars and idle persons, who are a great burthen and reproach to the kingdom, and that a numerous brood of such persons are daily increasing, who if they were set to work and bred to trades and callings, might not only cease to be a burthen, but might in a short time and upon far less expense become useful and profitable to the whole kingdom;" and further considering "that these good laws have been frustrated in consequence of there being no place provided wherein such poor people might be set to work, nor persons appointed to have the charge and oversight of them"—wherefore, with the advice and consent of parliament, it is ordained that the magistrates of the thirty-two principal burghs named in the Act shall, before Whitsunday of the next year, "provide correction-houses for receiving and entertaining of the beggars vagabonds and idle persons within

1672. Charles II., cap. 16. Sept. 4, No. 42.

Correction-houses to be provided.

[o] That is, the proprietors or owners of the property.

their burghs, and such as shall be sent to them out of the shires (which are also named), and that they appoint masters and overseers of the same, who may set these poor persons to work; and each house shall have a large close, sufficiently enclosed for keeping in the said poor people, that they may not be necessitated to be always within doors to the hurt or hazard of their health."

In case the correction-houses be not provided and in readiness at the time required, the magistrates of the burghs so neglecting are subjected to the penalty of five hundred marks Scots,[p] and a like sum quarterly until the houses are provided, to be paid to the commissioners of excise, who are empowered to enforce payment of the same by letters of horning and other execution against the defaulting magistrates, and to apply the amount towards building or purchasing houses for the above purpose. "And in the mean time, until the said houses be provided, the magistrates are required to dispose of the beggars and poor people who were either born within their respective burghs, or have haunted therein the last three years, in some convenient places, so that they may not go begging on the streets or at houses within the town." For enabling the burghs to bear the charge of these correction-houses, the contributions and allowances appointed by the Act of 1663[q] for maintaining the poor are to be applied to them, "whereby they shall have two shillings Scots per diem for each poor person that shall be sent to them, and entertained and bred by them for the first year, and twelve pennies Scots per diem for three years thereafter, together with the profit arising from their labour and work for seven years thereafter, which con-

Commissioners of excise to enforce penalty for not providing correction-houses.

---

[p] A mark or merk is 13*s*. 4*d*. Scots, equal to 13⅓*d*. English.

[q] Ante, p. 63.

tributions are to be paid by the parishes relieved of the said poor in manner contained in the said Act."

And in order that it may be known what poor persons are to be sent to the correction-houses, and who are to be kept and entertained by the contributions at the parish kirks, it is directed that the minister of each parish with some of the elders, or in case of vacancy of the kirk three or more of the elders, do make up an exact list of all the poor persons within their parish, with their age and condition, whether able or unable to work by reason of age infirmity or disease, where they were born, and in what parish they have most haunted during the last three years — intimation being always made to the heritors of the parish to be present, and see that the lists are rightly made up, and in order likewise that the heritors and occupiers of the land, who have to bear the burthen of maintaining such poor persons, may condescend (agree) upon such of them as through age or infirmity are not able to work, and appoint them places wherein to abide, that they may be supplied by the contributions at the parish kirk; and if the same be not sufficient to maintain them, that a badge or ticket may be given them, "to ask alms at the dwelling-houses of the inhabitants of their own parish, without the bounds of which they are not to beg, nor at all resort to kirks, markets, or other places of meeting, nor to marriages, baptisms, burials, or upon any other public occasion."

Lists of the poor to be made out.

Poor persons to be badged and licensed to beg.

It is likewise ordered that such of the said poor persons as are of age and capacity to work, shall be first offered to the heritors or inhabitants of each parish, "that if they will accept them to become their apprentices or servants, they may receive them upon their obligement to entertain and set to work the said poor persons, and to relieve the parish of them, for which cause they

The poor to be apprenticed or bound to serve heritors, &c.

shall have the benefit of their work until they attain the age of thirty years, conformably to the Act of James the Sixth[r] (1579); and the rest of such poor persons are to be sent to the correction-houses, "with clothing upon them to cover their nakedness," and a quarter's allowance is to be sent with them by their parish, and is thereafter to be paid quarterly in advance. The said commissioners of excise are also in each shire empowered to take an account quarterly of the performance of each parish in these respects, and in case of failure or neglect, to appoint other persons to make the said lists, and collect the said allowances; and the sheriffs, their officers, and mayors and constables, are required to be assisting in the same.

Vagabonds, &c., to be sent to the correction-houses and held to work.

In case the heritors shall find within their bounds any other vagabonds beggars or idle persons, not being in service nor having any visible means of maintenance, who were not born in the parish nor did formerly haunt within its bounds, they are empowered to seize upon all such and send them to the correction-houses, and to charge the magistrates or masters of the said houses to relieve them, without the advance of any allowance; but the magistrates or masters are notwithstanding empowered to charge the heritors of the parishes where these idle persons were born, or have most haunted the last three years, for the allowance of such of them as are not bred to work, and as to such of them as can work the benefit of their labour is to be taken in return for their meat. The masters of the correction-houses are charged to hold the inmates to such work as they find them most fit for, and in case of their disobedience the masters are empowered "to use all manner of severity and correction, by whipping or otherwise (except torture), and to detain them within the said correction-

[r] Ante, p. 16.

house or close thereof." And it is also provided, that in case any of the said poor persons "be suffered to escape to burthen the country of new," the magistrates are to relieve them again, without any allowance thereafter during the space of four years, under the pain of forty pounds Scots for each person so escaping. They are likewise empowered to receive disobedient servants, and to put them to work, and to correct them according to their demerits.

It is moreover declared to be lawful for "coal-masters, saltmasters, and others who have manufactories, to seize upon any vagabonds or beggars wherever they can find them, and to put them to work in their coal-hewghs or other manufactories, and to have the same power of correcting them, and the benefit of their work, as the masters of the correction-houses." And finally, the execution of the Act is committed to the privy council, with power to appoint all means and ways for making the same effectual; and the commissioners of excise in the several shires are to make returns to the privy council twice a year of the diligence observed in its execution, under penalty of forty pounds Scots.

Coalmasters, &c., may seize vagabonds and put them to work.

The enforced employment and species of slavery sanctioned by the Act of 1663 having failed, and a "numerous brood" of vagabonds and beggars continuing daily to increase, the king and parliament determined, seemingly as a last resource, upon establishing "correction-houses" for the reception and setting to work of such persons, taking the English Act, 7*th James* 1*st*, *cap.* 4,[8] as a model. The present Act is accordingly framed for the most part in accordance with that statute, differing only in such respects as the different circumstances of the two countries at the time seemed to render necessary. The powers given to the

[8] See 'History of the English Poor Law,' vol. i. p. 233.

magistrates of burghs appear to be sufficient, as do also the subordinate details for the government and upholding of the correction-houses, and for enforcing the provisions of the Act, first through the agency of the commissioners of excise (now first noticed in connexion with the Poor Law), and lastly by the privy council, specially empowered for that purpose.

The failure of manufacturing societies to seize and employ beggars and idle vagabonds under authority of the Act of 1663, is sufficiently intelligible; and the exercise of the powers which were conferred upon such associations, when the same were transferred to the magistrates of burghs by the present Act, although free from some of the previous objections, does not hold out much greater promise of success. The correction-houses could no doubt be provided with less difficulty and greater certainty than the manufactories, and would be less dependent upon the profits of the labour performed within them; but the labour would still be forced and artificial, adding in no way to the general wealth and productive powers of the country. We accordingly find that, "notwithstanding the penalties to which the burghers were subjected in the event of non-compliance with the provisions of this statute, they appear to have evaded performance so completely, that there does not exist in Scotland a single 'correction-house' applied to the purposes set forth in the Act"[t]—thus affording another instance of the futility of legislation when at variance with the wants and wishes of a community.

Correction-houses.

The power of correcting "disobedient servants," and the authorising coalmasters and saltmasters to seize vagabonds or beggars wherever they can find them, are new powers conferred by the present Act, and are obviously liable to be

Vagabonds and beggars may be seized, wherever found.

[t] See Dunlop, on the 'Poor Law of Scotland,' 1854, p. 20.

greatly abused. The latter is an extension of the power given to manufacturers by the Act of 1663, of which it may also be said to be an aggravation, inasmuch as the labour in coal-mines and salt-works is of a ruder and harder kind than that which is usually carried on in factories. The only limitation of punishment for disobedience or neglect of work is, that it must stop short of torture—up to which point whipping, &c., may be carried at the discretion of the master.

The ordinary or regular poor.

With respect to the infirm and impotent, or the "regular poor," as they are usually termed, the provisions of this Act are open to little objection. Lists of these are to be made out by the kirk session conjointly with the heritors, who are now for the first time empowered to take part in making out the lists and the other proceedings, because, as it is said, that "they and the occupiers have to bear the burthen." They are also to have a voice in assigning dwelling-places to such poor persons, wherein they may be maintained out of the contributions at the parish kirk; and if these should not prove sufficient, the heritors and kirk session are then to give them a ticket or badge with permission to beg from the inhabitants of the parish, but not beyond its limits. It has been surmised, from the possible insufficiency of contributions here noticed, that assessments for support of the poor under the Act of 1579 had not yet become general, and this was very likely to have been the case—it certainly was so in England long after the levying of assessments for the purpose had been required by law; and the backwardness in either case cannot be wondered at, the charge being a new one, and opposed to the notions and previous habits of the people. The badging of the poor now permitted, in proof of their being allowed to beg, differs little from what was practised in England under the *5th of Elizabeth*, *cap*. 3, except that it was there general, whilst here it is restricted to the parish.[u]

We find in these provisions another change made in the mode of dealing with the aged and infirm, or "regular poor." By the Act of 1579 their relief was committed exclusively to the magistrates. The Act of 1597 transferred it to the kirk session, to which the presbytery was afterwards added by the Act of 1600; and it thus remained until 1661, when the justices of peace were directed twice every year to make out lists of the poor, and to appoint overseers in each parish who were to make collections and distribute needful relief. By the present Act we find the duty of making out lists of the poor and administering relief again intrusted to the kirk session, with the assistance of the heritors, who are moreover empowered to grant permission to the poor to beg within their respective parishes when the collections are insufficient. These changes, like the changes which took place with respect to the poor in England, are indications that the previous legislation had proved defective, and required amendment. The same may be said of the various changes which, as we have seen, were made with regard to the vagrant classes; but as vagrancy in every shape was punishable as a crime, the power of the magistrates for its repression was always in force, whatever other provisions there might be respecting it. In the present Act, however, the powers conferred upon the newly created functionaries, the commissioners of excise, seem almost to supersede the authority of the magistrates.

This Act of 1672 must be regarded as of considerable importance, notwithstanding the little use made of the provision from which it takes its title, very few, if any, of the "correction-houses" having ever been established under it. The Act clearly points out the description of

---

[u] See 'History of the English Poor Law,' vol. i. p. 155.

persons for whom relief was chiefly intended, and it re-establishes the kirk sessions as dispensers of such relief, conjointly with the heritors—an arrangement that henceforward continued to be acted upon. The liability to furnish subsistence in return for the labour of idle vagabonds, &c. (that is for all unemployed persons), which is admitted by the tenour of the present and by several of the preceding Acts, although less binding and imperative than in the case of the aged and infirm poor, yet appears sufficiently indicated to warrant its being taken as amounting to a claim, and it is difficult to reconcile such indications with the assertion that in Scotland all claim for relief at the public charge is limited to the infirm and impotent poor. Whatever may have been the strictly legal limitation in this respect however, the practice, as explained by Dr. Robert Burns of Paisley, in his 'Historical Dissertation,' published in 1819, has not been opposed to the claim, although in the distribution of relief a clear and obvious distinction is, he says, made "between the *ordinary* poor, who are altogether incompetent at any time or in any circumstances to earn by their own exertions alone a subsistence for themselves, and the extraordinary or *occasional* poor, who by reason of temporary or local circumstances have been reduced to unlooked-for distress. In favour of the former class the provision is permanent. In regard to the latter class, such partial and temporary relief is given as may enable the unfortunate objects of it to regain the place they may have lost, and thus prevent them from becoming permanently a burthen on the public."

The occasional or irregular poor.

Dr. Burns of Paisley.

The death of Charles the Second in 1685, and the abdication of his brother and successor, James the Second, in 1688, followed by the accession of William and Mary in 1689, and (after Mary's death in 1694) the reign of William singly until 1702, when he was succeeded by Queen Anne, are historical incidents requiring to be here noticed only as giving a designation to the legislative enactments of the respective periods. For further mention of these events in connexion with our general subject, the reader is referred to the 'History of the English Poor Law.'

Between the passing of the Act of 1672, just commented on, and the Act of Union in 1707, there were several enactments of the Scottish parliament deserving of notice, although not immediately or exclusively appertaining to the poor. But it is thought better to carry on the narrative of Poor Law proceedings in an unbroken series, down to the Union of the two legislatures, after which the Acts referred to may be more conveniently brought under examination.

1695. William III., cap. 43. July 17, No. 74.

The first in the series of the Poor Law enactments to be noticed, is that of William the Third in 1695, entitled, an 'Act for reviving the Acts of Council anent the Poor.' It is very short, and merely declares that "our sovereign lord, with the advice and consent of the estates of parliament, doth hereby ratify, approve, and revive all Acts of Parliament, and Acts and Proclamations of Council, for maintaining the poor and repressing of beggars, and ordains them to be put to vigorous execution in all points." And it further empowers the privy council to take means for making the said Acts and Proclamations effectual, "conform to the true design thereof."

1696. William III., cap. 29. October 9,

In the year following another 'Act for the better providing the Poor and repressing of Beggars' was passed, as before ratifying approving and reviving all Acts and Proclamations for maintaining the poor and repressing beggars, and ordaining them to be put into full and vigorous execution. The Act further empowers the lords of the privy council, if they shall think needful, "to grant a commission to a certain number of persons to be supervisors and inspectors of the poor, either in particular shires and burghs, or over the kingdom, and to make and emit such acts and constitutions, not inconsistent with the standing laws, as shall be thought necessary for the more effectual employing and maintaining of the poor, and freeing the country of vagabonds and idle beggars;" which acts and constitutions of the privy council are to have the effect and force of law, until the next session of parliament. The king is likewise recommended "to cause visit all hospitals, and their rents and revenues, with their rights and foundations," to the end that whatever property or revenues belonging to them, and any way misappropriated, may be duly applied according to their foundations; as also to inquire after all mortifications, that they may be applied in conformity with the will of the mortifiers.

At the end of two years another 'Act anent the Poor' was passed, having the usual preamble. After referring to the Act of 1579, and the other Acts of James's reign for punishing masterful beggars, &c., it recites those portions of the Act of 1617, *No. 10*,[x] which provide for the putting out of poor children to service, and quotes the Act of 1663,[y] empowering the masters of manufactories to seize and employ idle vagabonds, &c.—and the Act of 1672[y] for establishing correction-houses, and also the two Acts last above inserted—after which it refers to the proclamations issued by the privy council, especially that of the 3rd of March immediately preceding, all of which acts and proclamations, with the alterations to be afterwards mentioned, are ordained "to be put into full and rigorous execution in all points." For the better and more effectual execution of the aforesaid acts and proclamations, the lords of the privy council are, as in the Act of 1696, empowered to appoint supervisors and

1698. William III. cap. 21. September 1, No. 40.

[x] Ante, page 37. [y] Ante, pp. 63 and 67.

inspectors of the poor, who are enjoined to cause the persons severally intrusted to do and perform their respective parts, and also to cause the burghs to build correction-houses in such order as they shall think fit. The privy council is likewise, as before, empowered "to make and emit such acts and constitutions, not inconsistent with the standing laws, as shall be thought necessary for the more sure employing and maintaining of the poor, and freeing the country of vagabonds and idle beggars;" and the same recommendation is again made with respect to hospitals, and their rights rents and foundations.

The procla-mations.

The proclamations adverted to and sanctioned in this and the preceding Act of 1696 are four. They were issued by the privy council in 1692, 1693, 1694 and 1698 respectively. The whole of this period, that is between 1692 and 1699, on account of the general failure of the crops, bears the designation of the "seven ill" or the "seven barren years."[z] The distress in England was very great, but in Scotland it was excessive, whole parishes having in some parts been nearly depopulated. The general distress caused an increase of mendicancy, and to mitigate the one, and as far as possible to prevent the other, the proclamations referred to were issued.

First procla-mation, August 1692.

The first is entitled a 'Proclamation of the Privy Council anent Beggars,' and is dated 11th August 1692. It refers in the first place to "the good laws which have been made for maintaining the poor, and relieving the lieges of the burthen of vagabonds"—in prosecution whereof the heritors ministers and elders of every parish are required to meet at their parish kirk, and there to make lists of all the poor within their parish, and ascertain the charge of entertaining them "according to their respective needs,"

[z] See 'History of the English Poor Law,' vol. i. p. 364.

one-half of which charge is to be borne by the heritors, and the other half by the householders of the parish. They are also to appoint two overseers to collect and distribute such maintenance, and likewise an officer to serve under the overseers for inbringing the said maintenance, and for "expelling stranger vagabonds from the parish;" and such of the poor as have not houses, the heritors are to provide with houses at the expense of the parish. In case any parish should fail in providing for its own poor, it is to pay the sum of 200*l.* Scots—one-third to the pursuer, and two-thirds to be applied to the maintenance of the poor of the parish, "and that monthly, as long as the parishioners fail in their duty." Mortifications are to be applied in like manner. The heritors and elders are to hold meetings in February and August of each year, "to consult and determine herein as shall be thought fit for every ensuing half-year, and to appoint overseers by the year or half-year as they shall conclude." All ministers are required to give information to the sheriff if any parish fails in performance of this Christian duty, and the sheriff is forthwith to summon the delinquents, "and fine them in double the quota which the minister shall attest to be wanting."

Heritors and elders to hold meetings in February and August.

If any of the poor are able to work, the heritors of the parish are required to put them to work according to their capacities, "furnishing them always with meat and clothes;" and if any child under the age of fifteen be found begging, any person who shall take him before the heritors ministers and elders, and engage to educate him to trade or work, "the said child shall be obliged to serve such person for meat and clothes, until he pass the thirtieth year of his age;" and all manufactories are declared to have the same privilege. Young persons above fifteen may voluntarily engage themselves upon like conditions. The masters are authorised to use correction as they

Poor persons, if able, are to be put to work.

judge expedient, life and torture excepted; but if the master shall exact inhuman or too rigid service, the sheriffs or the justices of peace, upon application of the servants, are to judge in the case.

All beggars are strictly commanded to repair to their several parishes, and to present themselves to the heritors and elders, that their names may be listed, and that they may be lodged and entertained accordingly. If found begging without the bounds of their parish after a certain date, they are to be seized as vagabonds, imprisoned, and fed on bread and water for a month; and if found vaguing a second time, they are to be marked with a hot iron on the face. All lieges are charged to apprehend such beggars as they find vaguing about after the time specified, and carry them to the principal heritor of the parish if it be in landward, and to one of the bailies in towns, who shall examine the beggar as to the parish where he was born, and shall direct him forthwith to the nearest parish that lies in the road to such parish, and deliver him to the nearest heritor that lies in that highway in the next parish; and so from parish to parish in the same road, until he arrive at the parish of his nativity, where he is to be listed and entertained among the poor. And whosoever after the time specified shall give alms to a beggar out of his own parish, and shall not seize him in order to his transportation as above said, is to be fined twenty shillings Scots, to be uplifted by the overseers, and applied to the use of the poor of the parish; and if the heritor to whom the beggar is brought fail in his duty of so sending him, he is to be fined twenty pounds Scots, to be applied in like manner.

Beggars to be apprehended and sent to their parish.

The Act of 1672[a] is then referred to, by which correction-houses are appointed to be erected in certain burghs for employing the poor, but

Correction-houses to be provided.

---

[a] Ante, p. 67.

which, it is said, have hitherto been too much neglected; and it is therefore directed that Edinburgh, Stirling, Dundee, Aberdeen, Inverness, Glasgow, Jedburgh, Dumfries, and Cupar in Fife, if they have not already, shall forthwith provide such houses, and receive such poor for work therein as shall be sent to them from any parish, in manner and on the conditions prescribed by that Act, and by the present proclamation, which is ordered to be openly published at the market cross in all the head burghs of the kingdom, "that none pretend ignorance."

Second proclamation, August 1693.

The second proclamation was issued on the 29th of August in the following year, and is headed the same as the one preceding. It commences by declaring that the intent of the former proclamation requiring all beggars forthwith to repair to their several parishes, hath been frustrated by the uncertainty of the parishes where the said beggars were respectively born, and also for want of suitable provision by the heritors and magistrates of the parishes where the said beggars have been born or had their last *seven* years' residence—wherefore it is strictly commanded that all beggars do immediately repair to the parishes where they were born, or if this be not certainly known, to the parish where they resided the last seven years, and there present themselves to the heritors and elders, "and where the parish is vacant and has no elders, to the heritors alone, who are required to make the provisions necessary for the said beggars, and to list their names among the poor of the parish, that they may be lodged and entertained accordingly." Persons found begging after a day named, are to be seized and imprisoned, &c., as is directed in the former proclamation.

Heritors and elders to make provision for the poor.

The magistrates of burghs are required to meet and stent themselves in conformity with the usage in laying on stents in the respective burghs, "and so may be most effectual to reach all the inhabitants." The heritors of vacant parishes are likewise to meet and stent themselves for maintenance of their poor, and appoint the ingathering uplifting and applying of the same, in the same manner as the heritors and elders are appointed in the former proclamation. The ministers are also in like manner required to inform the sheriff, if any parish or person shall fail in these respects. "And for preventing any question that may arise betwixt the heritors and kirk session, about the quota of the collections at the church doors and otherwise, to be paid to the heritors for the end aforesaid," it is determined that the same shall be one-half of the said collections, and the kirk session is to pay the same from time to time to the said heritors accordingly.

Half the church collections to be paid to the heritors and elders.

In the year following, another proclamation was issued "for putting former Acts and Proclamations anent Beggars in execution." The preamble declares that "many good laws have been made for maintaining the poor and relieving the lieges from vagabonds, in prosecution whereof several proclamations have been emitted by the Privy Council for the better putting the said laws in execution, notwithstanding which due obedience hath not been hitherto given to the same, so that the poor are not duly provided for in many places, nor the vagabonds restrained"—wherefore the ministers, heritors, elders, and householders of every parish, are respectively commanded to follow forth and obey the laws in these respects; and the sheriffs and their deputies, the justices of the peace, and the magistrates of burghs, are further commanded, within their several jurisdictions, "to take trial how far and in what manner the said Acts of parliament and proclamations have been obeyed and put to execution; and where any have been neglected, or been defi-

Third proclamation, July 31, 1694.

Sheriffs and magistrates to "take trial" as to the execution of the law.

cient in what is required of them, to amerce and fine them therefore, in the manner specified." If any difficulty should arise through what cause or occasion soever, not provided for by the said laws and proclamations, the same is to be represented to the privy council, " that such order may be given thereanent as may bring this good work of relieving the poor and restraining vagabonds to the desired issue"—for the better effecting of which, a committee of the lords of the privy council is appointed to receive any such representation, and likewise with power to call before them the sheriffs and other magistrates to whom the execution of the said Acts and proclamations is committed, and to examine and take trial of any negligence therein, and to report their opinion to a full council.

A committee of the privy council appointed.

The fourth and last " proclamation anent Beggars" was issued in 1698. It declares that " the many good laws for maintaining the poor, and suppression of beggars vagabonds and idle persons, have not hitherto taken effect, partly because there were no houses provided for them to reside in, and partly because the persons to whom the execution of these laws was committed have been negligent of their duty"—for remedy of which, it is ordained that the former proclamations be reprinted, and put in full and rigorous execution; and in order to make the said proclamations more effectual, so much of the Act of 1672[b] as relates to "correction houses" is revived, and they are ordered forthwith to be provided in the thirty-two burghs named in that Act, and the magistrates, with the advice of the presbytery, are to appoint masters and overseers for the same, to set the poor persons to work, " under the pain of 500 merks quarterly, until correction houses be provided." The

Fourth proclamation, March 3, 1698.

---

b Ante, p. 67.

sheriffs are likewise commanded to put the said Act in execution within their respective shires, and they are to give account of their diligence herein before the 1st of December following, under penalty of 500 merks for the use of the poor, and they are further "to be liable in 100*l.* weekly after the said day until they return an account of their diligence to the privy council, to be employed for the use aforesaid."

Sheriffs to see that correction houses are provided.

The several parishes within each shire and district are to send their poor to the magistrates of the towns where the correction houses are to be provided, against the 1st of November next; and in case the said houses be not ready to receive them on that day, the poor are to be maintained by the magistrates until the correction houses be provided, and that independently of the penalties imposed by the Act. "And because there may some questions arise in putting the said Acts in execution, for which there can be no general rule set down, in respect of the different conditions and circumstances of several places of the country," power is therefore given to the ministers and elders of each parish, with advice of the heritors assembled upon intimation for that purpose, "to decide and determine all questions that may arise in the respective parishes, in relation to the ordering and disposing of the poor, in so far as is not determined by the laws and Acts of parliament, and the former Acts of the privy council ratified by parliament."

Ministers and elders, with advice of heritors, to determine questions regarding the poor.

These proclamations were all confirmed and established as law by the Act of 1698.[c] It will be seen that they do not make any material change in the law itself, but are directed rather to supply certain deficiencies of detail, and to procure its being carried into operation with greater certainty and promptitude. This was no

---

[c] Ante, p. 77.

doubt necessary in the season of long continued dearth in which the proclamations were issued, when distress and privation were almost universal, and when the sufferings of the poorer classes must have been excessive. To mitigate these sufferings by providing at the common charge some speedy relief for the most destitute, was the main object of these proclamations. The necessity for relieving destitution had been recognised by previous statutes, but the means of obtaining or rather of administering relief were not so direct and efficient as the exigencies of the period called for, and the deficiency in this respect was therefore sought to be supplied. The chief change introduced by the proclamations was with regard to the heritors, or owners of property, on whom greater responsibility is thrown, as well as a larger portion of the charge. Much reliance appears to be still placed on "correction houses," although the little ground there was for such reliance is manifested by the fact of their never having been provided, notwithstanding the enactments to that effect in 1672 and 1698,[d] and the urgent directions and the penalties for noncompliance set forth in the 1st and 4th proclamations. The manner of removing beggars to the parish or place of their birth or accustomed residence prescribed in the 1st proclamation, is so nearly similar to what was a few years afterwards directed in England by the 11*th William* 3*rd*, *cap*. 18,[e] as to warrant the supposition of a common origin.

Object and effects of the proclamations.

The law in Scotland "anent the poor," may be said to have been settled by the Act of 1698, no change having been made between that and the Act of Union in 1707, and for a long period afterwards.

On a review of what has been cited in the preceding

---

[d] Ante, pp. 67 and 77.

[e] See 'History of the English Poor Law,' vol. i. p. 366.

pages, it will appear that the operative portions of the law are mainly derived from the Acts of 1579, 1597, 1672, the first proclamation in 1692, and the Act of 1698. The general provisions of these Acts devolved the relief of the poor in the several parishes upon the heritors and the kirk session, who were authorised to tax and stent the inhabitants, as well as to apply the church collections, mortifications, and other incomings for that purpose. The taxing is to be equally apportioned between the heritors and the householders of the parish, and a general power of supervision is given to the sheriffs, justices of peace, and magistrates of burghs. The persons to whom relief is to be afforded are of two classes—*first*, the aged infirm and impotent poor, to whom a right of maintenance and needful shelter and support is freely given; and *secondly*, the idle vagrant and mendicant poor, with respect to whom relief is to be coupled with employment, and in certain cases with punishment. They are not permitted to be idle, or to vaig or beg, but are to be compelled to labour. Were they permitted to wander about and beg, they might possibly obtain a living in that way; but as they are prohibited from so doing, and forced to work, the affording them the means of living in return seems to follow as a natural corollary, if not as an absolute right. The correction houses appear to have been considered, both by the Scottish legislature and the privy council, as likely to afford the least objectionable means of employing such persons, and indeed of all who were without employment, and who, whether on that account or any other, were found in a state of idleness; and hence, we may presume, the urgency with which it was endeavoured to enforce the provision of such establishments.

Summary of preceding enactments.

Supposing "correction houses" to have been provided, the degree of their usefulness, or whether useful at all, would of course depend on their management, and the manner in which they were applied. If used as places of confinement, to which vagrants might be sent and subjected to labour by way of punishment, there would be no more objection to them than to any other mode of imprisonment. If used for manufacturing purposes, and with the view of providing remunerative employment at the public charge, it is needless to say that they would fail of their object, and in the end be productive of evil. If used as a species of workhouse, and applied to test the actual destitution of the parties sent thither, as well as for relieving their necessities, they might prove beneficial; and that something of this kind was contemplated by the promoters of these intended institutions, may be gathered from the direction in the original Act of 1672, and which is repeated in the proclamation of 1698, "that each house shall have a large close, sufficiently enclosed for keeping in the said poor people, that they be not necessitated to be always within doors to the hurt or hazard of their health." As, however, the "correction houses" were never provided, we need not speculate further as to what might have been their effects.

The correction houses.

The kirk session of a parish in Scotland conjointly with the heritors, nearly assimilates to the old English vestry, and the functions of the two bodies with regard to the poor were likewise similar. Each was presided over by the minister of the parish, each had to decide upon the nature and amount of the relief in every case, and each also had to provide at the public charge the means for affording it. The kirk session was moreover, like the parish vestry, subjected to the supervision of a class of magistrates—in England to the justices of peace, in Scotland to the sheriffs and justices in landward parishes, and to the magistrates in burghs. This right of supervision as exercised

The kirk session compared with the parish vestry in England.

in England was productive of important consequences in regard to the expenditure for relief of the poor, the amount of which we have seen went on rapidly increasing from year to year, and the increase has been considered to have in a great degree arisen from the interference of the justices in questions of relief. Their right of interference had existed from an early period, and although restricted by *The 9th George 1st, cap.* 7[f] (1722), it was again largely extended by *The 55th George 3rd, cap.* 137[f] (1815), and continued to be exercised until the passing of the Poor Law Amendment Act in 1834, by which it was again restricted, and by which also justices were constituted ex-officio members of the boards of guardians. In Scotland the authority of the magistracy never extended beyond seeing that the laws were put in due execution—they had no power to interfere with the ordering of relief, which was exclusively vested in the heritors and kirk session; and to this, coupled with the determination strenuously adhered to of not admitting a right to be relieved on the part of any except the infirm and impotent poor, and the strict economy with which relief has been afforded to these, may be attributed the comparatively small amount of such relief in Scotland, as contrasted with that of England — a difference far greater than the actual state of the law in the two countries would seem to warrant or account for.

Settlement.

Settlement was in Scotland free from most of the complications by which it was encumbered in England—it there only depended on birth, or on a continuous although not necessarily a constant residence in a parish for seven years, as first enacted, a period which was afterwards reduced to three years, and then again extended to seven, by the second proclamation; but no one who did not beg or solicit alms was liable to be removed. In this respect the Scottish

[f] See 'History of the English Poor Law,' vol. ii. pp. 14 and 161.

law was always the same as what the English law was brought back to by *The 35th George 3rd, cap.* 101,[g] and had therefore not been productive of the same amount of evil which unquestionably ensued from removals in England: but it is nevertheless impossible to doubt, that in common with settlement of every kind where the power of removal is exercised, it must in many cases have caused great hardship, and that serious evils did practically ensue from the enforcement of the law.

The laws affecting the vagrant classes had in England from the time of *The 39th Elizabeth*[h] downwards, been kept distinct from the enactments regarding the poor, and were reduced into one statute,[i] known as the Vagrant Act in 1713. The case was different in Scotland. Vagabonds, "sorners," and masterful beggars, are included with the other poor in the Scottish Acts, although we do not find that the kirk session dealt with them in like manner. They in fact fell under the cognisance of the civil magistrate, and there must often have been great if not insuperable difficulty in distinguishing one class from the other—the indigent and more or less infirm poor from the vagabond—the employed and possibly industrious individual of one week, from the unemployed and therefore idle vagabond of the next. The line of demarcation between the two is continually changing, persons of one class to-day becoming merged in the other to-morrow. This difficulty of discrimination with regard to the poor exists in every state of society, but the condition of Scotland was calculated greatly to increase it, the vagabond classes being there exceedingly numerous. They were indeed so numerous and burthensome, as to lead Fletcher of Saltoun, whose

Vagabonds, &c.

---

[g] See 'History of the English Poor Law,' vol. ii. p. 118.
[h] Ibid. vol. i. p. 186.
[i] The 13th Anne, cap. 26. See 'History of the English Poor Law,' vol. i. p. 400.

liberality and patriotism have never been questioned, to advocate the subjecting of them to a species of slavery by way of remedy. But even this, he appeared to think would not be altogether effective, since the Highlands, being "possessed by a people who are all gentlemen only because they will not work, and who in everything are more contemptible than the vilest slaves, except that they always carry arms, because for the most part they live upon robbery, will always be an inexhaustible source of beggars." Wherefore he recommends their removal, and their place to be filled from other parts of the country; and further, "for example and terror," that "three or four hundred of the most notorious of those villains, which we call jockies, might be presented by the government to the state of Venice, to serve in their gallies against the common enemy of Christendom."[k]

According to the order of date, the Act of Union in 1707 would now be noticed; but there are a few Acts of the Scottish parliament, passed previous to 1698, the notice of which has been postponed, and which cannot be altogether omitted, as they throw considerable light upon the condition of the people and the general circumstances of the country.

1661. Charles II., cap. 19. June 12, No. 282.

The first of these Acts which I shall notice was passed in the first parliament of Charles the Second, and was entitled 'An Act against Swearing and excessive Drinking.' It recites that "our sovereign lord being desirous that all his subjects may lead a quiet and peaceable life in all godliness and honesty, and in order thereto having resolved to curb and suppress all sort of sin and wickedness, and especially the abominable and so much abounding sins of drunkenness and all manner of cursing and swear-

[k] See Andrew Fletcher's 'Second Discourse,' written in 1693, pp. 103 and 104 of the edition printed at Glasgow in 1749.

ing"—therefore it is enacted, that every person who shall blaspheme, swear, or curse, or who shall drink to excess, shall, if a nobleman, be fined twenty pounds Scots, if a baron twenty marks, if a gentleman heritor or burgess, ten marks, if a yeoman forty shillings, and if a servant twenty shillings; and if the offender be not able to pay the penalty, then to be exemplarily punished in his body according to the merit of his fault."[1]

Against drunkenness and swearing.

Eleven years afterwards another Act was passed confirming the above, and all other Acts "against cursing, swearing, drunkenness, fornication and uncleanness, profanation of the Lord's day, mocking or reproaching of religion and the exercise thereof;" and directing that the several penalties inflicted by the said Acts shall be exacted of the respective transgressors—for which purpose it is ordained, "that besides the exercise of church discipline, according to the laws and practice of the church," the lords of session, sheriffs, bailies, magistrates, and justices of peace, shall in the several parishes where they reside, "as shall be dilated to them by the kirk sessions," cause the several laws to be executed. Collectors are moreover to be appointed to levy the fines, to whom the kirk session and heritors may in each case assign such a portion thereof for his services as may be deemed right, and the remainder is to be applied to the use of the poor of the parish—one half to those in the "correction houses" for teaching them lawful trades, the other half to the aged and infirm poor appointed to be maintained by the contributions at the parish kirk.

1672. Charles II., cap. 18. Sept. 11, No. 58. Against profanation of the Lord's day &c.

The practices of the court little accorded with the spirit pervading these Acts, or with the elevated

[1] A shilling Scots is equal to 1*d.* English; a merk or mark Scots is 13*s.* 4*d.*, equal to 13⅓*d.* English; a pound Scots is equal to 20*d.* English.

although somewhat austere and rigid discipline of the Presbyterian church; and it is not improbable that the Acts may have been passed to mark the disapprobation of the clergy and better portion of the Scottish people, with regard to the lax and dissolute manners of the upper classes, on whom the example of the court and its satellites throughout Charles the Second's reign exercised a pernicious influence. Another 'Act against Prophaneness' was passed in 1690, confirming the previous statutes, and requiring them "to be put to exact and punctual execution;" but it does not contain any additional provisions, and requires no comment.

1662. Charles II., July 8, No. 17.

Against theft, robberies, and depredations.

An 'Act for suppressing of Theft, Robberies, and Depredations," was passed in 1662. It declares that notwithstanding the many laws made for suppressing these crimes, "yet some insolent persons have of late, and daily do, commit outrages, thefts, and robberies upon the persons and goods of divers his Majesty's faithful subjects, to the dishonour of religion, contempt of authority, and reproach of the nation." Wherefore in order to prevent such violences in future, "that so all his Majesty's good subjects may find the fruit of his happy restoration, in the safe protection of their persons and secure possession of their goods"—it is ordained, that whensoever any oppressions, hereships,[m] reiffs,[n] sornings,[o] thefts, robberies, or depredations shall be committed, the owner of the goods away taken is to give intimation thereof to the sheriff or his deputy, or to any justice of peace or constable, who is immediately, upon pain of being liable for restitution of the goods or payment of the value thereof, to "command and require all the fensible persons within the parish to go with them in pursuit of the said goods, and the waytakers thereof," which command the said persons are obliged

[m] Devastations. [n] Robberies with violence. [o] Obtrusions.

to obey under a like penalty. And in case the thieves and robbers shall pass through or rest in any other parish, the justices of peace, constables, heritors, wadsetters, and feuars are required, with their tenants and servants, and such as they can command, to make opposition and seize upon the goods and drivers thereof, and to restore the goods, and deliver or secure the waytakers, "that they may underly the law." If the depredators be so numerous and powerful that they cannot be stopped and mastered by the inhabitants of the said parish, then all the fensible inhabitants are to rise in arms and pursue them, requiring all the fensible persons in any other parish they pass through to join with them, that so the goods may be restored to the right owners, and the depredators punished according to law. It is further ordained, "that if the pursuer of the goods shall not be able after all his utmost endeavours, with concurrence aforesaid, to recover the said goods and apprehend the waytakers thereof, then the heritors, wadsetters, and feuars of the parish wherein the goods shall be found to have been disposed of or sparpalled,[p] shall be liable for the value according to their several interests;" and it is further ordained, that in case the parties whose goods are taken away, or those who are obliged to rise with them, shall happen to slay, hurt, or mutilate any of the waytakers thereof or their associates, they shall never be drawn into question for the same. And for the better suppressing of thefts robberies and depredations, the sheriffs and their deputes are strictly enjoined to put in execution the powers confided to them by the laws, for pursuing and apprehending robbers and thieves, with all other persons who have no certain residence nor known way of livelihood; and the inbringer of every robber and thief after he is outlawed and declared a fugitive, is to receive a reward of two hundred pounds Scots.

---

[p] Dispersed, scattered.

We here find proof of the depredations to which property was at that time subjected in Scotland. To raise the inhabitants of the plundered parish in pursuit of the depredators, and to require the inhabitants of other parishes to join in arresting them, was a natural remedy under the circumstances; but the necessity for having recourse to such a remedy shows the lawless character of the period, and the prevalence of illegal combinations for the purpose of plunder and devastation. These acts of violence were no doubt chiefly perpetrated by the Highland clans, in their raids upon the more industrious and orderly inhabitants of the Lowlands, as described by Fletcher of Saltoun; but they were not confined to them, similar violences being common in other parts of the country, arising often no doubt from party feuds, and aggravated by hereditary animosities.

1681. Charles II., Sept. 16, No. 103.

The masters of two sugar works established at Glasgow petitioned parliament in 1681, representing on behalf of themselves and their partners, "that they had employed a great part of their stocks and fortunes in setting up the said two works, which are now brought to that perfection that they are able and do sell the sugar at a third part cheaper than the same can be imported from abroad, by which many people are kept at work, and a great stock of money which used to be exported is kept within the kingdom"—and they therefore humbly supplicate that the said two sugar works may be declared manufactures, and enjoy all the privileges and immunities granted to manufactories by former Acts.[q] The supplication was favourably received by the king and the states of parliament, and after "report of the lords of articles thereanent," it is ordained that the petitioners and their successors shall enjoy all the privileges,

---

[q] See Acts of 1661 and 1663; ante, pp. 54 and 63.

freedoms, and immunities granted by the said Acts, and collectors are discharged from exacting any custom or excise or other public dues for any of the materials imported and used in or on any of the products of the said manufactures, for the space of nineteen years. Four years afterwards (in 1685) a similar favour was conferred upon the Greenland fishing, which is declared to be a manufactory, and exempt from duties of every kind—whereby it is supposed "vast sums of money will be kept within the kingdom, and by the export of oil and whalebone considerable sums of money will be brought into the kingdom." Like reasons were assigned for the encouragement given to the Greenland and Eastland trades by the 25*th Charles* 2*nd, cap.* 7,[r] in 1672. In the above instances, as in the case of that Act, it is impossible not to approve the solicitude manifested for extending the commercial resources of the country; although the mode in which this object was sought to be accomplished may be open to some objection.

The above enactments show that the pursuits of commercial industry had gotten to be appreciated by the Scottish legislature; and this is further proved by an Act passed eight years subsequently "for encouraging of foreign trade." It commences by declaring, that "our sovereign lord and lady the king and queen's Majesties, considering how much the improvement of trade concerns the wealth and welfare of the kingdom, and that nothing hath been found more effectual for the improving and enlarging thereof than the erecting and encouraging of companies, whereby the same may be carried on by undertakings to the remotest parts, which it is not possible for single persons to undergo"—wherefore, with the advice and consent of parliament, it is declared, "that merchants

1693. William and Mary, June 14, No. 50.

---

[r] See 'History of the English Poor Law,' vol. i. p. 323.

may contract and enter into societies and companies for carrying on trade to any kingdoms, countries, or parts of the world, not being at war with their Majesties; to which societies and companies, all powers rights and privileges as to their persons, rules, and orders are granted, that by the laws are given to companies allowed to be erected for manufactories"—and further, for their greater encouragement, their Majesties "upon the serious recommendation of the estates of parliament," promise to grant letters patent under the great seal, confirming the whole of the aforesaid powers and privileges, "with what other encouragements their Majesties shall judge needful." The Bank of England was established in the present year, and the East India Company was reconstituted[s]—events indicative of the enlightened interest taken by the government in promoting the general welfare, and of which the present Act affords another striking example.

1695. Bank of Scotland established.

Two years after the above, we find another instance of a like nature in the establishment of the Bank of Scotland, for which an Act was passed in 1695. It recites that our sovereign (William the Third),[t] "considering how useful a public bank may be in this kingdom, according to the custom of other kingdoms and states, and that the same can only be best set up and managed by persons in company, with a joint stock sufficiently endowed, and with the powers, authorities, and liberties necessary and usual in such cases, hath therefore, with the advice and consent of parliament, allowed a joint stock amounting to the sum of 1,200,000*l.*, to be raised by the company hereby established, for carrying on and managing a public bank." Twelve persons are then named, in whose favour the Act was immediately passed, five of them

---

[s] See 'History of the English Poor Law,' vol. i. p. 357.

[t] Queen Mary died at the end of December in the preceding year.

being described as resident in Edinburgh, and seven in London;[u] and they are authorised to receive subscriptions, "and all and every the persons subscribing and paying into the said stock as aforesaid, are declared to be one body corporate and politic, by the name of *The Governor and Company of the Bank of Scotland*, under which name they shall have perpetual succession."

Infanticide.

An 'Act anent murdering of Children' was passed in 1690. (July 19th No. 50.) It declares that the king and queen, "considering the frequent murders that have or may be committed upon innocent infants, whose mothers do conceal their being with child, and do not call for necessary assistance in the birth, whereby the new-born child may be easily stifled, or being left exposed in the condition it came into the world it must quickly perish"—for preventing which, it is with the advice and consent of parliament ordained, "that if any woman shall conceal her being with child during the whole space, and shall not call for and make use of help and assistance in the birth, the child being found dead or missing, the mother shall be holden and reputed the murderer of her own child," and is to be proceeded against accordingly. The object of this Act is the same as that of *James 1st, cap.* 27, in 1623;[x] but it aims at effecting the object with greater certainty, by declaring that the concealment of being with child, and not calling for assistance, shall in case of the child's being dead or missing subject the mother to capital punishment. The legal penalty for this most unnatural crime could not be carried further, and its entire prevention can perhaps only be hoped for through the

---

[u] One of these last is a *Mr. Thomas Coutis*—it is presumed Thomas Coutts, a name afterwards of great eminence in the banking world. The firm of Coutts and Co. has continued to be the London agents of the Bank of Scotland to the present day.

[x] See 'History of the English Poor Law,' vol. i. p. 245.

spread of education, and the beneficent influences of religion.

Our attention must now be given to the 'Act for settling of Schools,' which conferred the most important benefits on the Scottish people, and of which Scotland may be justly proud. The Act was passed in 1696, and recites that "our sovereign lord considering how prejudicial the want of schools in many places has been, and how beneficial the establishing and settling thereof in every parish will be to this church and kingdom"—therefore, with the advice and consent of parliament it is ordained, that there shall be a school established and a schoolmaster appointed in every parish, by advice of the heritors and minister thereof; and that the heritors do meet and provide a commodious house for a school, and settle a salary for a schoolmaster, of not less than one hundred nor over two hundred marks, to be paid to him half-yearly at Whitsuntide and Martinmas; "and that they stent and lay on the said salary, conform to every heritor's valued rent within the parish, allowing each heritor relief from his tenants of the half of his proportion, for settling a school and payment of the schoolmaster's salary." If the heritors shall not convene a meeting, or being convened shall not agree among themselves, then the presbyterie are to apply to the commissioners of the shire, who are empowered to establish the school and settle the master's salary within the above limits, and to stent the same upon the heritors, "which shall be as valid and effectual as if it had been done by the heritors themselves"—and for the better and more ready payment thereof, it is further ordained that if two payments run in arrear, the defaulters shall be liable to pay double their proportions then due, and double for every term's proportion that shall be due thereafter, until the schoolmaster be completely paid. "And that letters of horning, and all other executionals

1696. William, October 9, No. 26.

Parish schools established.

necessary, be directed at the instance of the schoolmaster for payment of the said stipend, and double of the proportions, in manner aforesaid."

We here see the origin of the Scottish parochial system of education, which has been carried into effect, and continued in operation, with singular judgment and perseverance during a long series of years; and the benefits arising from which, both socially and morally, can hardly be over estimated. To the general establishment of schools under the provisions of the above Act, and the consequent spread of education it is owing, more perhaps than to any or all other causes combined, that Scotland, a comparatively poor country in its natural resources, has attained the important position it now occupies as a member of the British empire, and that the Scottish people are second to none in moral qualities, or in the arts and refinements of life.

Results of preceding legislation.

The above is the last of the Acts prior to the Union which I think it necessary to notice as bearing upon the condition of the people, and the general state of the country. The inference to be drawn from these Acts seems to be, that the state of Scotland was then, on the whole, not materially different from the state of England on the accession of James the First to the English crown. The feudal powers of the Scottish nobles had been reduced, and brought within the limits of the general law, by the ascendancy the Crown then acquired, as the feudal powers of the English nobility had been reduced through the ascendancy acquired by the Tudor sovereigns in England; and the people in both countries were gainers by the change. The improvement of their condition was greatly accelerated by the Revolution in 1688, which, as Robertson remarks,[y] introduced new maxims of government into Scotland—" To increase the authority

---

[y] See Robertson's 'History of Scotland,' vol. ii. p. 840, of the edition of 1811.

of the prince, or to secure the privileges of the nobles, had hitherto been almost the sole object of the laws. The rights of the people were scarcely ever mentioned, were disregarded, or unknown." But thenceforward, he says, attention began to be paid to their welfare, "and as they came to enjoy more security and greater power, their minds began to open, and to form more extensive plans of commerce, of industry, and of police" —how greatly their progress in these respects must have been assisted by the means of education provided for the people of every class under the last cited Act, it would be superfluous to point out. This was however a privilege confined to Scotland—it unhappily did not extend to England, where the education of the great body of the people has continued to be very imperfectly provided for even to the present day, although considerable improvement in this respect has certainly taken place within the last few years.

The union of England and Scotland under one government, is obviously essential to the prosperity of both, and all the more eminent of the English sovereigns, from Edward the First downwards, sought to accomplish this object either by policy or by force. The union of the two crowns under James the First, seemed to afford increased facilities for effecting a union of the governments, and James continued throughout his reign to urge the adoption of such a measure; but he did not possess sufficient weight and consistency of character to bring it about. It was for a time accomplished by the iron will and strong arm of Cromwell, whose vigorous policy was everywhere successful; but the Restoration placed the two countries in the same relative position as before—not altogether antagonistic, it is true, but yet so incongruously joined as to render their junction a perpetual source of jealousy and dissatisfaction to each. From this state they were rescued by the Act of Union, in the reign of Anne.

To effect a union with Scotland, by bringing the affairs of the two countries into one common focus, was the object of Anne's government, as it had been of that of her predecessors, and the general popularity and early glories of her reign greatly facilitated its accomplishment. There was no doubt much preliminary negotiation, but the subject was formally opened by a letter from the queen to the Scottish parliament in 1705, in which she says—"We are fully satisfied (and doubt not but you are) that great benefit would arise to all our subjects by an union of Scotland and England, and that nothing will contribute more to the composing of differences and extinguishing heats that are unhappily raised and fomented by the enemies of both nations, than the promoting of everything that tends to the procuring the same." The parliament was therefore earnestly recommended to appoint a commission, as the English parliament had done, for treating of and effecting what is so desirable for both kingdoms, and to which the queen promises to give her best and hearty assistance. The commission was accordingly appointed, and after lengthened negotiations the treaty was brought to a close, and on the 16th of January 1707 it was solemnly ratified by the parliament; an 'Act for securing the Protestant Religion and Presbyterian Church Government' being at the same time passed. On the 19th of March following the ratification of the Treaty of Union by the English parliament was received and recorded, and the lord high commissioner,[z] by command of her Majesty, declared it to be "a great satisfaction to the queen that the Union is thus happily concluded in her reign, and that nothing should be omitted on her part to make the whole island feel the good effects of it."

1705. Queen Anne's letter to the Scottish parliament recommending a Union, read July 3.

1707. Anne—Treaty of Union. January 16, No. 6.

---

[z] The Duke of Queensberry.

On the 24th of March, "in the conclusion of the parliament," the following address to the queen was agreed to—"We your Majesty's most dutiful and loyal subjects, the noblemen and commissioners from shires and boroughs assembled in parliament, do with most humble thankfulness acknowledge that this nation has enjoyed many advantages under your Majesty's most happy government, but above all we beg leave to return our most humble and hearty thanks to your Majesty for the great care and concern you have shown to bring the Treaty of Union of your Majesty's two kingdoms of Scotland and England to a happy conclusion. This Union, which has often been attempted by your royal predecessors without effect, is by the special blessing of Heaven upon your Majesty's reign and your wise conduct now brought to perfection, which with the settlement of the succession in the Protestant line, has established a lasting monument of your Majesty's glory to all future ages, and laid a firm foundation of the security of our religion, and the peace and prosperity of this island." And finally, on the 25th of March, the lord high commissioner in putting an end to the session, declared—"I am persuaded that we and our posterity will reap the benefit of the union of the two kingdoms, and I doubt not that, as this parliament has had the honour to conclude it, you will in your several stations recommend to the people of this nation a grateful sense of her Majesty's goodness and great care for the welfare of her subjects, in bringing this important affair to perfection, and that you will promote an universal desire in this kingdom to become one in hearts and affections, as we are inseparably joined in interest, with our neighbour nation."

The above details regarding the Union are given somewhat at length, there being no other event in Scottish history which in its results affected in an equal degree the well-being of the people. "Since the Union,

(Robertson remarks) the commons, anciently neglected by their kings and despised by the nobles, have emerged into dignity; and being admitted to a participation of all the privileges which the English had purchased at the expense of so much blood, must now be esteemed a body no less considerable in the one kingdom, than they have long been in the other."[a] And he further observes that the people, "exempted from burdens to which they were formerly subject, screened from oppressions to which they had been long exposed, and adopted into a constitution whose genius and laws were more liberal than their own, they have extended their commerce, refined their manners, made improvements in the elegancies of life, and cultivated the arts and sciences." The testimony thus borne by so eminent a Scotchman, to the benefits conferred upon his country by the Union, is of much value; and it is confirmed by almost every other authority. The progress of Scotland since, and its condition at the present day, affords moreover proof of the advantages which followed the Union. Yet there was great opposition to it at the time, and the real patriots by whom it was promoted, were denounced as traitors to their country. Hence the heats and differences, to which, as we have just seen, the queen adverts in her letter to the parliament, and which long continued to exist, although happily with continually decreasing virulence, until at length the two nations became blended into one people, distinctions gradually disappearing, and the same manners habits sympathies and interests prevailing in all parts of our island.

This entire union and blending of the people did not however take place until after the Rebellion in 1745, when the defeat of the Pretender and his Highland followers, finally put an end to the hopes of the exiled family and their partisans, and to all pretences for dis-

---

[a] See Robertson's 'History of Scotland,' vol. ii. p. 842.

turbing the public peace. The steps subsequently taken by the government, in forming roads and opening out communications in the Highland districts, so as to render them generally accessible, changed the character of the Highlanders, and led to their adoption of more sober and industrious habits than had before prevailed amongst them. They ceased to be gentlemen and robbers, as described by Fletcher of Saltoun,[b] and became herdsmen and cultivators, their mountain slopes being converted into pasturage for sheep and cattle, and the lower levels to the raising of crops—a happy change for them, and for the country. Yet it was whilst this change was in progress that the poet lamented over the degradation of his country in the well-known strains[c]—

> "Mourn, hapless Caledonia, mourn
> Thy banish'd peace, thy laurels torn"—

so little is poetical testimony to be relied upon, whenever feeling or imagination takes the lead in depicting the stern realities of life!

After the Union, all separate legislation ceased. Scotland was then represented in the united parliament, and its affairs were discussed and settled with a view to general results, and as portions of the common interest. With regard to our immediate subject, the law remained unchanged for considerably more than a century, and the relief of the Scottish poor was founded upon the enactments which have been described, and a summary of which is given at pages 86 to 90. The practice adopted under sanction of the law, requires however at least equal attention with the law itself; and although the practice was varied and irregular, and often modified to meet local or special circumstances, its general character is well ascertained; and of this practice, it is necessary to afford some explanation.

Practical application of the law.

---

[b] Ante, p. 90.

[c] Smollett's 'Tears of Scotland.'

Assessments.

The power of assessment for providing the means of relief, we have seen was given by the Act of 1579[d] to magistrates in burghs, and to justices in landward parishes, which power was afterwards transferred to the heritors and kirk sessions; but until a comparatively recent period, this power of assessment was very rarely exercised, the funds for the support of the poor being raised (we may presume not always quite voluntarily) in the way of contributions at the parish churches, together with certain moneys arising from mortifications and other sources. On this point, the committee of the General Assembly, in their Report of 1839 on the management of the poor, remark—"It is true that a compulsory assessment for the support of the impotent poor, was at a very early period permitted in Scotland—but no assessment was imposed for upwards of a century afterwards; and when at length this measure became necessary in certain parishes, the use of it was confined to these parishes, the rule in practice which was acted upon having been, that an assessment is not to be laid on in any parish, while a sufficiency of funds for the maintenance of the poor therein is voluntarily contributed."

So likewise in a Report forwarded by the moderator of the General Assembly in 1818 (included in the Third Report of the Select Committee on the Poor Laws), it is stated to be a characteristic of the Poor Laws of Scotland, "that while they secure ultimately a certain provision for the poor, they do not imperatively require a regular and permanent annual tax or assessment to be levied for their support. They permit such a tax or assessment to be avoided entirely, if other parochial funds that are applicable shall be found adequate; and if from the occasional deficiency of these funds, any assessment may be found necessary, still the amount of

---

[d] Ante, p. 16.

it may be so limited, at the discretion of the heritors and kirk session, as to be merely sufficient for meeting the deficiency." It hence appears that at the end of two centuries and a half after the power was given by the Act of 1579, and more than a century after the Union in 1707, assessment for relief of the poor was little practised in Scotland—it in fact formed an exception, instead of being the rule, as was the case in England.

In the Report of 1818 above quoted, it is stated that prior to the year 1700, the number of parishes in which assessments had taken place was only three; between that and 1800 there were 93 more, and thence to 1817 not less than 49. The number at the date of the Report is stated to have been 152,[e] containing a population of 339,879. In the Report of 1839, also quoted above, the number of parishes at that time assessed is stated to be 236, with a population of 1,137,646, thus showing a steadily progressive increase, both in the number of parishes assessed and in the amount of their population, in the latter especially, assessments becoming indispensable in the large towns and manufacturing districts. A great diversity is described as existing in the mode of adjusting the assessment, but in landward parishes it is said to be for the most part levied one-half from the heritors and the other half from the tenants and householders, while in burghs the rate is levied from the inhabitants generally. Sometimes the assessment is fixed as a certain rate on the valuation, sometimes as a rate on the actual rental or value of the real property possessed by the ratepayers; "and sometimes as a rate on the estimated amount of their means and substance, or general wealth." In burghs the rate is sometimes

---

[e] In the Report of 1839 the number is said to have been 192, but there is much uncertainty in regard to these numbers, and I retain that which is given in Table No. 2 of the Appendix. It is however stated in a note, that 25 additional returns have been received, but too late to admit of their contents being included in the tables.

levied on the rental of the property, in others on an estimate of the means and substance of the occupiers "with different variations or modifications according to the particular usage of the burgh."

The entire amounts raised by assessment, and from other sources, appears by a supplemental return to parliament in 1820, to have then been as follows— Amount of relief.

| | | | |
|---|---|---|---|
| By assessment .. .. .. .. .. .. .. .. .. .. | £49,718 | 10 | 5¼ |
| By collections, voluntary contributions, and other means | 64,477 | 7 | 3¾ |
| | £114,195 | 17 | 9 |

equal to an average of 1*s.* 3*d.* per head on the population, according to the census of 1811.

The entire amounts raised by assessment and from other sources, according to the Report of 1839, was then, on an average of the three preceding years—

| | | | |
|---|---|---|---|
| By assessment .. .. .. .. .. .. .. .. .. .. .. | £77,239 | 19 | 0 |
| By collections, contributions, and sessional funds .. .. | 77,881 | 13 | 2 |
| | £155,121 | 12 | 2 |

equal to something above an average of 1*s.* 4*d.* per head on the population, according to the census of 1831.

The total number of poor persons receiving relief, is stated in the supplemental return presented in 1820 to have been 44,199, equal to about 2½ per cent. on the population, according to the census of 1811. In the Report of 1839, on an average of the three preceding years, the number of regular poor on the permanent roll is set down at 57,969, the occasional poor 20,348, and the lunatic poor 1112, in all 79,429, equal to about 3 per cent. on the population,[f] which had gone on steadily increasing from 1,050,000 at the period of the Union, and 1,805,688 in 1811, to 2,365,114 Numbers relieved.

[f] The decennial census in 1811 and in 1831 bear an equal proportion to the period of these and the preceding returns, being in each case six years anterior. The population would however appear greater, if estimated for 1817 and 1837, and would exhibit a somewhat less percentage of pauperism.

at the census in 1831. So that in the twenty years which intervened between the two returns of 1811 and 1831, the number relieved had it appears increased from 2½ to 3 per cent. on the population, and the amount raised for the purposes of relief, from 1*s.* 3*d.* to 1*s.* 4*d.* per head on the population.

Comparison of the pauperism of Scotland and England.

It may here be useful to contrast the condition of Scotland in regard to the relief of the poor, with what was the condition of England in this respect at nearly the same period—

| | Population. | Number relieved. | Amount of relief. | Proportion per cent. on population. | Rate per head on population. |
|---|---|---|---|---|---|
| | | | £. | | *s.* *d.* |
| England,[g] 1840 .. | 15,562,000 | 1,199,529 | 4,576,965 | 7¾ | 5 10½ |
| Scotland, 1837 .. | 2,500,000 | 79,429 | 155,121 | 3⅙ | 1 3 |

This comparison appears highly favourable to Scotland as regards the extent of pauperism, which in proportion to the population is less by one-half than what prevailed in England, and there is a still greater difference in the ratio of relief, which does not reach a quarter of the English amount. There may however be circumstances not only to account for the difference thus shown to exist between the two countries, but also to divest it in some degree of the favourable inferences as respects Scotland, to which the difference is calculated to give rise; for it by no means follows that the more limited extent of relief in Scotland, is a proof of the relief being better administered, or of the people being there better conditioned or less in need of it than was the case in England.

An intelligent writer, who appears to be thoroughly conversant with the subject,[h] declares "that the general deficiency of the allowances to the impotent poor in Scotland is habitually supplemented, not (or only par-

---

[g] See 'History of the English Poor Law,' vol. ii. pp. 375, 417, and Appendix No. 2.

[h] See Alison's 'Remarks on the Poor Laws of Scotland,' pp. 6 and 8, edition 1844.

tially) by assistance from relatives or friends, but in all parts of the country by *begging*, or one form or other of mendicity, *i. e.* by assistance given by persons who are either strangers to the suffering poor, or on whom they have no natural claim." And he likewise declares Scotland to be an example of the general fact, that wherever there is not an efficient legal provision for the relief of the poor, "the alternative practically found to exist is an extensive system of mendicity, under which there is much more misery disorder and vice, and such an extent and intensity of human suffering, as imposes a very heavy responsibility on the supporters of the voluntary system." He further remarks, that those who are entrusted with the management of the poor in Scotland, "profess to administer a law which binds them to provide for the needful sustentation of all poor and impotent persons, and defines what is meant by 'needful sustentation,' by specifying that it is that which the poor '*of their own consent*' shall be content to receive, and '*live unbeggand.*' They grant to the poor in almost all parts of the country an allowance utterly inadequate to their maintenance, knowing perfectly that the only means by which this deficiency can be supplied is common begging; and then they punish as criminals, persons who have been reduced to this degradation by their own maladministration of the laws designed for the protection of those very persons."

That the results should be as above described, in the absence of a general assessment or other certain and sufficient provision for the relief of the poor, cannot excite surprise; and the coupling of assessment with voluntary contributions, as we have seen to be the practice in Scotland, was certainly not calculated to remedy the evil, inasmuch as the one mode has invariably been found to interfere with and neutralise the other. Where destitution is not relieved, mendicancy must abound, violences will occur, and life and property be insecure. Where destitution is in some degree but not sufficiently relieved, life and property may be less insecure, but mendicancy must still more or less abound ; and the prevalence of a low standard of habits manners and mode of life in the mendicant classes, will operate injuriously upon and tend to depress the general character of the population. People become reconciled to what is common—to wretched dwellings where they inhabit them—to squalor filth and rags where they are perpetually presented to their view ; and they are themselves prone to sink to a level which they have thus ceased to regard with repugnance. That there was ground for apprehension on this score, in the case of Scotland, we have abundant proof.

In the Report for 1818, before quoted, it is stated that resolutions had been entered into by some counties for the suppression of mendicancy, but that these resolutions have not been carried into effect. Several of the ministers, it is said, consider "that the stranger poor carry away in the shape of alms from the parish, more in value each year than would support comfortably the whole poor on the parish roll ;" but there is nevertheless a diversity of opinion as to the expediency of putting an entire stop to begging. Some ministers deprecate its suppression "as likely to lead to the still more pernicious measure of compulsory assessments." Others think that the practice is attended with many hurtful effects, and some go so far as to consider begging "a violation of the whole provisions purposes and spirit of the Poor Laws, as a heavy loss to the community of productive labour, as encouraging the vices of those who are professionally pilfering vagrants, and as habituating generally the pauper to duplicity falsehood improvidence and dissipation." In some districts, it is said, the poor are limited to beg in their own parish only. In others they are not permitted to beg even within their own parish, without a licence from the kirk session, or a justice of peace; and instances are mentioned where they are restricted to beg on one particular day of the week: but "in a very few parishes only are badges worn by the begging poor." By such and similar limitations the practice of begging is said to be considerably checked, and an anticipation is held out "that it will soon be checked more extensively, and confined by such salutary and practicable regulations as the interests of public police and morals seem loudly to require."

The preventive and the remedy for the evils above noticed, would be found in a general assessment for relief of the destitute, who might then with perfect justice be restrained from begging; in which case the public would not only be relieved from the contaminating influence of mendicancy, but the burden of supporting the poor which before pressed injuriously upon industry, would be borne by the general capital of the country—a change on every account and to all parties beneficial.

# CHAPTER III.

Distinctive characteristic of Scottish Poor Law — Administration of relief — Settlement — Distress in Scotland — Schoolmasters' Act — Its effects — Distress at Paisley — Decision of Supreme Court — Scotch and English systems contrasted — Report on distress at Paisley — Extent and influence of distress — Report of Poor Law Inquiry Commission — Mr. Twisleton's 'Reasons of Dissent therefrom.'

THE chief characteristic of Scottish Poor Law administration, as contrasted with that of England, is the pertinacity with which all claim to relief on behalf of the able-bodied poor has been resisted. The General Assembly in their Report of 1839 however, admit "that the situation of people destitute of employment was not to be overlooked, and that many cases might occur in which men of this class ought to obtain temporary relief in times of occasional sickness or unusual calamity, although not as a matter of right." With this view, it is said, a certain proportion of the church collections has from an early period been placed at the disposal of the kirk sessions, "in order that they, at their discretion, may be enabled to afford assistance for a time to such industrious persons within their bounds as should happen, owing to temporary sickness, or to a casual failure of work, to be in difficulty and straits." This arrangement rested for a long time on usage only, but was at length sanctioned by the proclamation of 1693,[a] afterwards ratified by parliament, "by which one-half of the church collections was left to the disposal of the kirk sessions,

[a] Ante, p. 81.

for the purpose in part as has since been held, of being so applied." Such, it is further said, "are the rules of the law of Scotland on this subject—such the origin and foundation of the distinction between those who are called the '*ordinary*' and those who are denominated '*occasional*' poor. The latter receive temporary assistance only from the charity of the parish, bestowed at the discretion of the kirk session, during the pressure of want. Of the former a roll is made up, in terms of the Act of 1579 and subsequent statutes, and altered at stated periods according to circumstances by the kirk session in each parish, and such of the heritors as may act with them. The poor whose names are thus enrolled, are entitled to periodical allowances permanently and as a matter of legal right." [b]

Relief as practically administered.

The allowances to the parochial poor, are in the Report of 1839 said to be in all cases remarkably moderate.[b] The principle on which the amount is fixed, is—"that except in very rare instances of total and absolute destitution, the aliment to be provided by the parish is not such as would render the pauper independent of other resources—that in general poor persons are not so entirely destitute as not to be capable of procuring a part of their sustenance by their own labour, or by the assistance of relatives, or the benevolence of neighbours and others; and that it is only what may be necessary for their support, in addition to these separate means, that the parish ought to supply." A small sum in aid of their resources will, it is said, afford the relief that is necessary, and anything in addition would be adverse to the true interests of the parish, and the moral habits of the people. The relief afforded is therefore only supplemental to the earnings from all other sources, begging included, and amounts in fact to what was long known in England as "relief

[b] See the 'General Assembly's Report of 1839,' p. 7.

in aid of wages." The evils arising from such a practice would of course greatly depend upon the extent to which it is carried, and the persons to whom it is applied. If applied to the labouring classes, it would tend to divert them from a reliance upon their own industry, and also to lower the rate of wages—if to the infirm and disabled poor, the insufficiency of relief would not only cause them suffering and privation, but would also lead to their being depressed lower socially, than with a due regard to the general welfare it is right that they should be, whilst mendicancy would at the same time be sanctioned and perpetuated.

The foregoing extracts from the Report of 1839 explain the practice as regards the "occasional" or able-bodied poor, whose relief in any way is left entirely to the discretion of the kirk session, as a matter of charity. The relief of the "ordinary" or infirm poor, is imperative upon the heritors and kirk session conjointly; but in the Report of 1818, it is stated that in practice "the heritors seldom or never interfere in regulating the concerns of the poor, or the poor's funds, except in parishes where assessments are levied." In such cases "they meet on the first Thursday of August in each year, or oftener if they judge it expedient, and along with the kirk session examine and adjust the poor's roll, and fix the amount of the assessments required. In practice therefore, the heritors, we see, in no way interfere with the relief of the "occasional" or able-bodied poor; and only with that of the "ordinary" or infirm poor, where the parish has been subjected to an assessment. The reason for their then doing so is sufficiently plain, as they are required to pay half the levy; but the reason for their being exempted from interference with the relief of the "occasional" poor is not so clear, since the first proclamation (that of 1692[c])

[c] Ante, p. 78.

directs that "if any of the poor of the parish are able to work, the heritors of the parish are hereby authorised and required to put them to work according to their capacities, either within the parish or to any adjacent manufactory, as they shall find expedient, furnishing them always with meat and clothes." There is here no limitation as to the class of persons to be employed and furnished with meat and clothing, except their being poor, and capable of work, on each of which points the heritors appear to be the parties to decide, and to be responsible for putting the law in execution. It seems difficult therefore to understand the grounds on which a claim to relief was in practice limited to the "ordinary" poor, or on which the heritors were deemed to be restricted from relieving the wants of the "occasional" poor. We have seen however that both restrictions were practically maintained throughout a long series of years.[d]

Although the management of the poor and the administration of the funds are by law vested in the heritors and kirk session in landward parishes, and in the magistrates in burghs, the Report of 1839 declares that in the latter case the management generally devolves upon the kirk session; and it also repeats the statement made in the Report of 1818, to the effect, that in all cases where the poor are provided for by voluntary contributions, the management is left to the kirk session alone. But the heritors and magistrates are, it is said, always entitled to have an account of their administration from the sessions, even when the funds consist exclusively of church-door collections. When these "become inadequate, the heritors are called upon

---

[d] In his valuable work on Scotch Poor Law, Mr. Dunlop remarks that "the general tenor of our Scottish statutes applies solely to those who are permanently disabled; and although in many parishes, it was the practice to afford relief to persons labouring under temporary sickness, there seems to be no authority for considering that this was imperative on them."—*See p.* 33, *edition of* 1854.

to determine as to the course to be pursued; and whether they adopt the plan of a voluntary assessment, or impose a legal rate, they thereafter take a more active superintendence at the general yearly or half-yearly meetings of the joint board of heritors and session."

Practice as regards Settlement.

The Scottish law of settlement has already been briefly noticed.[e] The practice under it is to be gathered from the Reports of the General Assembly. That of 1839 states, that "the circumstances which entitle the impotent poor to demand parish relief are, that the claimant has had his residence or 'common resort' within the parish during the last three years immediately before he fell into a state of poverty and inability to support himself; and if he has removed from the parish, that he has not since his removal acquired a legal settlement in any other. If he has funds of his own, or relations who are bound in law and able to maintain him, the parish will be relieved of so doing." But it is added, "there is not and never existed by the law of Scotland, a power of removal of persons likely to become chargeable, such as was established in England by the *14th Charles 2nd, cap.* 12,[f] and which gave rise to so much litigation and oppression." The Report of 1818 remarks, that "it does not appear that there ever has been an instance of the removal of a pauper from one parish to another involuntarily, or by legal means. Even when the title of a pauper to maintenance has been contested at law between two parishes, he has been allowed to make his option of residence in either of them, and his allowance has been received by him in the usual way from the parish found liable to pay it. He frequently makes his option of residence in the parish where he can best find employment, when able to follow it, or where he happens to have relations

---

[e] Ante, p. 88.
[f] See 'History of the English Poor Law,' vol. i. p. 293.

living and who are able to contribute towards his support." This is practically equivalent to irremovability, and must have gone far in the then state of Scotland, to mitigate the evils necessarily inherent in a settlement law.

The description which has been previously given of the several legislative enactments regarding the poor, and the account here given of what has been the practice in this respect, chiefly founded on the representations contained in the General Assembly's Reports, will it is hoped enable the reader to understand both the state of the law, and the manner in which it was applied, throughout the long period extending from the Union in 1707 to the passing of the *Amendment Act 8th and 9th Victoria, cap.* 83, in 1845. Before entering upon a consideration of that statute, and the inquiries by which it was preceded, there are yet however a few matters which require to be noticed, as being essential to a right understanding of the condition of the people, more especially in the western districts.

1783. Great distress in Scotland.

In 1783 great distress prevailed in Scotland, especially in the Highlands, and a committee of the House of Commons was appointed to inquire into the circumstances. A good deal of evidence was taken, both oral and written, and reported to the house.[g] One of the witnesses stated—"that the season last year was very cold, and the harvest late—that the frost came on at the beginning of November very severe, and a great deal of snow fell at the beginning of the month—that at that time the corn in general was far from ripe, and only a small proportion of it was cut before the snow fell, and that the crop was very deficient." Another witness stated—"that during the early frost and fall of snow in November and De-

[g] See Report presented on the 28th May 1783, and subsequently printed by order of the House of Commons, dated 7th May 1846.

cember last, the crop of potatoes was entirely destroyed in most parts of the counties of Nairn Inverness and Murray—that the oats and barley were covered with snow before they were ripe—that the cattle in many parts were kept alive by pulling the green corn from under the snow, and that the frost kept the corn from filling so as to yield meal—that this is the second bad season, and the farmers had sold great part of their stock to pay their rent." The sheriff of the counties of Caithness and Sutherland wrote, stating—" that the condition of the north parts of Scotland is truly lamentable—In Sutherland and Ross shires many people have already perished for want of food—Caithness is not far removed from a similar disaster, and in Orkney they are still nigher to it." Another writer from Inverness, states—" I cannot express to you the miserable situation of this country—There are many good farmers with their wives and children begging in the streets—Last harvest has finished the most of them—meal or any kind of victuals cannot be had for love or money, and before the summer is over people will die in the fields for want."

Under these very distressing circumstances, the committee came to the resolution that Government should be enabled to allow the importation of corn for a time, not exceeding four months from the 3rd of September next, into the several counties named; and it was further resolved—" That it is the opinion of this committee, that the commissioners of land-tax of the said counties be enabled to levy a sum not exceeding 14*l.* Scots, on every 100*l.* Scots of the valued rent of the said counties, and to apply the same to the relief of such of the inhabitants as are or shall be reduced to poverty by the failure of last year's crop, and the scarcity and high price of corn occasioned thereby."

These resolutions were reported to the house by Mr. Pulteney, the chairman of the committee, who moved an address to the king, which was unanimously adopted, to the effect—"That it appears from evidence brought before this house that the inhabitants of the Highlands and northern parts of Scotland in particular, have suffered most severely from the lateness of the last harvest, whereby their corn while green was covered with snow, and in many places was not gathered in till the month of December, and then in a very bad condition. That the crop of potatoes on which the said inhabitants principally depend for support, was also destroyed by the frost. That many of the said inhabitants being thereby reduced to indigence, will either be constrained to migrate or be exposed to the danger of perishing for want of food, unless timely measures be devised for their relief. That the distresses occasioned by famine being generally most extreme in the summer months immediately preceding the new harvest, when this house may not be sitting"—his Majesty is besought to give such directions as may most effectually avert the evils apprehended from the above calamitous state of the northern parts of Scotland, and the house promises to make good the expenses incurred "in relieving the misery to which his Majesty's unhappy subjects may be reduced by this most deplorable calamity"—and the several provisions were forthwith embodied in an Act (*The 23rd George 3rd, cap.* 53) which immediately received the royal assent.

The distress at this time appears to have been very severe, and the removal of the restriction on the importation of corn was undoubtedly judicious under the circumstances. This was jealously done however, and limited both in duration and area—thus showing that the legislature did not omit other considerations in its sympathy for the distress of the people. The power given to the land-tax commissioners to "assess and levy upon all and every the heritors and landholders within the respective counties of Perth, Kincardine, Aberdeen, Inverness, Ross, Nairn, Cromartie, Argyle,

Forfar, Banff, Sutherland, Caithness, Elgin, Dumbarton, Orkney, and Zetland, a sum of money not exceeding 14*l.* Scots, on every 100*l.* Scots of valued rent," and to apply the same in relieving such of the inhabitants of these counties as have been reduced to indigence by the failure of the last year's crop, " in such way and manner as the said commissioners in their judgment and discretion shall think fit"—was a judicious measure, and calculated to afford immediate aid; but we have no means of ascertaining to what extent the power was exercised, or whether it was exercised at all. With a return of the usual seasons, it must be presumed that the distress subsided, at least for a time; but it will be seen that these districts were afterwards subjected to similar privations, arising from the same or a similar cause.

1803. 43rd George III., c. 54. Schoolmasters' Act.

The Schoolmasters' Act, 43*rd George 3rd, cap.* 54, also requires to be noticed, it being of very considerable importance, as well generally, as in connexion with our subject. It is entitled 'An Act for making better provision for the Parochial Schoolmasters, and for making further regulations for the better government of the Parish Schools in Scotland.' It commences by declaring that—" The parish schoolmasters in Scotland are a most useful body of men, and their labours have been of essential importance to the public welfare." The Scottish Act of William the Third[h] on the subject is then referred to, and its provisions for the salaries of the schoolmasters are recited, which it is said " by difference in the value of money, and change in the circumstances of the country, has become a provision altogether inadequate for a body of men whose labours are of so great public utility"—wherefore it is enacted, that except in certain cases mentioned, the salary of each parish schoolmaster shall

[h] Ante, p. 98.

not be under the sum of 300 merks,[1] nor above the sum of 400 merks Scots, per annum; and it is further directed, that within three months after the passing of the Act, the heritors and the minister of every parish are to hold a meeting (notice thereof being previously given) "and on due consideration of the circumstances of the parish in respect to extent population and valued rent, and the probable amount of the other emoluments of the schoolmaster's office," are to determine whether the salary shall be 300 merks, or 400 merks, or such other sum between the two as seems most suitable; and shall fix the amount of such salary by a resolution, to be signed by the preses of the meeting, and delivered to the schoolmaster, as his authority for collecting the same; which amount is to be paid by the several heritors, in the same manner as is prescribed by the former Act. But it is also provided—"that no salary at present payable to any schoolmaster shall be diminished," and in cases where any portion is payable in grain or meal, "it is so to be continued, with such additions in money as the meeting shall deem proper," and in determining the amount of such additions, the grain or meal making part of the salary is to be estimated at the rate of 200 merks per chalder. The salaries so fixed and determined, are to continue payable for five-and-twenty years after the passing of the Act; and within three years after the expiration of that period, the average price of a chalder of oatmeal for all Scotland is again to be ascertained, and is to form the rate according to which the schoolmasters' salaries are then to be fixed; and so on, for every succeeding twenty-five years—thus providing for the adjustment of whatever changes may take place in the successive periods.

---

[1] A merk is 13*s*. 4*d*. Scots, equal to 13⅓*d*. English. A salary of 300 merks Scots, is therefore 16*l*. 13*s*. 4*d*. sterling, and one of 400 merks Scots is 22*l*. 4*s*. 5*d*. sterling.

The Act further directs, "that in every parish where a commodious house for the school, and a dwellinghouse with a garden for the schoolmaster have not been provided, the heritors of every parish shall provide the same—the house for the residence of the schoolmaster not consisting of more than two apartments, including the kitchen, with a portion of ground for a garden from fields used for the ordinary purposes of agriculture or pasturage, as near and convenient to the schoolmaster's dwellinghouse as reasonably may be; which garden shall contain at least one-fourth of a Scots acre,[k] and be enclosed with such fence as is generally used for such purposes in the district where it is situated." The expense of providing schoolhouse dwellinghouse and garden, and supporting the same, is to be defrayed in like manner as is prescribed for providing a schoolhouse by the preceding Act of William's reign. Where a garden "cannot be allotted to the schoolmaster without great loss and inconvenience," the heritors, with the consent of the kirk session, may assign to the schoolmaster in lieu of such garden, an addition to his salary at the rate of eight bolls of oatmeal per acre." If the heritors neglect or refuse to provide the schoolhouse dwellinghouse and garden, or in case of the schoolmaster's not being satisfied with the accommodation afforded him, he may represent the same to the quarter sessions, whose judgment thereon is to be final—"provided always, that no justice of the peace who shall be an heritor in the parish of such schoolmaster, shall vote upon such representation."

Schoolhouse, dwelling-house, and garden, to be provided.

The schoolmaster is to be appointed by the heritors owning lands of not less than 100*l*. Scots, valued rental,[m] and the minister of the parish, at a meeting assembled

---

[k] An acre Scots is about an acre and a quarter English, twenty-three of the latter being equal to twenty-nine of the former, very nearly.

[m] Equal to 8*l*. 6*s*. 8*d*. sterling.

after due notice; and every schoolmaster so elected, is to carry the minute or a certified copy of the minute of his election to the presbytery, with an attestation of his having taken the oath of allegiance; "and the presbytery shall thereupon take trial of his sufficiency for the office, in respect of morality and religion, and of such branches of literature as shall be deemed most necessary for the parish." And provided they are satisfied with the same, he is to be furnished with an extract from their minutes, "bearing that he had appeared, produced the attestations required, and had been found on trial duly qualified for discharging the duties of the office to which he had been elected, which extract shall complete his right to the emoluments provided by the Act." The school fees are to be fixed as the heritors and minister shall from time to time direct, and a table of such fees is to be hung up in the schoolroom; but the schoolmaster is nevertheless bound to teach such poor children as the heritors, qualified as above, and the minister of the parish shall recommend.[n]

It is also provided that the presbyteries, in their visitations, shall have the power of regulating the hours of teaching, the length of the vacation, or anything that may be wrong or complained of in the management of the school; and the schoolmaster is required to conform to and obey all regulations so made, "under pain of censure, suspension from or deprivation of his office, as to the presbytery shall seem proper." The presbytery are also empowered, on complaint from the heritors minister or elders, charging the schoolmaster with neglect of duty, or immoral conduct, or cruel and improper treatment of the scholars, to take cognizance of the same, and either to acquit, or pass sentence of

Integration of Church, education + Poor Law

[n] In the 'General Assembly's Report for 1839,' it is stated that "a considerable number of children are, under this provision, educated gratuitously at the parish schools."

censure suspension or deprivation, as shall to them appear proper—"which judgement shall be final, without appeal to or review by any court civil or ecclesiastical."

It is impossible to read these carefully framed enactments for securing competent schoolmasters, and for providing them with suitable salaries and convenient dwellings in every parish, without feeling that the authors of the measure were earnestly solicitous for the education of the people, and for establishing a system that would be universally and at all times effective for the purpose. This was surely an enlightened policy, productive of a large amount of present good, and holding out a promise of still greater good in future—a promise which has been amply fulfilled, in the intelligence and general high character of the Scottish people.

Effects of the Schoolmasters' Acts.

The working of the present Act, and of the preceding Act of 1696, is described in the Report from the General Assembly to the Select Committee on the Poor Laws in 1818. There is, it is said, "reason to conclude from the reports of the ministers, that there is a school in every parish, competently endowed, as provided for by law, and in general supplied with a suitably qualified teacher. And the schools being under the immediate jurisdiction of the presbyteries, are regularly visited and examined each year by committees of their number." Few cases, it is stated, can exist, "where those who are willing to be taught, and reside within reach of a school, are left without the means of common education. The schoolmaster is by law obliged to teach gratis poor scholars recommended by the session;" and it is added, that "it is but justice to the schoolmasters to state, that many reports mention and applaud their disinterested readiness to receive indigent children on their list without fees." The practice in regard of education appears therefore to have come fully up to what the law required, whatever may have been the shortcomings in this respect with regard to the relief of the poor.

The stagnation of trade which took place in 1819, led to a general dearth of employment, and was the cause of much distress in all parts of the country. This was more particularly the case in the manufacturing districts, and at Paisley great numbers who were thus thrown out of employment, applied to the parish for relief. The heritors and kirk session however refused to comply with the application, on the ground that the applicants, being able-bodied, "did not fall within the class of poor for which the law provided." Application was then made to the sheriff, who adjudged the heritors and kirk session to meet and assess themselves for the relief of these persons. But on appeal to the supreme court, it was ruled that the determination of the questions—"1st, whether claimants of parochial aid are of the description of persons that are entitled to such relief, and 2ndly if they be of this description of persons, what shall be the amount of the assessment and relief—is vested in the heritors and kirk session of the parish, and that no control on the proceedings and determination of the kirk session in those particulars is committed to sheriffs or other inferior judicatures."

1819. Distress at Paisley.

Decision of supreme court in regard to relief.

This decision was considered to determine the rule of law with respect to other powers conferred upon heritors and the kirk sessions, and to have established the general principle, that in all "matters committed to their determination in the first instance, they are free from control by inferior judges, except where power to that effect is specially given by the legislature."[o] However intense or enduring the distress may be, or from whatsoever cause arising, its being relieved in any way depends therefore, we see, solely upon the will of the heritors and kirk session. There is no recognition of a right to

---

[o] See Dunlop's 'Scotch Poor Law,' p. 153, edition of 1854, from which this account of the Paisley case is abstracted.

relief, neither is there any power to enforce its being administered. The sufferers are restricted from begging, whilst they are without the means of living. They cannot obtain work, and they will hardly submit to starve. The alternative is obvious—property if not life will be put in jeopardy; and the danger can only be effectually met, by affording such aid as the occasion requires, subject of course to the condition of its being so given, as that whilst sufficient, it shall not be a temptation for resorting to it unnecessarily.

But to afford all the aid which would be required in cases similar to that which occurred at Paisley, even if its legality were admitted, would require a general assessment for the purpose, and to every form of assessment there was then the strongest objection. The General Assembly in their Report of 1818, declare their conviction "of the pernicious tendency of these compulsory taxations," the progress of which, they say, ought to excite the alarm of all who take an interest in the welfare of the country. Yet it is clear that the relief of general distress arising from the revulsion of trade, or any other wide-spreading and general cause, can only be fairly and fully met by a general taxation. Relief on these occasions is not a matter of charity, but is rather an effort of enlightened policy for the prevention of a greater evil; and to rely upon voluntary or purely charitable contributions in such a case, would be at once erroneous in principle and futile in practice. It would also be partial and unjust, for it would impose a burden upon the free and liberal minded, and would screen the selfish and the niggardly.

It may perhaps be said that stagnation of trade is not an uncommon occurrence, and that it ought to be provided against by the exercise of forethought and provident habits on the part of the working classes—No doubt it ought, as it ought also to be guarded against by the master and merchant class; yet how many of these do we see involved in difficulties on such occasions?—The law affords them a certain amount of relief and protection in their distress, and ought it not to be at least as careful of the operatives, who may be and often are great sufferers at such times, not so much perhaps through faults of their own, as through imprudent speculation and over-greediness of gain on the part of their employers. That the working classes are, as is asserted, less provident than they ought to be, may however be admitted, without removing the necessity for their being relieved when reduced to actual want—relief being then almost as essential for the general tranquillity, as it is for the distressed operatives themselves.

In rural districts, where the population is not excessive, and where employment is generally steady and continuous, it may perhaps be possible to dispense with assessment, and to rely upon voluntary contributions for the purposes of relief, without its leading to an extreme amount of suffering by any considerable portion of the people. But in districts where a dense population depends for its daily subsistence upon mercantile and manufacturing operations, changes in policy or in fashion, the discoveries of science, the inventions of the mechanist, or the outbreak of war, may suddenly and without warning plunge vast numbers of persons into deep and unavoidable distress, unavoidable at least by any effort or forethought of their own; and for these people there is surely a claim upon the community which has derived benefit from their exertions, for help to carry them through the present difficulty, and to prevent their sinking into desperate or evil courses, by which the public peace might be endangered and the community suffer injury.

Such however was not the view taken of this question in Scotland. Notwithstanding the growth of manufactures, and the consequent gathering together of large masses of the people into one focus, the non-relief of the able-bodied poor was strenuously maintained as the governing principle of the Scottish Poor-law, and was only so far departed from in practice, as when on some very peculiar occasion the kirk-session might deem it right to afford temporary relief to an individual sufferer of that class. But for general or extensive distress, no means of relief existed, either by law or established practice, notwithstanding the advance of the country in wealth and population, the latter having gone on progressively increasing at the following rates :—

| | |
|---|---|
| At the Union in 1707, the population was estimated at .. .. | 1,050,000 |
| In 1755, according to returns furnished by the clergy to Dr. Webster, it was .. .. .. .. .. .. .. .. .. .. | 1,265,380 |
| At the census of 1801 it was ascertained to be .. .. .. | 1,599,068 |
| " 1811 " " .. .. .. | 1,805,688 |
| " 1821 " " .. .. .. | 2,093,456 |
| " 1831 " " .. .. .. | 2,365,114 |
| " 1841 " " .. .. .. | 2,620,184 |
| " 1851 " " .. .. .. | 2,870,784 |

During the interval of nearly a century between 1755 and 1851, the population of the county of Lanark increased from 81,726 to 532,114, or to upwards of six times the amount at the first-named period; and there can be no doubt that this was accompanied by a corresponding increase of wealth, both the one and the other having their origin in the same cause, that is, the extension of manufacturing industry and commercial enterprise in the district. A great change has therefore evidently taken place, and a system of relief which may possibly have been sufficient at an earlier period, would be found insufficient at the latter, and would require to be adjusted to the altered circumstances in which the population was then placed, the two periods being in fact so dissimilar as to call for a very different mode of treatment.

It is not unlikely, that the dread which prevailed in

Scotland of the consequences that might ensue from recognising a right to relief on the part of the able-bodied poor, was in some degree caused by a knowledge of the abuses which had followed such a recognition in England. It is quite certain that the comparatively small amount expended on relief of the poor in Scotland was viewed with approbation, and aided the establishment of an amended system in England. In both instances however there was much exaggeration, as well as a disregard of the different circumstances of the two countries. It did not follow, because no relief was provided for the able-bodied poor in Scotland, that relief should not be provided for them in England; neither does it follow that because a lax and faulty administration of such relief was productive of mischievous consequences in England, similar consequences would necessarily ensue in Scotland. The superior wealth and population, and the nature and general organisation of society in England, combined with injudicious legislation, certainly did there lead to extravagant and ultimately even to fraudulent practices in administering relief.[p] But these abuses might have been avoided—they were excrescences rather than the natural or necessary growth of the system; and in Scotland, far poorer and less populous, and where the economical and prudent habits of the people are so marked as to be almost proverbial, needful relief in seasons of pressure and difficulty might surely have been imparted, free from the danger of such occurrences. Sound policy and humanity might have been satisfied by the mitigation of distress at the common charge, and the public might thus have been relieved from the frequently recurring spectacle of extreme destitution, not only without entailing evil consequences, but with

The Scotch and English systems contrasted.

---

[p] See 'History of the English Poor Law,' vol. ii. pp. 123 and 136, &c.

positive advantage to all parties, to the contributors as well as the receivers of the relief.

Doubts as to the sufficiency of the Scottish Poor Law for accomplishing the object for which it was designed, and dissatisfaction at the practice which prevailed under it, had been for some years becoming stronger and more general; and after the passing of the English Poor Law Amendment Act in 1834, and the Irish Poor Relief Act in 1838, together with the extensive inquiries by which these measures were preceded, and the numerous publications and the frequent discussions both in and out of parliament to which they gave rise, it was found no longer possible to avoid instituting an inquiry into the working of the Scottish law, with a view to its better adaptation to the wants and circumstances of the times. This inquiry was no doubt hastened by the distress which again occurred at Paisley, in the years 1840, 1841 and 1842, and which was so severe and so protracted as to call for the interference of government, and eventually for the raising of contributions in other parts of Scotland as well as in England for its relief. The funds thus obtained were confided to a local relief committee specially appointed, and the government sent a confidential agent to assist in the application of the money, and also to investigate the circumstances connected with the distress. Mr. Twisleton, the gentleman to whom these duties were confided, was well prepared for the task by the experience he had acquired as an assistant commissioner under the English Poor Law; and a comprehensive Report which he made on the occasion (and which my official position at the time enabled me to be cognisant of, although it was not published or generally known), affords proof of the efficient manner in which the task was executed by him. To a few of the matters contained in this Report, which is dated in June 1842, I will now advert; and

1840-42. Distress at Paisley, and contributions for its relief.

1842. Mr. Twisleton's Report.

there can be no impropriety in so doing, as although withheld from publication at the time, no inconvenience can possibly arise from its now becoming known, and it has an important bearing on the subject in hand.

The population of Paisley at the census of 1841 amounted to 48,416, nearly the whole of whom were engaged in the shawl manufacture, an occupation peculiarly liable to be affected by changes in fashion and fluctuations in trade. In 1819 we have seen that there was great distress at Paisley.[q] In 1826-27 severe distress again prevailed there, and also in 1837; and now the commercial difficulties which occurred between 1838 and 1843,[r] again subjected the manufacturers of Paisley to great pressure and privation. On all these occasions, recourse was had to extraneous aid, the local rates and contributions being insufficient for relieving the prevalent distress. The subscriptions during the preceding twelve months are stated in the Report to have amounted to upwards of 25,000*l.*;[s] and it is remarked that "nothing can more clearly show the inadequacy of a voluntary local subscription to meet such exigencies, than the simple fact that although it was agreed upon at a public meeting of the inhabitants in July last year, that the ratepayers should voluntarily assess themselves at the rate of 15 per cent. on their parochial assessment, the whole amount raised in this manner was only 574*l.* 1*s.* 11*d.*, and only 473 of the ratepayers contributed anything at all." It is further stated, that the whole sum raised in Paisley in the last year, whether by voluntary assessment or subscriptions, did not ex-

[q] Ante, p. 125.

[r] See 'History of the English Poor Law,' vol. ii. p. 373.

[s] Her Majesty and some of her ministers were contributors to the Paisley Relief Fund, in aid of which 4,715*l.* was also collected and transmitted from London, 960*l.* from Edinburgh, 500*l.* from Glasgow, and 440*l.* from Greenock. The Marquis of Abercorn subscribed 500*l.*, and the other landed proprietors of the country likewise contributed to the fund, which had been established in 1841.

ceed 1,227*l.* 14*s.* 8*d.*, whilst the number of persons depending for subsistence upon what they obtained from the relief fund, amounted in January 1842 to 12,703, and in June to 10,417.

Under such circumstances, we cannot feel surprised that the persons appointed by the relief committee to visit the dwellings of those to whom relief was afforded, should make representations of the following nature—"In many of the houses there is no furniture of any kind, except perhaps merely a box to sit upon—a great number of them have no regular bed or bedding, merely straw to lie upon on the bare ground." Another says, "I have visited 326 cases of females—In some of the houses there is no furniture at all—There is merely a small stool or a box to sit upon, and in two or three instances merely a large stone—The widows with families seemed the class worst off." Another says, "I have visited about 500 cases of men and women—The people are wretchedly poor—I have been in houses where there is not a single article, not a bed nor blanket—*They are very wretched*—The cases of the weavers are the worst; but the misery is very general." And the representations of the other visitors are all of similar import. The people are described in the Report as depressed in manner, and speaking despondingly of the future, and with the spirit of independence seemingly quite broken down—"the world was not their friend nor the world's law"—Their privations were extreme, their sufferings urgent and unavoidable, and there was no quarter to which they were entitled to look for assistance—how could they therefore be otherwise than spiritless and desponding?

Extent of distress, and its depressing influence on the people.

After noticing the general intelligence of the Paisley operatives, the Report states it to be universally admitted and deplored in Paisley, that the character of the weavers, particularly those of the rising generation, is much deteriorated, and this is said to be a consequence of the depressing circumstances in which they have for a long period been placed; for although adversity may under certain conditions lead to the improvement of character, it may, as is well remarked, "be doubted whether continued suffering in a community, when their physical comforts are curtailed by the operation of circumstances independent of their will, has not almost inevitably a tendency to impair their character." Under the influence of long-continued privations, it is further remarked "men lose self-respect, and become desponding and reckless. But this mood of mind is likely to prolong those privations, and is ill suited for steady industry thrift and foresight. The prolonged privations again reciprocally affect the mind; and the result is a vicious circle of action and reaction, in which the embarrassments and complications become at length so numerous, that escape seems hopeless"—and there is, it is added, reason to fear that the Paisley weavers are in this stage of downward progress. To what extent this social declension has been caused by the want of adequate relief in seasons of stagnation and pressure, it is impossible to say; but that such want was a prominent if not a principal cause, can hardly admit of question.

The management of the poor at Paisley was by law vested in the magistrates and the kirk session, but an arrangement had been made by which the latter retained the distribution of the church collections, mortuary fees, &c., and the former administered the money derived from assessments. But as under the Scotch Poor Law, able-bodied persons are not recognised as objects of relief, the funds derived from these sources were little affected by the severe distress which prevailed in the town, the average number of poor on the monthly roll during the year ending in June 1842 being somewhat over 700, and the entire cost of their relief amounting to 3,682*l.*—in neither case materially exceeding the ordinary amounts.

To maintain the exclusion of able-bodied persons from legal relief in cases like this of Paisley, is practically withholding it from the most distressed, who nevertheless must be supported in some way.—They cannot be left to starve; and such a system of exclusion will speedily become untenable, under the rude pressure of necessity. May we not ask then, whether provision ought not to be made for doing with equity and order, that which will otherwise be done inequitably and with disorder—whether relief should be provided promptly efficiently and fairly, rather than tardily partially and unequally?—The case of Paisley seems conclusive as an answer to the question; but however this may be, it undoubtedly hastened the inquiry into the general working of the Scottish Poor Law, which took place in the following year, and which now demands our attention.

1843. Commission of Inquiry appointed.

In January 1843 a commission under the great seal was issued, appointing seven gentlemen[t] of acknowledged competency to make "a diligent and full inquiry into the practical operation of the laws which provide for the relief of the poor in Scotland; and whether any, and what alterations amendments or improvements, may be beneficially made in the said laws, or in the manner of administering them, and how the same may be best carried into effect." As in the case of the English Poor Law inquiry, the commissioners were armed with powers to summon witnesses, and to require the production of accounts and other documents, and they were allowed a year for making their Report, which was not however

[t] The commissioners appointed were, Viscount Melville, Lord Belhaven, Henry Home Drummond Esq., James Campbell of Craigie Esq., Edward Twisleton Esq., and the Rev. Dr. Patrick Macfarlan, and the Rev. James Robertson.

delivered until the 2nd of May 1844; and to a consideration of this Report we will now proceed.

1844. Report of the Poor Law Inquiry Commission for Scotland.

In conducting their inquiry, the commissioners state that they examined either the minister or the session clerk of every parish, and any other persons who were suggested to them as likely to furnish information; and they have, they say, every reason to believe that the evidence taken by them "affords a fair general view of the state of pauperism and mode of managing the poor in each district." The witnesses whom they examined may, they remark, be considered as representing every class of society—Members of parliament, clergymen, country gentlemen, lawyers, medical practitioners, farmers, manufacturers, tradesmen, artisans, and labourers, all differing in education, feelings, habits and interests, and although exhibiting much diversity of opinion, yet substantially agreeing as to facts. The commissioners state that they personally visited the houses of many of the paupers in one or more parishes in each district, "to ascertain the condition of the inmates, and inquire into their means of subsistence," and they made notes of all such cases, which are appended to their Report: but the condition of the poor as described in these notes must, they observe, be judged of with reference to the condition of the working classes in the district, for "if this is not attended to, the notes, particularly those relating to cases in the Highlands and Islands, will convey an exaggerated impression of the discomfort of the poor."

With regard to the description of persons receiving relief, there is, it is said, a general uniformity of practice throughout Scotland. "The persons entitled to parochial relief, are those who are either wholly or partially disabled on account of age or infirmity, so as to be incapable of working and earning for themselves a sufficient maintenance—'cruiked folk, blind folk, sick folk, impotent folk, and weak folk,' in the terms of the Act of 1503 [u]—or 'aged, pure, impotent and decayed persons,' according to the Act of 1579 [u]—all persons in fact who do not come under the denomination of able-bodied." The commissioners accordingly found, that persons broken down or disabled by old age, or afflicted with any permanent disease incapacitating them for work, or who were insane or fatuous, and young children, whether orphans foundlings or deserted by their parents, or deprived of support from their father by his death transportation or imprisonment, were all considered proper objects of relief. But with respect to illegitimate children, the burthen of maintaining them was considered to be properly thrown upon the parents; and "unless constrained by the urgent necessity of the case, and the extreme poverty of the applicant, the parochial authorities do, as a general rule, resist all claims made on behalf of illegitimate children, from a desire to avoid the encouragement of vice by too ready advances made at the public expense."

The "regular" and the "occasional" poor.

In addition to the class of persons above enumerated, who are mostly termed the *regular or permanent poor*, from their being placed on the regular parish roll, there is another class usually denominated the *occasional poor*, who "being at other times able-bodied, receive occasional or temporary supply, when unable to work from sickness or other cause, during such time as their inability to work continues." The commissioners state, as the result of their inquiries respecting this last class, "that except in cases of fever or other epidemics, relief is seldom afforded, and when given, it is rather *ex pietate* than *ex lege*, more as a matter of compassion, than a matter of right." With regard to the labouring classes generally, the commissioners state, that "the

---

[u] Ante, pp. 11 and 16.

instances in which parish relief appears to have been afforded to able-bodied persons, on account of their inability to find employment, are of rare occurrence;" and they further say, that "the recent depression of trade, caused the question as to the right of able-bodied persons to demand relief, to be frequently agitated: but they found that the universal practice, with a few exceptions in one or two country parishes, has been to refuse relief in such cases; and the pressing wants of the able-bodied have been met by other means, such as subscriptions, or work furnished by proprietors in their neighbourhood at a reduced rate of wages." On this statement, it may be remarked, that the few exceptional cases in which relief was afforded to able-bodied persons "on account of their inability to find employment," might be expected rather to have taken place in towns than in country parishes; but "the work furnished by proprietors at reduced wages," may possibly in these rural instances have served as an inducement for breaking the rule.

Burghal, rural, and mixed parishes.

The parishes in Scotland are distinguished into burghal, landward or rural, and those of a mixed character, partly burghal partly rural. In burghal parishes, the duty both of raising the funds and of relieving the poor rests with the borough magistrates, who generally devolve the management upon a committee chosen for the purpose, the authority remaining nevertheless legally vested in themselves. In rural parishes, the kirk session and the heritors or landowners of the parish have conjoint control in all matters relating to the poor—They meet twice a year, the minister is ex-officio chairman, and the votes of the majority govern their proceedings. In parishes partly burghal partly rural, the administration is also vested in the heritors and kirk session, the borough magistrates taking part therein as heritors. It is said however, that "although legally the administrative body is the same in all parishes, whether purely landward, or partly landward and partly burghal, yet in practice, the management is different in different parts of the country."

Means of relief whence derived.

The fund from which the relief of the poor has been chiefly derived in Scotland is the church collections, the practice of contributing to which is said to be universally maintained, however small may sometimes be the amount realised. "Throughout the northern and western Highlands, and nearly the whole of the parishes in the synods of Shetland, Orkney, Sutherland, and Caithness, Ross, Glenelg, Argyle and Moray—comprising in extent almost one-half of Scotland, the church collections, with such small sums as may accrue to the kirk session from fees fines &c., aided in a few instances by occasional donations from heritors or casual visitors, form the only public fund to which the poor can look for relief." In other parts of the country, besides the church collections and sessional funds, many parishes derive a certain amount of income from mortifications, that is, money or land given in perpetuity by benevolent individuals. And in some parishes, the commissioners found that a small capital had been accumulated from donations or legacies, or savings in former years when the demand did not exhaust the income, the interest of which added to the church collections, formed a fund for the support of the poor.

The clergy opposed to assessment.

Where the moneys arising from these various sources proved insufficient for relieving the wants of the poor, the most obvious course would appear to be, as the commissioners remark, "to take immediate steps for raising the required sum by an assessment, regularly imposed, and leviable from the parties liable by law to contribute." But it is added, "a strong feeling in opposition to a legal assessment has existed in Scotland, and the clergy in general have strenuously exerted their influence, to prevent recourse being had to any compulsory mode of raising funds for the relief of the poor." In most of the unassessed parishes, all parties are said to regard assessment as an evil which ought to be avoided; and where the church collections and other ordinary funds prove inadequate, the heritors arrange to subscribe voluntarily among themselves, in order to supply the deficiency. Hence, it is remarked, have originated "the various forms of what is not unfrequently called a voluntary assessment," the contributions to which by individual heritors are sometimes said to bear little proportion to the value of their properties. Most frequently however, the money is, we are told, raised by the heritors agreeing to pay rateably, according to the rentals of their respective estates.

Notwithstanding what is said above, the commissioners state that the number of legally assessed parishes has been annually increasing, and they express their belief that the feeling against assessment is gradually diminishing. In most of the cities and large towns, they observe, "it has long been found absolutely necessary to resort to this mode of raising the required funds; and there is now hardly a considerable town or populous parish in Scotland, in which an assessment is not either in existence, or in contemplation. Even in Inverness, where an assessment was long resisted, it was in 1843 found to be inevitable." The mode of levying the assessment, is however said to be very different in different burghs; and in some instances, considerable difficulty is found in laying on an assessment that would in all respects be in strict conformity with the law.

Assessment adopted in most large towns.

After thus describing the mode in which they conducted the inquiry, the class of persons to whom relief was afforded, and the source whence it was derived, the commissioners next explain the nature and extent of the relief actually given.

In some of the larger towns, "where the number of aged and helpless individuals whose friends are unable or unwilling to undertake the charge of them is always considerable, it has (the commissioners say) been found desirable to provide a place into which persons of that description might be removed, and put under proper care and treatment." Such poor-houses, it is added, are under the control of the ordinary managers of the poor, and the expense attending them has been held a proper charge upon the poor's fund. A list of these establishments is given, amounting to thirteen in number, and their management is described, which appears to be very similar to that of the old English poor-houses; but in addition to these, the commissioners found "some approximation to a poor-house" in several other parishes, in which the more helpless of the poor were lodged and maintained.

Poor-houses.

The Scottish system is said however to be essentially one of out-door relief, administered in various ways, the most common mode being by an allowance in money, "either by the week, fortnight, month, half-quarter, quarter, or half-year." In fixing the allowance, the circumstances of individuals are separately considered—their claims on relations, the assistance they may receive from private charity, and every other possible source of income are taken into account. The relief given in the western Highlands is, the commissioners say, so small, as not to be of any material assistance in providing for the support of the poor. In the county of Sutherland such relief "was considered as an acknowledgment of poverty—that is, a sort of recognition of the claim of the party receiving it, to obtain charitable aid in whatever other way he can, from the benevolent individuals in the neighbourhood." In those districts, the allowances are sometimes as low as 2*s.* annually, and they seldom exceed 10*s.*, even in cases of special necessity. In other parts of Scotland,

Different modes of relief.

where the relief "is intended to be a real and substantial assistance to the recipients," there is a great diversity in its amount, and even within the same presbytery, the allowances given in one parish vary considerably from those in another. In some parishes there are two distinct classes of poor, who are under separate management. Thus in Glasgow there are "sessional poor," and "hospital poor," the former being under the kirk sessions of the several city parishes, who grant relief to the extent of 6*s*. per month; but if more be required, the applicant is transferred to the class of "hospital poor," who are under charge of the managers of the town's hospital.

The helpless and infirm poor, who are unable to take care of themselves, are usually boarded with relations or friends if they have any, or if not with other persons willing to take charge of them. Orphans foundlings and deserted children are usually provided for in the same way, and are represented as being generally well taken care of. Lunatics and fatuous persons are either sent to a lunatic asylum, or boarded in private houses—the latter mode being the least expensive, is generally adopted. Where the relief if given in money is likely to be misapplied, it is frequently given in victuals or clothing; and it is sometimes applied in payment of rents, which many persons consider an eligible mode of granting relief, although by others it is condemned. The commissioners however "do not find that any evil has arisen from this practice, or that it has been carried to such an extent as to afford encouragement for speculators to build pauper cottages, as is said at one time to have been the case in England." In Shetland the poor are said to be relieved by what is called "quartering," that is, by any one who is deemed a fit object for relief being assigned to a particular district of the parish, on which he is quartered; and it is considered obligatory on the inhabitants of that dis- "Quartering."

trict, in rotation, to furnish him with board and lodging for a certain number of nights, according to their several means. This is in fact equivalent to the levying of a poor-rate, and the practice is said to be strongly disapproved by the better class of householders.

Poor licensed to beg.

Another mode of providing for the poor is, by licensing them to beg within the limits of their own parish, in conformity with the Act of 1672;[x] and the commissioners accordingly found "that begging is in many places a recognised means of subsistence for paupers." In the parish of Campbleton, they say "forty nine persons were in October 1842, struck off the roll by a committee of managers of the poor, and badges were given to such of the number as chose to receive them as a licence to beg." And even without such badges, the commissioners found "that in most of the burghs and smaller towns the paupers are allowed to beg on one or more days in the week, as in Inverary, Dingwall, Thurso, Perth, Kirkcaldy, and many others."

The foregoing statements apply chiefly to the ordinary poor, who require regular relief, and are entitled to be placed on the permanent roll. But allowances are also granted occasionally out of the poor-fund for relief on account of sickness, for payment of funeral expenses, and for defraying the charge connected with removals.

Medical relief.

There is said to be scarcely any provision for medical relief in Scotland. This species of relief seems to be left almost entirely to private charity. Yet the commissioners state that the poor do not suffer materially from want of medical aid, there being in all the large and in many of the smaller towns, dispensaries supported by voluntary contributions, which supply the poor with medicines, and the officers of which give their attendance gratis. In rural districts the sick poor are

---

[x] Ante, p. 67.

generally attended without charge by the medical practitioners, who also in the great majority of cases furnish medicine—"extra diet and wine, if needed, must be obtained from the charity of wealthier neighbours of the poor." The medical men are naturally dissatisfied with this state of things. They are said not to be unwilling to give their attendance gratuitously, but they complain of being called upon to furnish medicine as well, and they moreover complain of the difficulty often experienced in procuring the necessary diet and stimulants for the sick. With regard to funeral expenses, it may be remarked, that the kirk session and other managers of the poor are held to be entitled to the effects of deceased paupers; but where the relations or friends undertake the expense of the funeral, the right is not enforced. This latter condition is however seldom attended to, and it may be said that the funeral expenses are almost invariably defrayed out of the poor-fund.

Funeral expenses.

Although there is in Scotland no power of removing a person against his will, from a parish in which he may have become destitute without having a settlement in it, the commissioners yet say that "considerable sums are expended yearly in sending home English and Irish paupers, and paupers belonging to other parishes in Scotland," the expense of which is charged to the poor-fund. The usual practice is to furnish the party with a pass, on the authority of which he proceeds to his parish, wherever it may be; and all the parishes on the road by which he travels, are expected to give him something for his support by the way. "Whole families are sometimes transmitted in this manner, and if there be invalids or children of the party they are removed in carts, and the expense of the conveyance is borne by the different parishes through which they pass on their road homeward." Passes of this description are said to be extensively granted in some parts of the country, and they are sanctioned by

Removals.

the Act of 1579, as well as by the proclamation of 1692.[y]

The foregoing is a brief summary of the practice described by the Commissioners of Inquiry, as actually pursued in Scotland with regard to the relief of the poor. The commissioners next proceed, in the terms of their commission, "to consider whether any and what alterations, amendments, or improvements may be beneficially made in the law, or in the manner of administering it, and how the same may be best carried into effect."

The commissioners explain the principle on which their recommendations will be founded.

The commissioners commence this portion of their subject by stating, that the points upon which they find it necessary to animadvert, do not arise so much from defects in the law itself, as from its being in many parishes either altogether inoperative, or else administered in a very insufficient manner. And therefore it has, they say, been their object to consider in what way the present law may be made to work most efficiently, without making any very material changes either in its letter or its spirit—keeping in mind that where a system of law and practice is in operation, to which a very large proportion of the inhabitants of the country have long been accustomed to look with respect, great caution is necessary in recommending measures the tendency of which might be entirely to subvert the existing order of things. They think it advisable therefore, that the efforts of the legislature should, at all events in the first instance, be directed to amend and repair the existing system, rather than to introduce what is altogether new and foreign to the habits and feelings of the community; and they would, they say, "consider that they were actuated by a false and ill-directed philanthropy, were they to recommend any measures likely to create an abatement of exertion on the part of the labouring classes, or a less independent feeling than

---

[y] Ante, pp. 16 and 78.

that which now exists, or which would lead them to rely on any other means of support than those derived from the exercise of their own energies—being convinced that such measures, however specious at first sight, would not be calculated ultimately to contribute to the happiness of the poor, or to promote their welfare."

After this exposition of their views, and the principle on which they purposed that any recommendation they might make should be founded—They first took into consideration the adequacy or otherwise of the relief then afforded to the indigent poor.

As to the adequacy of present relief.

On comparing the condition of the paupers on the roll, with that of independent labourers, the commissioners state that they found it but little inferior. The allowance made by the administrators of the poor's fund, it is observed, gives in most cases an imperfect notion of a pauper's means of livelihood. In the country parishes, there are few receiving relief who are not able in some way or other to earn a little; and the standard of living is said to vary so much in different parts of the country, "that with 1*s*. a week in one parish, a pauper may be in fully as good a condition compared with the independent labourer, as he would be with 2*s*. a week in another." But nevertheless there undoubtedly is, the commissioners remark, "abundant evidence to prove that the allowances are often inadequate, both in town and country parishes, and that the amount of relief given is frequently altogether insufficient to provide even the commonest necessaries of life." Where the funds are solely obtained from the church collections, the amount is often inconsiderable, and the same may be said of many of the assessed parishes, where the money raised is often inadequate to meet the claims on the fund. In the Highlands and Western Islands, when the poor have exhausted their small crop of potatoes, they are "forced to cast themselves on the charity of their neighbours, many of whom are nearly as poor as themselves. In other districts they may get assistance from the more wealthy classes, and in towns they generally have recourse to common begging." There can, the commissioners observe, be no question that it was the intention of the law that the poor should have adequate relief; and they now declare it to be their opinion—

> "That the funds raised for the relief of the poor, and "the provision made for them out of the funds "raised for their relief, is in many parishes through- "out Scotland insufficient."

The commissioners then remark, that since the commencement of the present century, great changes have taken place in the circumstances and general condition of the people. The impetus given by manufactures of various kinds, and the extended operations in the coal and iron districts have, they say, created an entirely new order of things. The annihilation of the kelp trade, and the alteration of the system of farming in the Highlands have also, it is observed, tended greatly to increase the amount of pauperism; and the sympathy which used to exist between the poor and the occupiers of land, exists no longer. Under these circumstances, a ready and accessible court of appeal might appear to be one of the first and simplest remedies for providing against the inadequacy of relief, and such a power has, the commissioners say, been recommended by many of the witnesses: but a right of appeal in regard to the sufficiency of relief, whether to the local magistrate or any other authority, would they consider be attended with very serious evils. They refer to the example of England, where for a long time the local magistrates exercised an appellate jurisdiction in regulating the amount of relief, the effects of which were found to be so prejudicial that the power was abolished, and there is now no appeal from the decision of the boards of guardians in England.

The commissioners finally declare themselves "so opposed to any court of appeal as to the amount of allowances, that instead of investing any new tribunal or board with jurisdiction in such matters, they are inclined to suggest that the appeal to the court of session should be taken away." If it be asked by what means due attention to the wants of the poor is to be secured, when the power of appeal is taken away, it may they think be answered, that the influence of good feeling, and the power of public opinion, which in many parishes have led to the poor being adequately provided for, will do this without the aid of compulsory measures, and they accordingly come to the conclusion—

> "That it is not desirable that there should be any
> "appeal from the decision of the parochial managers
> "as to the amount of advances."

Some persons had suggested the establishment of a compulsory assessment in every parish, in order to create a certain fund for the relief of the poor, which it was thought would lead to the allowances being fixed on a more liberal scale. But this, the commissioners observe, "would be an entire change of one of the leading characteristics of the Scottish system, which adapting itself to the varying circumstances of particular parishes at different times, admits of an assessment being either imposed or not, as the managers of the poor may judge expedient; and such a change, without some certainty of its being productive of beneficial results, they are not disposed to recommend." A pauper has, they say, the same right to relief whether his parish be assessed or not, and there are many unassessed parishes in which the allowances are more liberal than they are in others where an assessment has been established. On the whole therefore, they consider that it ought to be left to the parish authorities to provide the funds for the relief of the poor, either by assessment or otherwise, as they may deem expedient—at the same time remarking however, "that the voluntary method of providing these funds, to which a preference is still given by a large portion of the intelligence of the country, has appeared to them in a great variety of instances to work in a satisfactory manner, and to be productive of beneficial effects."

The commissioners are of opinion, that means should be taken for subjecting the proceedings of parochial managers to a strict review at stated periods. Hitherto, they say, the necessary facilities have not been afforded for enabling the public to form a judgment as to the working of the present system, and the influence of public opinion on the management of the poor has therefore not been practically felt. The present inquiry has, it is observed, already proved beneficial, by "fixing the attention of many influential parties on the important subject to which it refers, and thus causing the actual state of pauperism to be thoroughly investigated, and the provision made for its relief to be carefully inquired into." There would, it is considered, be no difficulty in establishing a board of supervision in Edinburgh, on some such footing as the present General Prison Board, to which reports from every parish might be made at stated periods, and the board itself reporting annually to the secretary of state. The commissioners do not think it expedient that such board "should have any power of interfering with the management of the parochial boards, except by representation or advice; but they are decidedly of opinion that it should have full power to require the parochial boards to furnish it with every information regarding the management of the poor in their respective parishes"—and they therefore propose—

Board of supervision.

"That a board of supervision, all the members of "which should be unpaid, shall be esta- "blished for a limited period, to which "board reports shall be made at least twice in the "year from the parochial boards, stating specially "the numbers and condition of the poor in each "parish, and the amount of relief, in such form as "shall be prescribed by the board of supervision; "that complaints may be made to such board, and "that such board shall have the fullest power of "inquiry and remonstrance. That the board of "supervision shall make a report annually to the "secretary of state on the condition and manage-"ment of the poor throughout Scotland."

If such a board of supervision be instituted, it will be necessary that a responsible officer should be appointed in each parish to make the requisite reports, and give the information which may be required. The advantage of having such an officer, would it is believed be great, "as he would be officially bound to have a knowledge of the whole poor, and to make himself acquainted with the circumstances in each case." The feeling of responsibility which would attach to him would also, the commissioners consider, be in the highest degree beneficial; and they accordingly further suggest—

A paid clerk to be appointed in every parish.

"That the heritors and kirk-session or other "managers of the poor in each parish, "shall be bound to appoint a salaried clerk "or other officer, who shall be required "to make the reports to, and to conduct the "correspondence with, the general board of super-"vision; and that the remuneration which such "officer shall receive shall be fixed by the paro-"chial board of management."

Parochial board of management.

The constitution of the several parochial boards of management next occupied the commissioners' attention. In the unassessed parishes of the rural districts, "where a primitive simplicity of manners continues to prevail," the present administrative body must, it is considered, generally speaking, be the parties best fitted for performing the duties of a responsible board of management; and in such parishes the commissioners therefore "doubt the propriety of removing the funds for the relief of the poor from the control of the heritors and kirk-session, under whose joint management they at present are." But where an assessment is levied, some alteration may it is thought be advantageously made in the constitution of the board, by allowing those who pay assessments, but who are not heritors, to have a voice in the administration of the funds. If the ratepayers as a class were permitted to have a voice along with the heritors and kirk-session, it might tend to inspire confidence; but such an alteration would, it is said, require to be accompanied with some provision "by which the number of persons entitled to vote as heritors at the parochial meetings may be limited." The "*feuars*," or owners of small tenements, are in some places very numerous, and if assessed they would all be entitled to vote equally with the heritors. The commissioners consider it expedient therefore, that in matters concerning the poor there should be a limitation in this respect, and they recommend—

> "That those persons only are to be considered "heritors, and held entitled to vote as such, who "have a valued rent to the amount of 5*l*. Scots."

And subject to this limitation, the commissioners also recommend—

> "That in rural parishes in which assessment is "raised, the body to be entrusted with the power "of imposing such assessment and administering "the funds, shall consist, in addition to the heritors "and kirk-session, of a certain number of persons

" to be chosen by the ratepayers, not being heritors
" as above defined."

The law applying to parishes of a mixed character, partly burghal and partly rural, is the same as in the case of purely burghal parishes. They are subjected to one managing body, consisting of the heritors and kirk-session, the burghal magistrates being entitled to act and vote as heritors. But in Dundee and certain other places, this mode of administration having been found inconvenient, had been abandoned, and committees of management were appoinied in its stead by the heritors and the magistrates. Without expressing any opinion as to the expediency or legality of these changes, the commissioners "assume it to be generally admitted, that in places where the population has become excessive, the separate parochial system can be no longer effectively carried out." A person may, they observe, reside for many years in a town consisting of two or three different parishes, without acquiring a settlement in any one of them, the individuals most likely to come on the poor-roll being in the habit of frequently shifting their residences from one part of the town to another. The commissioners are therefore of opinion—

Town parishes to be united under one board of management.

"That it is desirable that all parishes which either
" in whole or in part, are situate within
" the parliamentary boundaries of any
" burgh, should be united and held to be
" one parish for the purposes of providing for the
" poor, and of settlement."

And they further recommend—

"That the managers of the poor in such united
" parishes, should consist wholly or chiefly of
" managers to be elected by the ratepayers, and
" also of the provost or chief magistate ex officio—

"The number of votes which each ratepayer shall "have, being regulated by the amount of the pro- "perty on which he is assessed."

Having stated their views with regard to the constitution of the managing boards in rural and town parishes, the commissioners next advert to the question of poorhouses. In parishes having no poorhouse, paupers incapable of taking care of themselves are, it is said, usually boarded with relations, or other persons disposed to take charge of them, but in neither case are they always properly treated. The same may be said with respect to orphans foundlings and deserted children, who in populous places are moreover exposed to the influence of bad example, and the risk of contracting evil habits. Cases of the above description can only, it is considered, be properly treated within a poorhouse, and the commissioners therefore think it "highly desirable, that in every parish having above a certain amount of population, a poorhouse should be established under proper regulations, for the reception of aged and helpless persons, incurables, orphans and deserted children, and the dissipated and improvident poor." No precise amount of population is named, but where a parish contains more than 6000 or 8000 inhabitants, the necessity for a poorhouse will it is thought be generally apparent; and it is added— "indeed there are few parishes having a population of upwards of 5000, in which an establishment of this nature is not desirable." The commissioners nevertheless do not propose to make the erection of poorhouses compulsory, as they "confidently anticipate that the administrative bodies constituted as has been proposed, and acting under the influence of public opinion, will of themselves take steps for the accomplishment of this object in all the more populous parishes." This recommendation of poorhouses, is however qualified by the commissioners declaring, that they do not wish to do

Poorhouses.

away with the present system of out-door relief to helpless individuals who can otherwise be properly cared for, their object being, they say, "to provide for the greater comfort of the paupers, and to secure for them the certain means of proper treatment, if they cannot obtain it elsewhere." A poorhouse will also, it is observed, be advantageous in another respect, as it will assist the parochial board in determining the amount of allowance for out-door relief. The pauper's right to be relieved extends to nothing beyond "needful sustentation," and the rate of out-door relief ought therefore never to exceed the cost of maintenance in the poorhouse. On all these considerations, the commissioners recommend—

> "That requisite powers should be given for two or
> " more contiguous parishes to unite for the pur-
> " pose of building a poorhouse."

Medical relief.

The question of medical relief is next considered. The defective practice in this respect which prevails in all parts of Scotland, has been already noticed.[z] But the authority for affording medical aid to persons afflicted with temporary sickness, out of funds raised by assessment, is deemed to be very questionable; and the commissioners consider it necessary that "the managers of the poor in each parish should have full discretionary power by law, to afford medical relief in all cases where it may seem to them desirable." Parishes might, it is said, be often gainers by promptly granting efficient medical aid, as temporary sickness may else grow into a permanent malady, and become an occasion of expense to and a burden on the parish funds. The commissioners wish medical relief to be understood as comprising "the supply of nutritious diet, wine, or cordials, where deemed necessary for

---

[z] Ante, p. 142.

the proper treatment of the case; and also the vaccination of children when necessary;" and they propose—

> "That medical relief should be supplied more extensively to the poor, and that this should form a proper charge upon the poor-funds."

They also further recommend—

> "That in those parishes in which it is found expedient to build poorhouses, the managers of the poor should in connexion with the poorhouses provide accommodation for dispensaries for the poor."

Pauper lunatics.

The next subject to which the commissioners direct their attention, is the condition of the pauper lunatics. Great improvement has, they say, taken place in the treatment of insanity in Scotland within the last twenty or thirty years, lunatic asylums having been erected in Edinburgh, Glasgow, Aberdeen, and several other towns; but the accommodation is nevertheless still very inadequate. In some of the parishes which they visited, the commissioners found pauper lunatics under most improper treatment, and they describe a few of the most flagrant cases, which are exceedingly revolting. They think it important that the parochial boards should take measures for sending insane paupers to an asylum, immediately on the appearance of the disease, and they recommend—

> "That where an insane person is in receipt of parochial relief, it shall be imperative on the managers of the poor to send such insane person forthwith to a lunatic asylum, unless authorised by the board of supervision to treat him otherwise."

The commissioners next advert to the case of "applicants for relief, who have no settlement in the parish to which they apply, but are otherwise proper objects for parochial aid." The rule in such cases is understood to be, that the managers of the poor are bound to relieve persons in distress, even although they have no settlement in the parish; but the commissioners express themselves satisfied from the inquiries they have made, "that the practice is often at variance with this rule." The practice in the larger towns has been, (as is before stated[a]) if the applicant appeared to belong to some other parish, to give him a pass or certificate, under authority of which the bearer is held to be entitled to pass from parish to parish on his road homeward, and to obtain such assistance as he can from the different parishes through which he travels. These passes, it is observed, are subject to great abuse, and they serve as a cloak for vagrancy and imposition. Their number is also very great. Those given by the city parish in Edinburgh during the year 1843 amounted to 771, and from Dundee alone during the year 1842, the inspector of the poor stated that he had given no less than 1913. "The complaints against them are loud and general, especially on the part of the country parishes." Although the system of passes is sanctioned by the Act of 1579,[b] and the proclamation of 1692,[b] it cannot, the commissioners observe, be supposed that the legislature intended to countenance the abuses to which it has given rise. Before granting a pass, they consider that means ought to be taken for ascertaining the parish to which the applicant belongs, and in cases of sickness a medical certificate ought to be obtained before the applicant is removed. The law, they say, provides that the parish furnishing interim relief, may recover the outlay from the parish liable for his maintenance; and they therefore consider "that there can be no hardship in enacting, that the parish

Non-settled paupers.

---

[a] Ante, p. 143.

[b] Ante, pp. 16 and 78.

in which a person is found destitute shall be bound to afford relief, until the parish of his settlement be ascertained." Wherefore it is recommended—

> "That in all cases the parish in which a pauper "is found destitute, should be required to relieve "him forthwith, provided he be a proper object of "parochial relief; and that such relief shall be "continued until the pauper's parish of settlement "be ascertained, and his claim admitted or esta-"blished, the expenses of interim maintenance "and other expenses being recoverable from the "parish ultimately found liable."

Interim relief.

In order to enable a parish which has advanced money by way of interim relief to a pauper belonging to another parish, to recover the amount without delay, some additional facilities are considered to be necessary. Several cases were submitted to the commissioners, in which applications for repayment of such outlay have either been left unnoticed, or refused on the ground of want of funds. "It appears indeed from the statement of several of the clergy in the Highlands, that it is a common practice there to pay no regard to such applications." The commissioners therefore recommend—

> "That an officer should be appointed for each paro-"chial board, in whose name the managers of the "poor should pursue and defend actions."

Power of removal.

In connexion with this subject, it is further stated, that a considerable number of English and Irish immigrate into Scotland in search of employment, some of whom occasionally become objects of relief before they have acquired a settlement; but such persons cannot at present be removed without their own consent—"there being no means of compelling them to return home, and seek relief in their own country." It is also felt to be a hardship, that an Englishman may by an industrial residence of three years acquire a settlement in a Scottish parish, while a Scotchman can never by mere residence acquire a settlement in England. The commissioners consider therefore, that if the power of removal now possessed by parishes in England be continued, a reciprocal power ought to be vested in the parish authorities of Scotland; and it is accordingly proposed—

> "That a power of removing English and Irish paupers "should be introduced into Scotland, similar to that "which now exists in England with respect to "Scotch paupers."

With respect to the education of pauper children, the commissioners remark—"it may seem surprising that any doubts should exist as to the legality of dedicating a portion of the poor-fund to purposes of education, for the culture of the mind would appear to be as necessary, where a destitute child is dependent on the parish for relief, as the supply of food and raiment is for the body." Such doubts did nevertheless appear to exist, although in most parishes provision of some kind or other, is said to be made for the education of pauper children. But the commissioners think that there should be a regular and certain provision for the education of these children, and that the parochial boards should be empowered to make the necessary arrangements for this purpose; and they accordingly recommend—

Education of pauper children.

> "That in each parish the board of managers should "be required to defray from the funds provided "for the relief of the poor, the expenses of educating "pauper children."

Cases of desertion of wives and families are said to have increased of late years, and an additional burden has thence been thrown on the parochial

Desertion of wives and families.

funds. "The law at present provides no means of punishing criminally a husband guilty of an act of this kind. When a family is abandoned by their father, and relief supplied by the parish, there is no other mode of proceeding against the father than by a civil action, at the instance of the parish authorities, to recover the amount expended;" and this proceeding is said to be seldom attended with success. The commissioners therefore recommend—

> "That in addition to such civil remedies as now exist, "husbands or fathers neglecting to maintain their "wives or families, be punishable criminally by a "summary process, in the event of the wives or "families becoming chargeable on the parish. And "that in like manner, fathers of illegitimate "children, where such fathers admit their liability, "or have been found liable by decree of a competent "court, shall be punishable criminally by a summary "process, if they neglect to pay the aliment, and "the child become chargeable."

The commissioners next proceed to offer suggestions on certain other matters connected with the subject of their inquiry, commencing with the church collections, one half of which may, it is observed, be by law applied to occasional purposes, whilst the other half merges in the common poor-fund. "The evidence of all who have had practical experience in the management of the poor, (they say) demonstrates the advantages which arise from affording assistance to persons who have been reduced by temporary calamity, so as to save them from sinking in the world, and losing their position in society. Small sums, bestowed privately by the minister or elders, whether by way of charity or loan, will often help to rouse the dormant energies, and sustain the drooping spirit; and by such well-timed assistance a man may be enabled to get over his diffi-

Church collections.

culties, and resume his station in the world, without the consciousness of having been degraded to the state of a pauper." The commissioners can conceive nothing more correct in principle, than that the means of relieving such cases should be furnished by voluntary benevolence, " nor could any more fitting almoners be found for dispensing such charity than the ministers and elders of the church :" wherefore they are of opinion—

> " That in every parish where an assessment for the
> " poor is imposed, the collections in the churches
> " should be left at the disposal of the kirk session
> " of each congregation."

Where the church collections are entirely separated from the funds raised by assessment for the poor on the common roll, and their administration is entrusted to the kirk session, the commissioners confidently anticipate that the amount of such collections will be greatly enlarged, " and that the results in regard as well to the character as to the condition of the poor, will be highly beneficial." Wherefore they propose, firstly—

> " That all capital sums whatsoever, and all other
> " funds than church collections, in the hands of
> " the heritors and kirk session, or either of these
> " bodies, for the use of the poor, not specially
> " destined to other purposes, should, where an
> " assessment is imposed, be transferred to the
> " managers of the poor, and be at their disposal."

And secondly—

> " That all funds for behoof of the poor arising from
> " mortifications or bequests, as to which no special
> " mode of investment is prescribed, and that all
> " floating funds not required for immediate use,
> " should be lodged either in a chartered bank, or
> " invested in government or heritable security."

On settlement.

The subject of settlement is next considered, and it is regarded by the commissioners as "one of the most important questions submitted to them." The present law establishing settlement by a residence of three years in a parish is, they say, complained of by a large class of persons, as being partial and unjust. It is alleged that there is a constant influx from rural parishes into the towns and large villages, which thus become unduly burdened. To this allegation however the commissioners attach little weight, the inquiries which they have made as well as their own observations having led them to the conclusion, that generally speaking the condition of the poor in the Lowland parishes is superior to what it is in the towns, and that even in many parts of the Highlands the poor are better provided for than in Edinburgh or Glasgow. Wherefore they consider that there is nothing to induce such an influx into the towns, and that the allegations that such is the case are unsupported by evidence, and without foundation. With regard to the period of residence for conferring settlement, and a right to relief in a parish, the commissioners observe, that it was fixed at seven years by the Act of 1579,[c] which was altered to three years by the Act of 1672,[c] and although seven years is again named in the proclamation of August 1693,[c] it has, they say, "long been established that three years' residence is sufficient to constitute a settlement." They adduce various reasons however in favour of the longer term, and recommend—

"That the period of residence for acquiring a settle-
"ment be extended to seven years; and that in-
"dustrial residence by means of which a settlement
"may be acquired, shall be understood to mean
"residence, where a party maintains himself without

---

[c] Ante, pp. 16, 67, and 81.

"parochial relief, or having recourse to 'common
"begging,' either by himself or his family."

And they further recommend—

"That a settlement by residence shall only be acquired
"by natives of Scotland."

There are two other points connected with the law of settlement which were at that time involved in some uncertainty, and with respect to which the commissioners recommend—

Firstly—"That a child *foris familiated*, after the age
"of fourteen, shall, in the event of the father
"having acquired a new settlement by residence,
"be held to have a settlement in the parish of the
"father's settlement at the period of *foris familia-*
"*tion*, and that illegitimate children shall, under
"all circumstances, follow the existing settlement
"of the mother, until they have acquired a new
"settlement for themselves."

Secondly—"That a child whose father is dead, shall,
"while under fourteen and unemancipated, follow
"the settlement of the mother, if she shall have
"acquired a new settlement, either by residence or
"by subsequent marriage."

In illustration of the practice for which the last recommendation is intended as a remedy, the commissioners state the case of an Irishman, who had died without having acquired a settlement, leaving a widow and children. The widow, it is said, continued to maintain herself and her family for upwards of three years, and then applied for relief on account of her children. But as the father had no settlement, the children were not held to have any claim, and the parish authorities offered to remove them to Ireland. "Had the mother been also removed to Ireland, she might have been refused relief there on the plea of her Scotch settlement, and the result would have been a separation of the children from their surviving parent."

The commissioners here conclude their observations on the several points with regard to which they think it desirable that some change should be made in the existing law; but there are, they say, two questions remaining which they cannot pass over unnoticed, although they are not prepared to make any suggestions respecting them. "The first and most important of these questions is, the propriety of granting relief to able-bodied persons when unable to procure employment. The second is, the expediency of making a change in the present mode of imposing assessments for the relief of the poor."

The able-bodied poor.

With respect to the first question—The relief of the able-bodied poor, it is observed, "involves points deeply affecting the fundamental principles of the whole system of Scottish Poor Laws;" and at the present time, owing to long-continued depression of trade, the question is invested with peculiar interest. The claims of the impotent poor to be relieved, are said to be recognised as a right, but there is no such recognition with regard to the able-bodied poor, neither are the parochial boards authorised to levy assessments on their account. The commissioners then enter into an elaborate exposition, filling seventeen closely printed folio pages, of the various arguments connected with this question; and they finally arrive at the conclusion, that on the whole, as regards the rural parishes, "the present law makes as near an approach as is attainable under existing circumstances, to the system of relief which sound principle points out as applicable to the case of the able-bodied poor." Whilst with regard to town and manufacturing populations, they consider "that the present laws, if amended as they have proposed, will be found sufficient for their purpose, and therefore that relief to able-bodied persons from funds raised by assessment, is neither necessary nor expedient."

With respect to the second question, that of assessments—it is admitted that they are raised in a very irregular and disorderly manner. "Almost every burgh has some peculiar established usage as to the mode of carrying the general law into effect; and as might be expected, there are in every burgh parties ready to express their dissatisfaction with the existing order of things." The commissioners however see great difficulty in applying any legislative remedy in this case. There will always, they say, be found persons ready to complain of the principle on which a tax is imposed. But they consider the prevalence of any usage for a length of time, sufficient to create a presumption of its being in accordance with the feelings of the majority; and influenced by this sedative, and seeing that parishes are at present enabled to raise the requisite funds for the relief of the poor, the commissioners "are not prepared to recommend any alteration with regard to the mode of imposing assessments."

Assessments.

The Report would seem naturally to end here; but the commissioners cannot close it, without adverting to the great prevalence of mendicity in Scotland. The evil they say is most observable in towns. In some of the country districts it has been checked by the establishment of a rural police, but it is still very prevalent in many parts of the country. The law relating to vagrants is said not to be clearly defined, and the practice varies in different counties, which it is thought may have some influence in preventing the application of an effectual remedy. Few things, it is remarked, operate more strongly in promoting immorality, than the encouragement of common begging, with all its train of self-abasement, dissimulation, and fraud. "The low lodginghouses which beggars frequent, and the bad habits of the class of per-

Mendicancy.

sons with whom they necessarily associate, soon familiarise their minds with vice and debauchery; and if such (it is asked) be the effects upon those of mature years, what must be the result with children, whom it is the common practice for the parents to send to beg?" —Begging is, the commissioners observe, often a profession, and frequently a very lucrative one; and it will never be altogether abandoned, until people are induced to refrain from indiscriminate charity, which (it is added, quoting from evidence in the cases of Selkirk and Kelso) "they will always do, if they can excuse their consciences by knowing that the parties have a place of refuge to go to."

Some observations are then made in reference to publichouses, pawnbroking, savings-banks, friendly societies, emigration, and lastly education. But it is not necessary to follow the commissioners on either of these subjects, with respect to which they advance nothing new, or which has an important bearing on the general question.

The commissioners conclude by declaring that they cannot expect their recommendations will give universal satisfaction, neither can they hope that a complete remedy for the evils complained of will be provided by legislation. They have, they say "been unwilling rashly to propose innovations which they did not feel convinced would be improvements, and they have rather been anxious to preserve what are deemed the peculiar merits of the Scottish system." They believe "the suggestions which they have made to be both safe and salutary, and at the same time calculated to relieve much of the wretchedness which had been brought under their notice."

Thus ends the Report of "The Poor Law Inquiry Commission for Scotland," of which it has here been endeavoured to give a faithful although necessarily a condensed summary. The original wording of the most important portions has been adhered to as closely as possible, in order that nothing of the spirit and intention might be lost or perverted; and with respect to the entire Report, it is hoped that enough will have been retained to enable the reader fully to comprehend its import, and to form a judgment on the several points which it seeks to establish.

It is however necessary to state, that the Report did not receive the signatures of all the seven commissioners. Mr. Twisleton, one of the number, and of whom mention has been made in connexion with the distress at Paisley in 1841-42,[d] not only declined signing the Report, but he recorded his reasons for dissenting from his colleagues in the conclusions to which they had come. These reasons are stated under eight separate heads, and it is right with regard to the important bearing which they have upon the recommendations made in the Report, as well as due to the part taken by Mr. Twisleton in the investigations on which it is founded, to place his dissent in juxta-position with the foregoing summary of the Report itself, in order that both may be considered together.

'*Reasons of Dissent from the foregoing Report.*'

*First.*—" Because the proposed alterations in the Scotch Poor-Law are, I am afraid, insufficient to remedy the defects which are admitted to exist in their administration.

*Secondly.*—" Because, while it is admitted that the provision at present made for the relief of the aged and infirm poor is in many parishes of Scotland inadequate, the main reliance for the supply of this deficiency seems to be placed on a proposed board of supervision, or standing commission of inquiry, with ample powers of inspection, but with no administrative control or direct authority. But it appears to me, that the striking inadequacy of the allowances at present made to the aged and infirm poor in a large proportion of the unassessed rural parishes of Scotland, arises not so much

[d] Ante, p. 130.

from ignorance of facts as from want of funds, which again is owing in no small degree, to theories respecting the effect of any provision for the poor, even when it is restricted to the relief of the aged and the infirm. And any statements made annually in reports tending to show that this class of poor are in a destitute condition, will be met by the usual answer, that the only cure for such evils is in the moral and religious education of the young; and that a provision for the poor creates much of the misery which it relieves, but does not relieve all the misery which it creates.

*Thirdly.*—" Because no proposal is made for requiring the managers of the poor in unassessed rural parishes to assess themselves for the relief of the destitute aged and infirm poor, using these terms in the most comprehensive sense, as including all those who are entitled to relief under the present law. It appears to me that the mischiefs which have been attributed to assessments for this class of poor have been remarkably exaggerated, even although they may not be altogether visionary. On the other hand, this mode of providing for the aged and the infirm is the most equitable which can be adopted; its general tendency as distinguished from its invariable result, is to ensure an ampler supply of funds than can be raised by voluntary contributions; and it reaches non-resident heritors, and others who may give either nothing or comparatively little, in aid of the church collections.

*Fourthly.*—" Because it is not proposed to render it compulsory on managers of the poor to provide medical attendance for paupers. The arrangements for medical relief and the power of fixing the scale of remuneration to medical practitioners, are to be left exclusively to the local authorities, who may deem that they have a direct pecuniary interest in fixing the scale of remuneration as low as possible, or in throwing altogether upon medical practitioners, as is frequently the case at present, the burden of attending the sick poor gratuitously.

*Fifthly.*—" Because it is not proposed to authorise, or to render it compulsory upon the managers of the poor in large towns, to provide houses of refuge or poorhouses, with wards for able-bodied persons. But establishments of this kind, which are in fact identical with English workhouses, appear to me essential to the proper management of the poor in large towns; and without them I do not see how the begging which prevails to such a great extent in the chief towns in Scotland can be suppressed, consistently with humanity, or in accordance with public feeling.

*Sixthly.*—" Because, while in reference to towns with a population above 5000 inhabitants, the advantages of poorhouses for the reception of certain classes of poor, entitled to assistance under the present Scotch Poor Law, are clearly pointed out, as subsidiary to out-door relief; yet the erection of such poorhouses is proposed to be left entirely to the discretion of the local authorities. But while I admit that the arrangement of various details may be safely vested in the managers of the poor in each particular town, it is my opinion that the *principles* of dealing with a subject so difficult as that of administering relief, should be settled by the enlarged wisdom of parliament. And a matter of such importance as the erection of poorhouses, ought not to depend either on the honest judgment, or possible caprice, partial knowledge, or narrow views, of accidental majorities in particular localities.

*Seventhly.*—" Because no proposition is made for dealing with the case of large towns, when during seasons of depression of trade, large bodies of operatives are thrown out of employment, and become dependent for subsistence upon public charity. It seems to me desirable that in all large towns which have a poorhouse with wards for able-bodied men, the managers of the poor should have a discretionary power, with consent of a board of supervision, to assess the inhabitants for the purpose of setting to work destitute unemployed persons, without requiring them to enter such poorhouse. The aid of a poorhouse with wards for able-bodied persons, materially facilitates the operations of those who, in periods of depression of trade, undertake the duty of giving out-door relief to a certain number of that class.

*Eighthly.*—" Because no alteration is proposed in the Scotch law of rating, which is peculiarly anomalous and defective. The usual mode of levying the rate on what is called ' means and substance,' is similar in its main features to the income-tax, but it is unaccompanied by those safeguards with which the levying of the income-tax has been surrounded by the wisdom of parliament. Either, therefore, safeguards should be introduced for the purpose of ensuring secrecy and fairness, or the attempt to assess supposed means and substance should be abandoned, and the mode of levying poor-rates in Scotland should be assimilated with that which is in operation in all other parts of the United Kingdom."

# CHAPTER IV.

The lord advocate's speech on introducing the bill 'for the Amendment and better Administration of the Laws relating to the Relief of the Poor in Scotland'—Summary of the Act—The board of supervision constituted—Its first, second, and third Reports.

THE commissioners' Report, of which a summary is given in the last chapter, together with the appended dissent of one of their number, must be presumed to have received from the government all the consideration which the importance of the subject demanded; and in the following session (1845) a bill for 'the Amendment and better Administration of the Laws relating to the Relief of the Poor in Scotland' was introduced by the lord advocate,[a] who in an able speech very clearly explained the existing state of the law, the mode of its administration, and the defects which the bill was intended to remedy. In doing this, he relied almost exclusively on the commissioners' Report, which he highly commended as comprising all the information that could be desired on the subject, and on which the bill was accordingly founded. The dissent appended to the Report was not once noticed, and little weight appears to have been attached to its representations in framing the measure.

1845. A bill is introduced.

The several portions of the subject were discussed by the lord advocate in the same order in which they stand in the Report. They were likewise handled in the same spirit. He made the same admissions as to the defects, and the same assertions as to the

The lord advocate's speech.

[a] Duncan McNeill Esq.

merits of the existing system; and he also proposed the same remedies for the one, and the same means for extending and perpetuating the other. His speech was in short little more than a lucid summary of the Report itself; and it is therefore not necessary, as it else might have been, to go through it in detail, or to do more than extract the sketch which he gave towards the conclusion of his address, of what was intended to be the operation of the measure. He believed, he said, that the leading benefits it was calculated to confer on the poor, were—

"1st. Compelling periodical and constant attention to "their condition, and preserving a record of what "had been done or refused to be done.
"2nd. Giving speedy and effectual redress against "wrongous refusal of relief.
"3rd. Also against illusory or inadequate compliance "with the right to relief.
"4th. Requiring relief to be given in the parish where "the pauper was found, leaving to the parish, not "to the pauper, to find out the liability of another "parish.
"5th. Authorising the poor-funds to be applied for "procuring medical relief.
"6th. And for the education of poor children.
"7th. And for the relief of occasional claims.
"8th. Facilitating compulsory assessments for all those "purposes.
"9th. Authorising assessments for the erection of poor-"houses.
"10th. Uniting burghal parishes, so that settlement by "residence shall not be interrupted by removal from "one parish to another in the same town, and by "which other advantages will also be gained.
"11th. Requiring that insane paupers shall be sent to "asylums, except in special cases."

The bill for effecting these several objects, was introduced on the 2nd of April, and after considerable discussion was read a second time and committed on the 12th of June. It was considered in committee and various amendments were made on the 3rd, 11th, 17th, and 21st of July, on the last of which days it was read a third time and passed. On the 28th of July the amended bill was, on the motion of the duke of Buccleugh, considered and read a second time in the Lords, and on the following day it was read a third time and passed without further amendment. On the 4th of August the bill received the royal assent, and became law, under the title of 'An Act for the Amendment and better Administration of the Laws relating to the Relief of the Poor in Scotland' (*8th and 9th Vict. cap.* 83.)

1845. The 8th and 9th Vict. c. 83.

This Act, like the English Poor Law Amendment Act of 1834, was founded on the recommendations of a commission, specially appointed to inquire into and report upon the subject in all its details; and it would seem impossible to devise a better mode of procedure for effecting the object, or one less open to objection. The chief difference between the circumstances into which the two commissions had to inquire was, that in one case there had been a profuse and lavish administration of relief, whilst in the other relief had been insufficiently administered, or altogether withheld; and against these opposite defects of stringency and laxity, of parsimony and profusion, it became in each case the commissioners' duty to devise a remedy. In the case of England, what was done in the way of amendment has already been shown;[b] and with regard to Scotland, it is now in the first place proposed to give a summary of the new Act (in framing which the Irish Poor Relief Act was obviously kept in view[c]), and then to describe the

---

[b] See 'History of the English Poor Law.'
[c] The 1st and 2nd Vict. cap. 56, passed 31st July 1838.

steps taken for carrying its provisions into effect, together with a detail of the results from year to year down to the end of 1852-3.

*Summary of the 8th and 9th Victoria, cap.* 83, (4th August 1845,)

'For the Amendment and better Administration of the Laws relating to the Relief of the Poor in Scotland.'

*Section* 1.—Contains the preamble, declaring it to be "expedient that the laws relating to the relief of the poor in Scotland should be amended, and that provision should be made for the better administration thereof;" and also the interpretation of certain words and expressions used in the Act.

*Section* 2.—Appoints a "Board of Supervision for Relief of the Poor in Scotland," consisting of the lord provost of Edinburgh, the lord provost of Glasgow, the solicitor-general of Scotland, the sheriffs depute of the counties of Perth Renfrew Ross and Cromarty, together with three other persons to be appointed by the crown.

*Sections* 3, 4.—Provide that one member of the board of supervision, to be named by the crown, shall be paid a salary, and likewise the secretary; but that all the other members are to act gratuitously.

*Sections* 5, 6.—The board of supervision are to hold two general meetings in each year, on the first Wednesday in February and August respectively, and may adjourn and hold meetings from time to time as they shall see fit, three constituting a quorum. The board may also appoint two or more of their number as a committee for the purposes of the Act. The paid member is not only to attend the general and special meetings, but is also "to give regular attendance for the purpose of conducting the business of the board."

*Sections* 7, 8.—The board may, subject to the approval of one of her Majesty's principal secretaries of state, make general rules and regulations for conducting the business, and for exercising the powers and authorities thereof. A record of all their proceedings is to be kept, and once in every year they are to submit a general report, to be laid before parliament, containing "a full statement as to the condition and management of the poor throughout Scotland, and the funds raised for their relief."

*Sections* 9, 10, 11.—The board are empowered "to inquire into the management of the poor in every parish or burgh in Scotland," and to require answers and returns on all matters connected with or relating to the same; and also to summon and examine upon oath such persons as they think fit, "and to enforce the production of all books, contracts, agreements, accounts, and writings in any wise relating to any such question or matter." The board may appoint one of its members to conduct any special inquiry, with power to summon and examine witnesses on oath, and may likewise with consent or by direction of a secretary of state or the lord advocate for the time being, appoint one or more persons (not being members of the board), "to act as commissioners for conducting any special inquiry, for a period not exceeding forty days;" and may delegate to the persons so appointed, such powers as the board shall deem necessary.

*Sections* 12, 13, 14.—The board may allow such expenses of witnesses, and with regard to the production of books &c., as they think reasonable. Persons giving false evidence are to be deemed guilty of perjury; and any person who shall refuse to produce books &c., or shall disobey any summons or order, "or be guilty of any contempt of the said board or committee or member or commissioner," is for the first offence liable to forfeit 5*l*., and for the second and every subsequent offence will be liable to forfeit not exceeding 20*l*, nor less than 5*l*.—The board are moreover empowered to appoint "such clerks messengers and officers as they shall deem necessary," the salaries being regulated by the treasury.

*Section* 15.—The members of the board and the secretary are authorised to attend the meetings of parochial boards for the management of the poor, and to take part in the discussions, but not to vote; and the same privilege is extended to any clerk or officer of the board duly authorised by them for the purpose.

*Section* 16.—Where the parochial boards of two or more parishes deem it expedient to combine for the administration of the laws for the relief of the poor, and where the board of supervision is satisfied of the expediency, the board are empowered "to resolve and declare that such parishes shall thenceforward be combined, and shall be considered as one parish, so far as regards the support and management of the poor, and all matters connected therewith." But it is provided that any adjacent parish may, upon application, be added thereto, if the board of supervision see fit, "due regard being had to the circumstances of the case."

*Sections* 17, 18.—In every burghal parish or combination of parishes, there is to be a parochial board of managers of the poor, in whom the whole administration of the laws for the relief of the poor is to be vested, and on whom is devolved all the powers and authorities in this respect hitherto exercised by magistrates or other functionaries. The managers are to be elected by the persons assessed to the relief of the poor, and the parochial boards are to consist of such number of managers not exceeding thirty, and possessing such qualifications, "as the board of supervision, having due regard to the population and other circumstances, may from time to time fix, such qualification being in no case fixed at a higher annual value than 50*l*." The magistrates of the burgh, and the kirk session of each combined parish, are likewise severally empowered to nominate four persons to be members of the parochial board. The board of supervision are to fix a day for the election of managers, and are also to fix the time for the magistrates and the kirk sessions "to nominate the persons to be by them respectively nominated to be members of the parochial board," all of whom "shall be entitled to act for the period of one year, and may be re-elected or re-appointed."

*Section* 19.—At the election of managers of the poor, the votes are to be taken in such manner as the board of supervision may direct, every person assessed for the support of the poor being "entitled to vote, whether such assessment be made in respect of ownership or occupancy of lands and heritages, or in respect of means and substance." The number of votes is regulated according to the following scale—

| | |
|---|---|
| Owners of lands and heritages of the annual value of less than 20*l*., are each to have .. .. .. .. .. .. | One vote. |
| Ditto of the annual value of 20*l*. and under 40*l*. .. .. | Two votes. |
| Ditto ,, ,, 40*l*. ,, 60*l*. .. .. | Three votes. |
| Ditto ,, ,, 60*l*. ,, 100*l*. .. .. | Four votes. |
| Ditto ,, ,, 100*l*. ,, 500*l*. .. .. | Five votes. |
| Ditto ,, ,, 500*l*. and upwards .. .. | Six votes. |

Persons assessed as the occupants of lands and heritages, or assessed on means and substance, are each to have the same number of votes as an owner of lands and heritages assessed to the same amount would have. Where an occupant is also the owner, and assessed in both capacities, he will be entitled to vote as well in respect of his ownership as of his occupancy; and so likewise where a person is assessed on his means and substance, if he be also assessed as an owner of lands and heritages, he will be entitled to vote in respect of both—provided that no person shall have more than six votes, and that no one shall be entitled to vote who has been exempted from the payment of his rates, or who shall not have paid the rates due from him at the time of voting.

*Sections* 20, 21.—The board of supervision are empowered to divide a burghal parish or combination into wards, for the election of managers, and to apportion the number of managers to be elected by each ward, "having due regard to the population and the value of property therein." But residents only are entitled to vote for managers in the ward, or have a right to vote in respect of ownership or occupancy of lands and hereditaments within it—neither shall "any person give in the whole of the wards into which a parish may be divided, a greater number of votes than he would be entitled to give if the parish had not been so divided." The books of the collector of the assessment for the poor are to be taken as evidence for ascertaining the number of votes to which each person is entitled.

*Sections* 22, 23, 24.—Parochial boards for the management of the poor, are also to be constituted in the parishes which are not burghal or in combination. Where no assessment has been made, the parochial board is "to consist of the persons who, if this Act had not been passed, would have been entitled to administer the laws for relief of the poor in such parish." Where an assessment has been made, the parochial board is to consist of the owners of lands and heritages of the yearly value of 20*l.* and upwards, and the provost and bailies of the royal burgh, if any, and if assessed in such parish, and the kirk session of the parish (not exceeding six) together with a certain number of elected members. All persons who are assessed in the parish, and who are not members of the parochial board, are to elect so many of their own number to be members thereof as shall "be regulated and fixed from time to time by the board of supervision, due regard being had to the amount of the population, the number and residence of the other members of the parochial board, and the special wants and circumstances of each particular parish." The scale of voting is the same as prescribed in Section 19.

*Sections* 25, 26.—Corporations and joint stock companies may vote by their officer, or one of their body nominated for the purpose. Any member of the parochial board, being a heritor, may appoint another to act and vote for him in his absence, and husbands are entitled to act and vote in right of their wives.

*Sections* 27, 28, 29.—All disputes touching the election of a member of the parochial board are to be determined by the sheriff of the county, and pending such decision the person returned is entitled to act. A returning officer wilfully making a false return, is liable to a penalty of 50*l.*

*Sections* 30, 31, 32.—Parochial boards are to fix certain days and places for holding general meetings, and may adjourn such meetings as they think fit; but two general meetings at least must be held yearly, one on the first Tuesday of February, and the other on the first Tuesday of August, or as soon thereafter as may be, "or at such other stated times as may be approved by the board of supervision." Special meetings may also be held, and power is given to appoint committees to act on behalf of the whole board. A chairman is to be elected annually, and is to have both an original and a casting vote in case of equality. "A roll of the poor persons claiming and by law entitled to relief, and of the amount of relief given or to be given to each," is to be made by every parochial board. These boards are also to appoint inspectors of the poor, and fix the amount of their remuneration, and report the same to the board of supervision.

*Sections* 33, 34, 35.—Parochial boards may, after due notice, resolve that the funds required for relief of the poor shall be raised by assessment, reporting the same to the board of supervision; and thereafter "it shall not be lawful to alter or depart from such resolution without the consent and authority of the board of supervision." The parochial board may resolve that the assessment shall be imposed half upon the owners and half upon the tenants or occupiers within the parish, or one half upon the owners and the other half upon the whole inhabitants according to their means and substance —or may resolve that the "assessment shall be imposed as an equal percentage upon the annual value of all lands and heritages within the parish, and upon the estimated annual income of the whole inhabitants from means and substance;" and in either case the resolution is forthwith to be reported to the board of supervision for approval. If the same be disapproved, the parochial board are "to meet and resolve upon another mode of assessment consistent with the law," and report as before; and if the board of supervision shall then approve, the resolution is to be acted upon, and not thereafter altered or departed from without the board's consent. If the assessments have hitherto been imposed under any local Act, "or according to any established usage," the parochial board may resolve that the same shall continue, subject in like manner to the approval of the board of supervision.

*Sections* 36, 37.—The parochial board, with consent of the board of supervision, may classify lands according to the purposes for which they are used, and may fix such rate of assessment upon each class respectively as seems just and equitable. "In estimating the annual value of lands and heritages, the same shall be taken to be the rent at which, one year with another, such lands and heritages might in their actual state be reasonably expected to let from year to year, under deduction of the probable annual average cost of the repairs, insurance, and other expenses, if any, necessary to maintain such lands and heritages in their actual state, and all rates taxes and public charges payable in respect of the same." [d]

*Sections* 38, 39, 40.—Where assessment is adopted, the parochial board is to cause a book to be made up " containing a roll of the persons liable to payment of such assessment, and of the sums to be levied from each of such persons, distinguishing the sums assessed in respect of ownership or occupancy, or means and substance; and the book or roll so made up shall be the rule for levying the assessment for the year or half-year then ensuing." The parochial board is also to appoint a collector or collectors, and fix the amount of remuneration; and the same person who is an inspector of the poor may likewise be appointed collector of the assessments. After the assessment roll is made up, the collector is to intimate to each person the amount to be levied from him, and the time when the same is payable. Parochial boards may correct any error or omission in the assessment, and persons aggrieved may obtain remedy by law, as before the passing of the present Act.

*Sections* 41, 42, 43, 44.—If the assessment in any year or half-year proves insufficient, the parochial board may impose such further assessment as is necessary; and they may exempt from payment of the assessment, or any part thereof, " to such extent as may seem proper and reasonable, any person or class of persons on the ground of inability." Where half the assessment is imposed on the owners and half on the tenants, the collector may levy the whole from the latter, " who shall be entitled to recover one half thereof from the owners, or to retain the same out of their rents." And where houses have been built under a building lease, the tenant is to be deemed the owner.

*Sections* 45, 46, 47, 48, 49.—Where a canal or railway is situate in more than one parish, the value on which assessment is to be made " shall be according to the number of miles or distance which such canal or railway passes through or is situated in each parish, in proportion to the whole length." The same property is not liable to assessment in more than one parish. Where an assessment is imposed on means and substance, individuals or companies carrying on business in a parish, are liable to be assessed on their means and substance derived from such business, although none of them may be actually resident in the parish; but they are not liable to be

---

[d] This is taken nearly verbatim from the Irish Act.

assessed upon the same means and substance in any other parish; and if any person shall be liable to be assessed as an inhabitant of more than one parish, he may determine in which he will be assessed on his means and substance derivable elsewhere. No person is liable to be assessed on means and substance, unless the estimated annual value thereof exceeds 30*l.*; and clergymen are not liable to be assessed in respect of their stipends.

*Sections* 50, 51.—The privilege of exemption from assessment heretofore enjoyed by the members of the college of justice, and the officers of the queen's household in Edinburgh, is not to apply to assessments under the present Act; and no assessment is to be rendered void by "any mistake or variance in the name or designation of the person chargeable therewith."

*Sections* 52, 53, 54.—Parish property of every description, whether heritable or moveable, "or under any law or usage, or in virtue of gift, grant, bequest or otherwise, for the use or benefit of the poor," is to become vested in the new parochial boards, and be by them administered for behoof of the poor of the respective parishes. All sums of money or other funds given, mortified, or bequeathed for the use of the poor, if not specially directed otherwise, are to be lodged in a chartered bank, or placed at interest on government or heritable security; and the board of supervision may require returns from time to time as to all such money or funds. But all moneys arising from ordinary church collections in a parish, whenever an assessment has been imposed, are to be at the disposal of the kirk session, who are however "bound to report annually or oftener if required to the board of supervision, as to the application of the moneys arising from church collections."

*Sections* 55, 56, 57, 58.—The inspector of the poor is to have the custody of all books writings accounts and other documents relating to the management or relief of the poor, and is to make himself acquainted with the circumstances of each of the poor persons receiving relief, and keep a register of such persons and of the sums paid to them, and of all persons who have applied for and been refused relief, with the grounds of refusal; and he is to visit and inspect personally, "at least twice in the year (or oftener if required), at their places of residence, all the poor persons belonging to the parish in receipt of parochial relief—provided that such poor persons be resident within five miles of any part of such parish." But in populous and extensive parishes, the duties of inspecting and visiting the poor may be performed by assistant inspectors, for whose conduct and accuracy the inspector of the poor is nevertheless responsible to the board of supervision, who may suspend or dismiss any inspector deemed by them to be incompetent. An action may be brought, and may also be defended, on behalf of a parish by the inspector of the poor, and actions brought by or against any inspector of the poor in his official character, are to be continued by or against his successors in office.

*Section* 59.—The inspectors of the poor are required to report to the board of supervision all cases of insane or fatuous persons chargeable as paupers, who are to be conveyed to and lodged in some establishment legally authorised to receive lunatic patients; and if this be not done within fourteen days, the board of supervision are empowered to take measures for effecting the same, and to recover the whole expense from the parochial board.

*Section* 60, 61, 62, 63.—" For the more effectually administering to the wants of the aged and other friendless impotent poor, and also providing for those poor persons who from weakness or facility of mind, or by reason of dissipated and improvident habits, are unable or unfit to take charge of their own affairs" —it is enacted, that whenever the inhabitants exceed 5000, the parochial board may, subject to the approval of the board of supervision, erect a new or enlarge an existing poorhouse. And with the concurrence of the board of supervision, two or more contiguous parishes may unite in building a common poorhouse, the expense to be borne proportionally, as shall be agreed upon. The parochial boards are likewise empowered to borrow money for building and enlarging such poorhouses, and to charge the future assessments with the amount; but the principal sum so borrowed is in no case to exceed three times the amount of the assessment raised for the relief of the poor during the year preceding, and the loan borrowed is to be " repaid by annual instalments of not less in any one year than one-tenth of the sum borrowed, exclusive of the payment of the interest on the same." But no poorhouse is to be built, altered, or enlarged, nor money borrowed for such purpose, unless the plans be approved by the board of supervision.

*Sections* 64, 65.—The parochial boards are required to frame rules and regulations for the management of the poorhouses, for the discipline and treatment of the inmates, and for affording them religious assistance, such rules and regulations being subject to the approval of the board of supervision. Poor persons of one parish may be accommodated in the poorhouse of another, on payment of such a rate of maintenance as the board of supervision approve.

*Sections* 66, 67.—The parochial board are to appoint a properly qualified medical man to attend the inmates of the poor-house, and assign him a reasonable salary; and are to make arrangements for dispensing and supplying medicines to the sick poor, under regulations to be approved by the board of supervision, who are moreover empowered to suspend or remove any medical man that appears to be "unfit or incompetent, or neglects his duty." Parochial boards may likewise subscribe such sums as to them may seem reasonable or expedient, "to any public infirmary dispensary or lying-in hospital, or to any lunatic asylum or asylum for the blind or deaf or dumb."

*Sections* 68, 69.—All assessments levied for relief of the poor, are applicable to the relief of occasional as well as permanent poor—"provided that nothing herein contained shall be held to confer a right to demand relief on able-bodied persons out of employment." The parochial boards are required "to provide for medicines, medical attendance, nutritious diet, cordials and clothing for such poor, in such manner and to such extent as may seem equitable and expedient." They are also empowered "to make provision for the education of poor children, who are themselves or whose parents are objects of parochial relief."

*Sections* 70, 71, 72, 73.—Inspectors of the poor are bound to furnish applicants for relief who are legally entitled thereto, but who have not a settlement in the parish, with sufficient means of subsistence until the next meeting of the parochial board, and such interim maintenance as may be adjudged necessary is to be continued, until the parish to which the poor person belongs is ascertained, or until he is removed. The amount disbursed on behalf of such poor persons is recoverable from the parish of their settlement, provided it do not exceed the rate expended for relief of the poor in the relieving parish. If relief be refused, application may be made to the sheriff, who if he consider the poor person "legally entitled to relief," may make an order upon the inspector of the poor, directing him to afford relief until he have stated in writing why the relief was refused, and until such statement be answered on behalf of the applicant. But the sheriff has no power "to determine on the adequacy of the relief afforded, or to interfere in respect of the amount of relief in any individual case."

*Sections* 74, 75.—If any poor person considers the relief granted him inadequate, he may lodge a complaint with the board of supervision, who are required to investigate the case, and if the complaint appears to be well founded, the board "shall by minute declare that in the opinion of the board such poor person has a just cause of action against the parish from which he claims relief;" and a copy of such minute being furnished to such poor person, will entitle him "to the benefit of the poor's roll in the court of session." But no court of law can entertain or decide any action relative to the amounts of relief granted by parochial boards, "unless the board of supervision shall previously have declared that there is just cause of action, as hereinbefore provided."

*Sections* 76, 77, 78, 79.—No person is to be held to have acquired a settlement by residence in any parish, unless he has resided for five years continuously therein, and "have maintained himself without having recourse to common begging, either by himself or his family, and without having received or applied for parochial relief." And a person who has acquired a settlement by residence in a parish, "shall not be held to have retained such settlement, if during any subsequent period of five years he shall not have resided in such parish for at least one year." Settlements acquired previous to the passing of the Act, are specially exempted from its operation. Natives of England, Ireland, or the Isle of Man, not having acquired a settlement, and who are "in course of receiving relief in any parish in Scotland," may upon complaint by the inspector of the poor, and after examination before the sheriff or any two justices of peace, and by order under their hands, be removed at the expense of the complaining parish, to England Ireland or the Isle of Man respectively—a certificate by a regular medical practitioner that the health of the parties will admit of such removal being first obtained, and the removing officer is to have the power of a constable whilst effecting the removal. If any person who has been so removed return to Scotland, and apply for relief, or again become chargeable, "such person shall be deemed to be a vagabond under the provisions of the Act of 1579, cap. 74,"[e] and may be apprehended and prosecuted criminally at the instance of the inspector of the poor of the parish to which he shall have so applied or become chargeable.

*Section* 80.—Every husband or father who deserts, or neglects to maintain his wife or children, being able so to do, and every mother and every putative father of an illegitimate child, after the paternity has been admitted or otherwise established, who refuses or neglects to maintain such child, being able to do so, whereby such wife or child becomes chargeable to any parish, "shall be deemed to be a vagabond under the Scottish

---

[e] Ante, p. 16.

Act of 1579, cap. 74,"[f] and may be prosecuted criminally at the instance of the inspector of the poor of such parish, and if convicted is punishable by fine or imprisonment with or without hard labour, at the discretion of the sheriff.

*Sections* 81, 82, 83, 84, 85, 86.—The penalties imposed by this Act may be recovered by summary proceeding in the name of the secretary to the board of supervision, or of any agent appointed by the board. And the sheriff by whom any such penalty is imposed, is to award the same to the poor of the parish where the offence was committed, and order the amount to be paid over to the inspector of the poor. Ratepayers are to be deemed competent witnesses in any proceeding for the recovery of a penalty, and any person summoned to give evidence in any matter under the provisions of this Act, who neglects or refuses to attend, or to be examined on oath for that purpose, is to forfeit a sum not exceeding 5*l.* for every such offence. No proceeding for recovery of penalties under this Act is to be set aside for want of form, nor be removed by appeal or otherwise into any superior court. Actions are to be brought within three months after the fact committed, and at least one month's notice of action and the cause thereof is to be given to the defender; and no pursuer is to recover in any action for irregular or wrongful proceedings, if tender of sufficient amends be made.

*Section* 87.—In case any parochial board shall refuse or neglect to do what is by law required of them, or in case any obstruction arises in the execution of this Act, the board of supervision are empowered to apply by summary petition to the court of session, or in its vacation to the lord ordinary, "which court and lord ordinary are authorised and directed in such case to do therein, as to such court or lord ordinary shall seem just and necessary."

*Section* 88.—All the powers and rights of issuing summary warrants and proceedings, and all remedies and provisions for collecting and recovering the land, assessed, and other public taxes, are made applicable to assessments for the relief of the poor; "and the sheriffs, magistrates, justices of peace and other judges, may grant the like warrants for the recovery of all such assessments in the same form, and under the same penalties, as is provided in regard to such land, assessed, and other public taxes." In cases of bankruptcy or insolvency, assessments for relief of the poor are to be paid out of the first proceeds of the estate, in preference to other debts of a private nature.

---

[f] Ante, p. 16.

*Section* 89.—If any parochial board finds it necessary to make disbursements for the relief of the poor, beyond the amount received of the assessment for the year, or the half-year, the board may borrow on security of such part as is still due, not exceeding one half the amount of such part; and until this be repaid, no money is to be borrowed on any future assessment.

*Section* 90.—In all cases where notice or intimation is required to be given by this Act, without prescribing the particular form, the board of supervision are empowered "from time to time to fix the form of such notice or intimation, and the manner in which the same is to be given."

*Sections* 91, 92.—All laws statutes and usages, so far as they are at variance or inconsistent with the provisions of this Act are repealed, but they are to continue in force in all other respects. "The debt owing by the charity workhouse of the city of Edinburgh" is exempted from the operation of the Act. And section 92 provides that the Act may be renewed or repealed during the present session.

The Act, of which the foregoing is a comprehensive summary, contains many important provisions, and no doubt goes far to remove some of the uncertainties, and to supply several of the deficiencies, which existed under the old Scottish law with regard to the relief of the poor. By establishing regularly constituted parochial boards of management, and a board of general supervision, a machinery is moreover created competent to the discharge of all the duties imposed by the Act, and of still more extensive duties should such hereafter be required; whilst the power of levying assessments, and of combining parishes for the erection of poorhouses and providing medical relief, together with the appointment of inspectors, and the more certain provision for relief of the lunatic casual and unsettled poor, and for the purpose of education, are all exceedingly valuable additions to the former system, and cannot fail of being productive of much benefit.

The Act makes no change in the description of persons legally entitled to relief under the old law. In

England all destitute persons are so entitled, but in Scotland the right is still, in conformity with the recommendation of the commissioners of inquiry, limited to the aged and infirm poor. The functions of the board of supervision are chiefly suggestive or corrective —the commissioners may inquire and call for returns, or may recommend a course of procedure, but are not empowered to take the initiative. If invoked, they may combine parishes for providing a poorhouse; but unless applied to by the local boards they have no power to direct this to be done, and can only require them to meet and consider the question; and so in other matters. Their usefulness in securing an effective administration of relief, must therefore be necessarily less than it would be if they were not so restricted, and the new law will perhaps work less efficiently in consequence. With respect to the vexed question of settlement, the term of residence for conferring a right, is fixed intermediately between the three years of the former practice, and the seven recommended by the inquiry commissioners; and the continuance of the right, is made to depend upon the party not applying for relief or resorting to common begging, and also on his residing in the parish continuously for one year at least, during any subsequent five years.

No further observations appear to be at present called for in regard to the provisions of this important Act, and we will now therefore proceed to describe the steps which were taken for carrying it into effect, and the general results attending its application.

The 'Act for the Amendment and better Administration of the Laws relating to the Relief of the Poor in Scotland,' was passed on the 4th of August 1845; and on the 4th of September following *the board of supervision* constituted under it met in Edinburgh for the transaction of business, *Sir John McNeill, G.C.B.* being appointed the paid commissioner and chairman

The board of supervision.

of the board, and *William Smythe Esq.* secretary. At the end of a year, that is in August 1846, the board, as required by the *8th section* of the Act, made their Report, in which they give a full statement of the proceedings for bringing the law into operation. Of this first Report, and of the others subsequently made in like manner, it is proposed in the following pages to give a summary, omitting only the merely technical and less important matters; but still affording such explanations as will enable the reader to judge of the progress and the effects of the new law.

1846. First Report of the board of supervision.

One of the first duties required from the board of supervision, was to afford assistance and information to the several parishes in constituting the new parochial boards, and in appointing inspectors of the poor, there being, it is said, "in many parishes a misapprehension as to the objects of the legislature in respect to these matters, and a diversity of opinion as to the mode of proceeding to effect them."

Parochial boards.

The constitution of the parochial boards, on whom the administration of relief to the poor exclusively devolved, was no doubt an object of primary importance; and although provided for with great minuteness in the *17th and following sections* of the Act, there were yet certain things left undetermined, and subject to the directions of the board of supervision, who lost no time in preparing the necessary instructions and regulations on every point requiring the exercise of their authority. The board opened its communication with the several parishes by addressing a letter to each, pointing out what was required under the *32nd section* of the Act, and advising the parish authorities as to their holding meetings, making up a roll of the poor, appointing inspectors, and settling the mode of raising the necessary funds. Most of the persons named as inspectors, were necessarily "unacquainted with the duties of the office, and the system of management they were called upon to carry out was new to them all." The commissioners therefore framed rules for their guidance, and to which after being approved by a secretary of state, the inspectors were bound to conform. At the end of the first year, every parish in Scotland had, we are told, named an inspector; and the commissioners observe, that due allowance being made for inexperience, the duties have generally been well performed.

Assessments.

After making up the poor's roll, and appointing an inspector, the parochial boards had next to determine whether the funds required for the relief of the poor should be "raised by voluntary contributions or by legal assessment." Both modes were practised under the old law, but the former was the one most generally adopted. Out of the 878[f] parishes into which Scotland was then divided, only about 230 were legally assessed in 1842-3. The number which however, at the date of the commissioners' Report, had resolved to raise the funds for relief of the poor by assessment, was increased to 448, being something more than one half of the entire number.

Under the old law, all the inhabitants of purely burghal parishes were assessed "according to the estimation of their means and substance," in terms of the statute of 1579;[g] but in landward parishes "half the burden was laid on the owners of lands and heritages within the parish, and the other half on the whole inhabitants according to their means and substance." By the new Act three modes of assessment are provided, and it is left to each parochial board to adopt whichever of the three may be considered best suited to the circumstances of the parish.[h] Half the assessment may be

---

[f] In the second Report the number is stated to be 880, and the number of assessed parishes is stated to have been 451.

[g] Ante, p. 16. [h] Ante, p. 175.

imposed upon the owners, and half upon the occupiers; or one half upon the owners, and the other half upon the whole inhabitants, according to their means and substance; or the whole may be imposed as an equal percentage on the annual income derived from both sources indifferently. Whenever the first mode is adopted, the 36*th section* empowers the parochial board "to distinguish lands and heritages into two or more classes according to the purposes for which they are used or occupied, and to fix such different rates of assessment on the tenants and occupants of each class as may seem just and equitable." In all these modes, the commissioners remark, "that which may be regarded as the national principle, that each man shall be assessed in proportion to his means, has in effect been preserved." And they further add, that "none of the modes established by usage are opposed to the principle of the old law under which they were adopted, neither are any of the local Acts at variance with the principle on which the law was founded."

In determining the mode in which a parish should be assessed, the parochial board had not therefore to consider the principle as to whether each man should be assessed according to his means, but whether the assessment should be imposed directly upon his estimated means and substance, or indirectly by assuming that the house or lands occupied by him represented his means and substance proportionally with the other ratepayers. In a great majority of parishes, the commissioners say, the indirect mode of estimating means and substance, by taking annual value or rent as the criterion, has been preferred, the numbers being 379 for that mode of assessment, and 66 for the other modes; and they "think it not very unlikely that the second and third modes of assessment mentioned in the Act, may gradually be abandoned, and the first mode, with or without classification, adopted by all or nearly all the parishes in Scotland."

At the date of the Report, all the parishes in Scotland had either by assessment, church collections, contributions, or other means, provided the funds required for the relief of the poor, and it is satisfactory to find that in no case had the commissioners found it necessary to avail themselves of the power given them by the 87*th section*, of applying by summary petition to the court of session in case of refusal or neglect in doing what the law requires.

The 16*th section* of the Act empowers the board of supervision, either on application or otherwise, to require the parochial boards of two or more adjoining parishes to meet and consider the expediency of their combining for the management of their poor, and if it be resolved that it is expedient and proper for them so to combine, the board of supervision may declare such parishes to be thenceforward combined accordingly. It appears however that only two applications had yet been made for this purpose, and that the commissioners were enabled to exercise the power confided to them in one only of these, by combining the three parishes of the island of Islay which belonged almost exclusively to one proprietor. The requisite consent of all the parishes was not given in the other case.

Combination of parishes.

The practice of giving passes to poor persons, authorising them to ask relief in the places through which they passed in their way to their own parish, had long prevailed under sanction of the Act of 1579.[i] But there was no certainty that the person receiving the pass had a settlement in the parish to which he represented himself to belong, and the pass often became a cover to fraud, and a warrant for mendicancy. A poor person legally entitled to relief has, under the new law, a right to claim such relief in any

Pauper passes and removals.

[i] Ante, p. 16.

parish where he may apply for it;[k] and the relief is to be continued until the parish of his settlement be ascertained, by which parish the cost of such interim relief, and the expense of the pauper's removal, is to be borne. The ground for granting such passes therefore no longer existed, and steps were taken for putting an end to the practice. The commissioners say that the rule they endeavoured to enforce was, "that a poor person, who has applied for relief in any parish, is not to be removed, or provided with the means of removal, to any other parish in Scotland than that which has been ascertained to be the parish of his settlement." English and Irish paupers will, they add, under this rule, "be removed from the parish in which they may apply for relief, to their native country, instead of being passed on as heretofore from parish to parish." But to protect English and Irish paupers from unnecessary hardship in their removal, a letter was addressed to the inspectors of the poor of the parochial boards, recommending attention to the health and comfort of all such paupers, and also recommending that those who are to be removed by sea, should be conveyed to a port with which there is such regular communication as may afford the greatest likelihood of their speedily reaching the place of their destination.

Increase of the casual poor.

The facility of obtaining relief under the new law by persons legally entitled to it, elsewhere than in the parish of their settlement, is said thus early to have considerably increased the charge of the casual poor. The cost of the relief afforded to non-settled Scottish paupers, is recoverable from the parishes to which they belong. The number of English paupers is noticed as being comparatively small. "But the number of natives of Ireland, or of their families, who receive casual relief, and who are removed to Ireland at

[k] See the 70th and two following sections, p. 179.

the cost of the different parishes in Scotland, especially Glasgow and other towns on the west coast, is very considerable." A table in the appendix to the Report shows the number of persons so removed from Glasgow, between August 1845 and 25th July 1846, to have been 1949, at a cost of 133*l.* 16*s.* 9*d.*

With respect to the important question of poorhouses, the erection and management of which are provided for by the 60*th and four following sections* of the new Act, it is stated that several parishes, either singly or conjointly with contiguous parishes, have taken into consideration the expediency of erecting poorhouses; but hitherto, the commissioners say, "no resolution to erect a poorhouse has been transmitted to us by any parochial board." It appears however that certain parishes in the counties of Caithness and Ross proposed to erect poorhouses, if the commissioners were prepared to admit the right of the parochial boards to refuse relief to any poor person who might refuse to enter the poorhouse. But the commissioners were of opinion, that they "had no power to sanction the abolition of out-door relief in any parish, and that they must judge of the propriety of refusing to relieve a pauper otherwise than by admitting him into the poorhouse, with reference to the circumstances of each case." The question whether a parochial board could legally refuse relief except in the poorhouse might, the commissioners believed, come to be decided in a court of law, and therefore it would be wrong in them to give an opinion with regard to it.[m] Some communications which had taken place with certain parochial boards on the subject

Poorhouses.

---

[m] A case involving this question did in fact subsequently arise at Glasgow, —a person entitled to relief was offered admission to the poorhouse, and was refused other relief. An action was brought against the parish for illegally refusing relief, but the sheriff held that the parish had not acted illegally in the matter, and dismissed the case. It appears therefore, as the commissioners remarked at the time, that the only question the sheriff has to decide is, whether the claimant is or is not entitled to relief—he is not empowered to judge of its adequacy or fitness.

of poorhouses are then noticed, after which the commissioners conclude this head of their Report by declaring, that although they have been strongly impressed with the advantages which both the poor and the ratepayers in many parishes would derive from the erection of poorhouses, they have nevertheless abstained from pressing this opinion on any parochial board—"We do not," they say, "doubt that experience will lead them to the same convictions that have forced themselves upon our minds, and in any event we are satisfied that it is more advisable to leave them to pursue the course that may to them appear the most expedient, than to press upon them measures involving a considerable present expenditure, to remedy evils which they have either not yet experienced or not fully appreciated, and for which it will not be too late to provide a remedy when they have become urgent."

Medical relief.

By the 69*th section* of the new Act, parochial boards are required to provide medicines, medical attendance, nutritious diet, cordials, and clothing for the sick poor, "in such manner and to such extent as may seem equitable and expedient." Before this there was no provision for medical relief, and the assistance the sick poor received, was for the most part afforded gratuitously by the resident practitioners in the several parishes. The commissioners very early called the attention of parochial boards to this section of the Act, and they likewise, in framing the rules for the inspectors of the poor, made it their duty "in all cases of sickness or accident befalling persons entitled to relief," and also "in every case of sickness or accident of any person in receipt of parochial relief," not only to take measures for procuring without delay such medical aid as can be obtained, but as soon as may be, and from time to time afterwards, "to visit the home of such sick person, and supply him with such articles as may seem necessary, until the case shall have been reported at the next meeting of the parochial board." This was probably, under the circumstances, all that the commissioners could directly do towards securing needful relief for the sick poor, although their influence would no doubt be still further exerted in forwarding that object. It appears that in a large majority of the parishes, no salary had yet been assigned to a medical officer. In a considerable number this had however been done, and in some instances parishes situated near towns in which there were hospitals or dispensaries, had subscribed thereto on behalf of their sick poor. The commissioners are, as was to be expected, far from thinking "that the medical relief afforded to the poor in Scotland, more especially in the rural and remote parishes, is on a satisfactory footing." In some of the town parishes, and in a few of the rural parishes, medical relief is, they say, adequately provided for; but in a great majority of parishes much yet remains to be done. They hopefully add however, that "the intention of government to contribute from the public funds a considerable sum towards defraying the cost of medical relief in Scotland, will afford an opportunity of revising the whole system, and of placing it on a much more satisfactory footing than it has hitherto been."

Insane and fatuous paupers.

Parochial boards are required by the 59*th section* of the Act, to remove all insane or fatuous paupers to an asylum, unless the board of supervision, under special circumstances, dispense with such removal, in which case the paupers are to be provided for in such manner as the board of supervision shall approve. By returns which the commissioners obtained, it appears that the number of lunatic paupers not accommodated in any asylum, amounted to 1621, whilst according to another return, there was only available accommodation for 82 in public asylums, and for 52 in private establishments, making together 134 vacancies; so that not even a tenth part of the entire number of pauper lunatics could be dealt with as required by the Act. The commissioners therefore insisted on the removal of such only, as they had reason to believe from the reports of the medical men were likely to be benefited by being sent to an asylum, or who might become dangerous or offensive to decency; and they expressed their regret "that the accommodation in Scotland for lunatics generally is so limited, and that the existing asylums are for the most part filled with incurable patients, to the exclusion of recent cases, many of which are curable."

It is impossible not to participate in the regret here expressed. The state of the lunatic asylums is everywhere the same. In England and in Ireland, as well as in Scotland, they are not only insufficient in number, but those which exist are clogged with incurable cases, to the exclusion of numbers who by suitable treatment in a well-managed asylum might be restored to health, and again become useful members of society. The obvious if not the only remedy for this state of things, would be, to establish subsidiary asylums for chronic and incurable cases, in connexion with the ordinary asylums, which would then be left free for the treatment of the curable, and for the application of whatever medical science could devise in mitigation of one of the heaviest afflictions with which humanity is visited.

Inadequate relief.

If in any case the relief afforded to a poor person is deemed by him to be inadequate, the 74*th section* of the Act provides that he may "lodge or cause to be lodged a complaint with the board of supervision," which is without delay to investigate the same; and if the complaint appears well founded, the board is to record a minute declaratory of its opinion that such poor person has a just cause of action against his parish, which will entitle him without further proceedings "to the benefit of the poor's roll in the court of session." The board of supervision is thus made the channel through which the person complaining of inadequate relief has to seek redress, and it became the duty of the commissioners therefore to afford every facility for the transmission and adjudication of such complaints. Forms of application were accordingly prepared, and placed in the hands of the inspectors of the poor, with directions to deliver one to every poor person on the parish roll who might demand it, and also if required to fill up the form in any terms the applicant might desire. After the form has been filled up with the statement of the applicant, it is to be delivered open to the inspector for him to insert such remarks thereon in the way of explanation as he may think fit, and it is then to be transmitted to the board of supervision for decision or further inquiry as may be judged expedient.

When the information thus obtained led the commissioners to consider that the relief complained of was inadequate, the case was remitted to the parochial board for reconsideration. If the relief was then adequately increased, the ground of complaint was held to be removed; but if the relief was not increased, or was not adequately increased, the parochial board was then called upon to state the grounds on which they held the relief to be adequate; and if they failed to do this, or if the grounds stated were deemed insufficient, it was then intimated to them that unless the relief were adequately increased, a minute declaratory of the board's view in the matter would be recorded against them. In all the cases thus remitted to the parochial boards, the commissioners have, they say, been satisfied by the information furnished to them, that the relief complained of was adequate, or that the additions subsequently made thereto were such as to remove the grounds of complaint. It is then with great propriety remarked, that these decisions on complaints of inadequate relief, not only affect the comfort and well-being of the applicants, but must also influence the scale of relief to the poor generally; and the commissioners declare that they have felt the full weight of this responsibility, and have given the most careful consideration to the cases that have come before them. "To have sanctioned illusory or inadequate relief, would (they say) have been unjust to the poor. To have exacted more than needful sustentation, would have been unjust to the ratepayers and to the independent labourers, and injurious to the community."

The condition and habits of the people, and the cost of their ordinary subsistence, are so different in different parts of Scotland, that no unvarying rule could be laid down for adjusting the amount of relief. A weekly allowance which would be fully adequate in the Highlands and Islands, would be inadequate in the southern counties. Even in the same parish, the commissioners observe, it rarely happens that any two cases are precisely similar; and they are satisfied therefore, that the only safe course is to consider each case with reference to its own peculiar circumstances. But although it might be impossible to fix any one standard of adequacy for the whole country, it was necessary to endeavour to ascertain the cost of subsistence in the different districts, so as to enable the commissioners to judge of the adequacy or inadequacy of the allowances in case they should be complained of. After much anxious deliberation and inquiry on this point, they have, they say, "come to the conclusion that the safest guide to a right estimate of what constitutes '*needful sustentation*' in any parish, is to be derived from a knowledge of the earnings on which industrious labourers are able, in that parish, to maintain themselves and their families without parochial aid;" and they add, "that it would be a fatal error, even in Scotland, where such persons only as are incapacitated by physical or mental disability from maintaining themselves are entitled to parochial relief, to make the condition of the pauper more desirable than that of the independent labourer"—a proposition which no one will be disposed to controvert.

The number of cases of paupers complaining of inadequate relief which had come before the board of supervision, down to the date of the Report, was 597,—of these 303 were dismissed on the information contained in the schedules, and 94 after communication with the parochial boards. In 182 cases remitted to the parochial boards, the allowances were so far increased as to remove the ground of complaint; and 18 cases remained undisposed of. The discontent which led to the transmission of so many complaints was, the commissioners say, "not caused by urgent destitution, and still less by any unfavourable change in the complainants' condition since the new Act came into operation, for their condition had been greatly improved; but was to be attributed chiefly to the exertions of certain persons to excite discontent amongst them, and to the extravagant expectations that had been raised of the advantages which the Act provided for them."

Complaints of inadequate relief.

According to a return of the applications made by poor persons to the sheriffs in the several counties, under the 73*rd section* of the Act, on account of their being refused relief, it appears that the entire number of such applications during the fifteen months in which the new law had been in operation, amounted to 456, of which 184 were from the counties of Ross, Sutherland, and Caithness. Upon this the commissioners remark, that where the change was greatest, the applications would necessarily be the most numerous, and the labours of the sheriffs are said in some instances to have been very considerably increased thereby. The duty of deciding moreover, the commissioners observe, must often be painful and perplexing. Where the applicant is both wholly disabled and wholly destitute, a parochial board can hardly fail of at once affording the relief which there is then no

Application to sheriffs on refusal of relief.

ground for refusing. But it is in cases of doubt as to the applicant's right to be placed on the roll, that the sheriff is likely to be applied to, and these are generally cases of partial disability, or partial destitution, in which it is obvious that questions of extreme nicety must occasionally arise, in ascertaining the precise point at which an individual may have become entitled to relief. The commissioners suggest what would seem the right method of solving such questions, by remarking, that "were poorhouses universally established, they would afford a ready means of testing the exigency of such claims;" and they support this suggestion by declaring that in parishes where poorhouses exist, the same difficulties have not been experienced in dealing with applicants of whose claims doubts were entertained by the parochial board, an offer to receive an applicant into the poorhouse having been held to be sufficient to justify the refusal of other relief. This testimony as to the insufficiency of individual judgment, and the importance of an established test, for determining the claims of applicants for relief, is of great value, coming from such a quarter; and we may presume, can hardly fail of leading eventually to an increase in the number of poorhouses, the want of which thus appears to be already felt.

Amount of expenditure on relief of the poor.

Accuracy and uniformity had not yet been established in registering the poor who were in receipt of relief, nor in the accounts of the expenditure for that purpose; but according to the best returns which the commissioners could obtain from the several parishes,

| | £. | s. | d. |
|---|---|---|---|
| The amount expended in relief of the poor between the 1st of February 1844, and the 1st of February 1845, was .. .. .. .. .. .. .. .. .. .. .. .. | 258,814 | 19 | 11 |
| The amount expended in relief of the poor between the 1st of February 1845, and the 1st of February 1846, was .. .. .. .. .. .. .. .. .. .. .. .. | 295,232 | 8 | 1 |

The shortness of the time since the new Act came

into operation, and especially since arrangements were made in accordance with the 54th section, for placing certain funds at the disposal of the kirk sessions, made it impossible to obtain separate returns of the expenditure by that body, and the whole amount expended on relief of the poor, from whatever source derived, is therefore included in the above statement.

It appears from returns obtained in 1843, that the money raised from all sources for the relief and management of the poor in Scotland, amounted—

| | | | |
|---|---|---|---|
| In 1836 to | £171,042 | In 1839 to | £199,660 |
| „ 1837 „ | 180,123 | „ 1840 „ | 202,812 |
| „ 1838 „ | 192,829 | „ 1841 „ | 218,481 |

In February 1846 the amount expended is above stated to have been 295,232*l.*; but the amount raised in that year was 306,044*l.*, being, as compared with 1836, an increase in ten years of 135,002*l.*, or nearly 79 per cent., upwards of a fourth part of which increase had, it is to be remarked, taken place in the last year.

Amounts of property, and population.

The annual value of real property in Scotland, according to returns laid before parliament in 1843, was 9,320,794*l.*

The population of Scotland at the periods of the census in 1831 and 1841 was—

| | |
|---|---|
| In 1831 .. .. .. .. | £2,365,114 |
| „ 1841 .. .. .. .. | 2,620,184 |

Thus exhibiting an increase of population in ten years equal to 10·7 per cent.

Number of persons relieved.

The number of poor on the rolls of all the parishes for the year ending 1st February 1845, was 63,070, or about 1 in 42 of the population. For the year ending the 1st of February 1846, the number on the rolls was 69,432, or about 1 in 38 of the population; but the imperfect manner in which the parish rolls were kept, deprives these numbers of any pretension to exactitude.

The commissioners conclude this their first Report

with the declaration, that they are deeply impressed with the importance of the duties assigned to them, and the weight of the responsibility involved in the administration of the Poor Law. They have however, they say, felt that the responsibility did not rest with them alone, but was shared by the parochial authorities of the country; and they bear testimony to the honourable and humane spirit in which the heritors and parochial boards generally, have endeavoured to give effect to the provisions of the 'Act for the Amendment and better Administration of the Laws relating to the Relief of the Poor in Scotland.'

Conclusion of the First Report.

Such was the first Report of the board of supervision, of which it has been here endeavoured to give the condensed substance, and on all material points as far as possible in the words of the Report itself; for it was felt to be important that in a matter so peculiar and beset with so much difficulty as the new Scottish Poor Law, the views of the commissioners charged with the duty of superintending its introduction should be so stated, as to leave no doubt of the grounds of their proceeding in any case, or of their decision upon any point, whether of practice or principle.

The first year's experience of the working of the new law, was generally held to be satisfactory. The administration of relief was more orderly, its amount approximated more nearly to the wants of the recipients, and the charge was more equally spread over the whole community. The means of further improvement had been provided for by the organisation of parochial boards with inspectors of the poor, and by the various regulations promulgated by the board of supervision—all tending to the establishment of one comprehensive system throughout the country, varied only in its application by the different circumstances of the districts where it had to be applied. For the details of such application in carrying out the law, and for the results which ensued, we must turn to the second and subsequent Reports of the commissioners.

1847. Second Report of the board of supervision.

The second Report of the board of supervision was made in August 1847. The period was one of much distress and difficulty, owing to the almost universal failure of the potato crop. Some details of this calamity, as it occurred in England and Ireland, are given in the Histories of the English and Irish Poor Laws.[n] In Scotland the pressure caused thereby was exceedingly severe, especially in the Western and Highland districts, which were again reduced to a state similar to that which occurred in 1783.[o] The Report states that "the failure last year of the potato crop which had hitherto furnished probably about two-sevenths of the food consumed by the population of Scotland, and the high price of every description of grain, demanded increased allowances to the poor." As soon therefore as it was ascertained that the failure "had been almost universal and complete," the commissioners called upon the parochial boards to consider the propriety of increasing the allowances, and recommended that the increase should be made in the form of a separate extraordinary allowance in food, rather than an increased allowance in money. They were aware, they say, that in certain of the poorer parishes, advantage might be taken by dealers to exact exorbitant prices, or to adulterate the food; and they therefore recommended the parochial boards of such parishes to lay in stores of meal on their own account, from which the extra allowances should be issued to the poor: but as the commissioners had no means of ascertaining in what parishes a regular supply of food at fair prices could be safely relied upon, they left each parochial board to the exercise of its own discretion as

Failure of the potato crop.

[n] See 'History of the English Poor Law,' vol. ii. pp. 391, 392, and 393. Also 'History of the Irish Poor Law' during the years 1846 and 1847.

[o] Ante, p. 117.

to laying in stores, or trusting to the ordinary course of trade for a supply.

Distress in the Highlands.

The Appendix to the Report contains long and minute statements made by officers whom the board of supervision, on the failure of the potato crop, had sent to the distressed districts of the western Highlands and Islands, with directions to visit the several parishes, and examine into the condition of the poor; and it appears from these statements, that although the labouring classes endured much privation in most of the parishes, "the poor who were dependent on parochial relief had been provided with the necessaries of life at least as amply as in the most abundant of former years." The commissioners also remark, that "taking into consideration the shortness of the time that has elapsed since any systematic attempt has been made to give effect to the legal provision for the poor in those districts, and the very severe test to which the efficiency of the law and of the machinery by which it is to be carried out have been exposed during the last year, they think they are justified in expressing a confident hope that the recent statute will be found adequate to accomplish the benevolent objects contemplated by the legislature." They further express their satisfaction at being able to state, "that after a careful investigation they have been unable to discover any case in which it can be clearly established that want of food was the immediate cause of death"— doubtless a subject of gratulation, as the reverse was to be expected under the very trying circumstances of the period. But considerable mortality did nevertheless ensue, want and disease having on this as on other occasions maintained their accustomed relations of cause and effect; and the commissioners express their regret at having "to report the death of several very efficient inspectors and assistant-inspectors, and more than one medical officer, from fever caught in discharge of their duty amongst the poor."

The Scottish Poor Law, we have seen, excluded able-bodied persons, that is in fact all the class of labourers, from participating in its benefits, or availing themselves of its protection in seasons like the present. It is true that famine, or a failure in the usual supply of food, is an event so far exceptional as scarcely to admit of being provided against by any description of Poor Law; but like other visitations it has its degrees of severity, and the sufferers under it have their different claims for sympathy and assistance. To exclude formally and entirely, whatever might be the circumstances, any one class or section of the people, whilst all requisite support is furnished to another section, does not seem to be consistent with justice, and can hardly be defended on the score of policy.

The failure of the potato crop was known so early as the month of August in the preceding year. The failure was very general, but in the western Highlands and Islands where the potato constituted the chief food of the people, it was nearly entire, and the distress was there proportionally great. The board of supervision, as already stated, took steps for securing a sufficient supply of food for those of the poor who were legally entitled to relief; but with regard to the rest, for all were poor, assistance had to be sought elsewhere. Government was early applied to, and an experienced commissary[p] was sent to ascertain the state of things in the western districts, and to organise the means for supplying the wants of the population. Extensive inquiries were likewise instituted into the state of the crops, and the condition of the people, in other parts where a dearth of food was apprehended. The distress was referred to with expressions of "the deepest concern" in the Royal speech on the assembling of parliament, and in answer to inquiries afterwards made, the

Government aid.

---

[p] Sir E. Coffin.

home secretary stated that in order to mitigate the distress, government had made advances under the Drainage Act of last session (*9th and 10th Vict. cap.* 101), which in their results were highly beneficial, increasing the value of the land to the proprietors, and affording extensive relief to the distressed labourers. The government had moreover, he said, established depôts for the sale of food, one at Tobermory and one at Skye, in addition to which commissariat officers had been sent in government steamers to make inquiries, and to give such assistance as was necessary. These measures had, he believed, been the means of supplying the people of those districts with food, who otherwise would have been in want of the necessaries of life. Grants had moreover been made in a few instances "to meet local subscriptions, and to relieve distress, where the Scottish poor law had been found to be inefficient; and he hoped that by these means the severity of the calamity in Scotland might not only be mitigated, but that by the exertions of the landed proprietors, who showed every disposition to meet the misfortune, Scotland would be brought safely through the present crisis." [q]

Parishes assessed.

Of the 880 parishes existing in Scotland, the number which, down to the end of June in the present year, had resolved to raise the funds for relief of the poor by assessment was 558; of these 431 were assessed according to the first of the three modes pre-

[q] See Sir George Grey's speech on the 1st of February 1847, as given in Hansard. I have examined the voluminous correspondence which took place at this time between the government and various parties in Scotland, and extracts might be given as in the case of 1783 (see ante, p. 117) showing the extent of the distress, and the sad condition to which the people were reduced, in the Highland districts especially; but all that is necessary for our present purpose seems to be comprised in the speech of the home secretary, the substance of which is here given. "The British Association" remitted 77,683*l.* for relief of the distress in Scotland, that being one-sixth of the amount of subscriptions received by them. The other five-sixths were appropriated to Ireland. The conduct of the landed proprietors of Scotland on this occasion was generally admirable. They appeared to feel the duties appertaining to their position, and promptly and liberally responded to its claims.

scribed by the recent Act, 37 according to the second, 34 according to the third, and 56 according to local Acts or established usage; whilst 76 of the parishes assessed according to the first mode, had classified lands and heritages in the terms of the 36*th section* of the statute. The commissioners had sanctioned changes in the mode of assessment at first adopted in several of the parishes, and also in regard to the classification; and on a review of the number of parishes assessed according to the different modes, and of the changes from one mode of assessment to another which had been resolved upon by the parochial boards, they are, they say, led to the conclusion, "that the general feeling of the country is not yet favourable to the application of one mode of assessment to all the parishes in Scotland."

Election of managers of the poor.

In the great majority of the assessed parishes the elections appear, notwithstanding the novelty of the operation, to have been conducted in a satisfactory manner. The managers were generally returned without opposition, and no instance of irregularity or confusion was reported to the commissioners, who moreover remark that "they have reason to believe the introduction of a limited number of elected members into the parochial boards, has afforded greater facilities for obtaining an accurate knowledge of the condition of the poor, and has generally been conducive to the better administration of the laws for their relief and management."

Inspectors of the poor.

The inspectors of the poor are highly important functionaries in Scotland, and on their zeal integrity and efficiency the successful administration of the law must mainly depend. The inspector has to perform the duties of the clerk, the relieving officer, and indeed of all the other officials of the English unions, for he is the sole executive of the parochial board. The commissioners say that the inspectors have generally performed their duties in a creditable manner, although there were some instances to the contrary. Several of them had resigned, some on account of the onerous nature of their duties, and some from impaired health or other causes. There was however reason to believe that some of the inspectors were interested in supplying provisions and other articles to the poor, and an order was therefore issued, prohibiting these officers from deriving any profit or emolument directly or indirectly from such dealings; and in transmitting the order to the several parishes, the commissioners took advantage of the opportunity to point out to the parochial boards "the very questionable propriety of employing their own members to supply food or other necessaries to the poor, or any articles to be paid for out of the parochial funds of which they had the control." There could be no doubt as to the impropriety of such a practice, and it might perhaps have been better at once to prohibit it, as in the case of the inspectors; but the commissioners seem to have been doubtful either of the power of enforcing, or of the policy of issuing such an order with regard to the members of parochial boards, and therefore only ventured to call attention to what they designated the "questionable propriety" of the practice.

The distress in the western Highlands engaged the commissioners' earnest attention, and the inquiries which they instituted made them aware, that in some of the more remote parishes and islands, the inspectors were not only very imperfectly acquainted with the details of their duties, but were also "under the impression that distance and the unfrequency of intercourse placed them beyond the reach of observation." Yet the commissioners declare their gratification at finding, that except in a few of the more remote parishes, "the parochial boards and the inspectors, in the midst of the distress and suffering with which they were surrounded, and the difficulties attending the first introduction of compulsory systematic relief to the poor, had discharged their duties in a spirit that does them credit." The inquiries which had been made however tended, the commissioners think, to establish greater regularity in conducting the general business connected with the relief of the poor than had before prevailed, and they are of opinion that it may be necessary to institute similar inquiries from time to time in all parts of the country.

Increase of the casual poor.

The dearth of food in Ireland, and in some parts of Scotland, has this year it is said "greatly increased the number of casual applicants for relief, first in those towns on the west coast which have a regular communication with Ireland, and next in almost every considerable town in the country, as well as in some of the rural parishes, to which these immigrants had proceeded in quest of work or alms." The sickness which generally prevailed, particularly among the Irish labourers on some of the lines of railway, had also caused a considerable increase of this class of paupers in Edinburgh, and in most of the towns in the neighbourhood of those lines, everywhere bringing an increased burden upon the rates. The want of suitable accommodation for the casual sick poor, is said to be a serious evil in many places. "The dread of infection shuts against them the doors of those houses in which the parochial officers have usually found temporary accommodation for the casual poor, and hitherto few parishes have provided any separate house for their reception." The consequence has been "that some have remained in their huts by the railway, and some have unavoidably been lodged in outhouses and other places unfavourable to their recovery, and from which their condition made it impossible to remove them." The parochial boards where these difficulties have occurred, ought not, the commissioners think, to be blamed because they were unprepared for such a state of things, although it is doubtless their duty to take measures for preventing its continuance; and several parochial boards had accordingly, on finding that they could not get the casual poor accommodated, "applied for and obtained the commissioners' sanction for the erection of a building at the cost of the parish, in which this class of paupers may be lodged and attended to."

Vagrants.

The increase of the casual poor, almost necessarily led to an increase of vagrancy. The commissioners say that they have no means of ascertaining the number of vagrants in Scotland, but they believe it to be large. It is only with those who are in receipt of relief, that the poor-law authorities have any power to interfere; and these will notwithstanding sometimes resort to vagrancy, through early habit or immoral tendencies. In some of the remote parishes also, where the Poor Law is imperfectly administered, begging within the parish is said to be still sanctioned by the parochial boards; "but the great body of vagrants in all parts of Scotland, and almost all those who pass from parish to parish, and county to county, are not recipients of parochial relief." Where vagrancy occurs among those who are in receipt of relief, it has, the commissioners say, been found extremely difficult to put an end to the practice. Some parochial boards have attempted to check it by diminishing the allowance, with a promise of its being again restored when the pauper relinquished begging; but the diminution was found only to give the pauper an additional pretext for following the practice. Other parochial boards proposed to withhold the allowance altogether, unless the pauper desisted from mendicancy; and this course appears to be sanctioned by the law, which makes provision for the poor in order that they may not be driven to beg. But if the allowance be withheld, the pauper will necessarily be thrown upon the charity of the public, and he will thus probably be enabled to indulge the inclination to vagrancy with a better chance of making it a profitable occupation. To remove from the roll a pauper who has a habit of begging, would therefore, it is said, "be in many cases a reward rather than a punishment."

The commissioners close this head of their Report by declaring, that "the only efficient means of checking vagrancy in poor persons already on the roll of a parish, without the aid of the police, would be to erect a poorhouse, in which habitual beggars amongst the poor on the roll could be relieved, and restrained from wandering through the country." But it is added, that as no parish whose population does not exceed 5,000 can raise by assessment funds for the erection of a poorhouse, unless in combination with some of the adjoining parishes, there are "many cases in which the parochial authorities cannot effectually check vagrancy even amongst the poor on the roll." Such is no doubt the case, and where the want is so obvious, and the remedy so easy, we must believe that sooner or later it cannot fail of being applied; and that in Scotland as in England, parishes will be united for effecting an object in common, which could not be so well accomplished by them singly, or which might be too weighty for them singly to undertake or sustain.

Poorhouses a remedy for vagrancy.

Some progress seems to have been made towards a more efficient provision of medical relief for the poor, although in most parishes it is said to be still very defective, whilst in some of the remote parishes where there is no resident practitioner, the means of affording medical relief do not exist. The amount expended for medical relief had however increased from 4,055*l*. in 1846, to 12,879*l*. in 1847, thus showing that the want had to some extent been supplied, and showing likewise how urgent it must previously have been.

Medical relief.

The mode in which the board of supervision dealt with complaints of inadequate relief has been already explained.[r] The number of such complaints in the present year amounted to 673. Of these 226 had been dismissed on the information contained in the schedules, and the commissioners state that in 262 cases remitted by them to the parochial boards, the allowances had been increased to such an extent as to remove the ground of complaint; whilst in one case, the ground of complaint not having been so removed, they had issued a minute declaring that the applicant had a just ground of action against the parochial board. The matter was however subsequently arranged without further proceedings, and the result of these appeals seems on the whole to be satisfactory.

Complaints of inadequate relief.

It appears that between the 1st of July 1846, and the 30th of June 1847, the number of applications at the sheriffs' courts under the new law was 1043,[s] of which 778 were so far substantiated that an order for interim relief was made. In 305 of these cases the order must have been acquiesced in, as in 473 only were answers lodged by inspectors. In 287 the answers lodged were successful, and in 174 the proceedings were either abandoned or no decision had been pronounced. The commissioners here remark, "that although it cannot be argued upon the data thus furnished, that there has been any unnecessary opposition on the part of parochial boards or their officers to the admission of claims, where the parties were justly entitled to parochial relief, the results show that the provisions of the statute which confer on sheriffs a power to give redress, and order immediate relief, are neither injudicious nor unnecessary"—and

Application to sheriffs on refusal of relief.

---

[r] Ante, p. 192.

[s] In ten months of the previous year, the number of applications was 456—ante, p. 195.

it seems impossible not to concur in the justice of this observation.

Prosecution of fathers of illegitimate children.

The commissioners express their satisfaction at the effective working of the 80*th section* of the Act.[t] The greater number of the prosecutions under this section have, they say, been instituted against the fathers of illegitimate children, and against husbands for deserting their wives and families, but chiefly the former. Attempts were frequently made to throw the burden of maintaining illegitimate children upon the parish, and if the parochial authorities had not strenuously resisted these attempts, and enforced the law, the evil might have grown to a serious amount. As it was, there appears during the year ending on the 30th of June to have been 370 prosecutions, and 224 convictions. Both these numbers however fall short of the actual number against whom proceedings in some shape were taken, the parties having in many cases settled with the parish, either before or immediately after the commencement of the prosecution; and the commissioners declare their belief, " that the law has been brought to bear upon offenders in even a more powerful and extensive manner than the returns exhibit, and that the operation of this portion of the statute has been highly beneficial."

In order to secure uniformity in the returns connected with the relief of the poor, which is so essential for affording accurate means of comparison, the commissioners issued minute regulations on the subject, and directed that the returns should be made up at Whitsunday, or the 15th of May in each year. The following statement will therefore be for the year ending on the 14th of May 1847, the interval between the 1st of February and the 15th of May 1846 being on this occasion altogether omitted—

---

[t] Ante, p. 180.

1847. Amount of relief.

| | |
|---|---|
| The sum *raised* for the relief of the poor in the year ending the 1st of February 1846, was .. .. .. .. .. .. | £306,044 |
| The sum *raised* for the relief of the poor in the year ending the 14th of May 1847, was .. .. .. | 435,367 |
| Increase raised in the year .. .. .. .. | £129,323 |

| | |
|---|---|
| The sum *expended* for the relief of the poor in the year ending the 1st of February 1846, was .. .. .. .. .. .. .. .. | £295,232 |
| The sum *expended* for the relief of the poor in the year ending the 14th of May 1847, was .. .. .. .. .. .. .. .. .. | 433,915 |
| Increase expended in the year .. .. .. | £138,683 |

| | |
|---|---|
| The sum *raised* for relief of the poor in 1836 was, as has been before stated, 171,042*l.*,[u] equal according to the census of 1831, to .. .. .. .. .. | 1*s.* 5¾*d.* per head on the population. |
| The amount *raised* in the year ending the 1st February 1846, was according to the census of 1841, equal to .. .. | 2*s.* 4*d.* per head on the population. |
| And the amount *raised* in the year ending the 14th May 1847, was nearly equal to .. .. .. .. .. .. .. | 3*s.* 4*d.* per head on the population. |

Thus showing a continual increase both in the actual and in the proportional amounts, an increase still however falling short of what the necessities of the poor required, and the order and social well-being of the community called for.

Church collections.

The church collections in assessed parishes during the year ending 14th May 1847, amounted to 17,095*l.*, one half of which or 8,587*l.* is stated to have been expended on the relief of the poor. In many parishes these funds were, it is said, handed over to the parochial boards, although under the recent statute the whole of the church collections are left at the disposal of the kirk sessions, in parishes in which assessments are established. A portion of the above 8,587*l.* must therefore be included in the amount of receipts returned by the parochial boards; but the precise amount, or what was the additional relief derived from

---

[u] Ante, p. 197.

church collections, there were no means of ascertaining. —It is remarked however, that "the recipients were probably for the most part not strictly speaking legal objects of parochial relief."

| | Numbers relieved. |
|---|---|
| The number of poor on the parish rolls in all Scotland, on the 1st of February 1845, was .. .. .. .. .. .. | 63,070, or 1 in 42 of the population. |
| On the 1st of February 1846, the number was .. .. .. .. .. .. .. | 69,432, or 1 in 38 of the population. |
| On the 1st of May 1847, the number was .. .. .. .. .. .. .. | 74,161, or 1 in 35 of the population. |

In the latter year the number of casual poor, or persons relieved by the inspectors without orders from the parochial boards, was 60,399; but these were not cases of regular or permanent relief, and therefore cannot be ranked with the above. It may moreover be remarked, that the returns of the numbers relieved do not appear to have been made with such exactitude as to entitle them to implicit reliance, although they may be sufficient for the general purposes of comparison.

In reference to the foregoing statements, the commissioners observe that "the large increase in the amount expended on the relief and management of the poor in Scotland, exhibited in the returns for this year, may be regarded as sufficient evidence of the readiness with which parochial boards generally have met the demands caused by the failure of the potato crop and the high price of grain;" and they further observe, that "after deducting the portion of this increase which may fairly be attributed to the increased cost of food during six months of the year, there will remain a large amount which cannot be attributed to that cause, and which must be regarded as a permanent addition to the sum annually expended on the relief and management of the poor."

Such were the results at the end of the second year of the new law. It is impossible to deny that it was put to a severe trial by the scarcity which occurred, or that the credit claimed for it by the commissioners of being successful within the limited sphere of its operations is well founded; and for an account of its further development and more effective working, we must continue our examination of the reports annually made by the board of supervision, the third being the next in order.

1848. Third Report of the board of supervision.

The commissioners' third Report is dated in August 1848. In a great majority of the cases in which elections had taken place in the past year, the parties nominated for managers of the poor are said to have been unanimously elected. Some of the parishes had been divided into wards for the purpose of election, and a more equal representation of the ratepayers was thus obtained, especially where one estate happened to comprise a majority of the votes, or where the urban ratepayers outnumbered the rural population, and excluded them from a fair share in the management. The rapid increase of the expenditure for relief of the poor is said to have raised the value, in the estimation of the ratepayers, of their right to elect their own representatives; and the commissioners express their conviction, "that the introduction of a limited number of elected members into parochial boards, had been conducive to the better administration of the law;" although the result of their investigations in certain suburban parishes in Glasgow and Edinburgh, satisfied them that it will be necessary to extend their inquiries to other parishes similarly situated.[x]

Election of managers.

Inspectors of the poor.

The inspectors are again reported to have generally performed their duties in a creditable manner, although there were some instances of misconduct and inefficiency. Of the many complaints against

[x] The "Feuars" are numerous in some parishes, and if assessed, would be entitled to vote equally with the heritors.

inspectors which the commissioners had been called upon to investigate, the great majority proved to be unfounded, or to have proceeded from misapprehension; and with great propriety it is observed, that "in the difficult and often invidious position in which these officers are sometimes placed, they require protection and support, as well as control and supervision."

Parishes assessed.

Since the date of the last Report, 44 parishes in which the funds for relief of the poor were raised by voluntary contributions, had resolved to raise the money by assessment. The number of parishes assessed was now 602, and the number unassessed 278. The parochial boards of 27 parishes had requested the commissioners to sanction a change in the mode of assessment or of classification previously adopted. In 15 of these cases the request was complied with, and in 12 it was refused. The manner in which the funds for relief of the poor were now raised in the different parishes, is stated to be as follows—

| | | |
|---|---|---|
| First mode prescribed by the Act, with classification | 85 | |
| Do. do. without do. | 386 | |
| | | 471 |
| Second mode prescribed by the Act .. .. .. .. .. .. | | 40 |
| Third mode do. .. .. .. .. .. .. | | 36 |
| According to established usage .. .. .. .. .. .. .. | | 55 |
| Total assessed parishes .. .. .. .. | | 602 |
| By voluntary contributions, &c. .. .. .. .. .. .. .. | | 278 |
| Total number of parishes in Scotland .. | | 880 |

Poorhouses.

The commissioners had approved the plans and specifications for eight new poorhouses, to be erected for twenty-three parishes singly or in combination, having an aggregate population of 175,065. The houses collectively were designed to accommodate 2,310 inmates, so that poorhouse accommodation would thus be provided for 1 in 75 of the population in these parishes. Plans and specifications were likewise approved for adding to and enlarging poorhouses in Edinburgh and Glasgow; and five other parishes containing a population of 20,986, are also said to have resolved to erect poorhouses, but had not transmitted their plans for approval at the date of the Report.

The casual sick poor.

The want of suitable accommodation for the casual sick poor, had been remarked upon in the last Report,[y] and the want was now more urgently felt on account of the spread of fever, the invariable accompaniment of distress among the poor. The commissioners therefore addressed a circular to the several parochial boards, calling their attention to this particular portion of the Report, and pointing out that poor persons disabled by sickness "cannot with propriety be placed in common lodging-houses, where they rarely meet with the quiet and attention their cases require; and that to place paupers suffering from fever in a lodging occupied by the healthy poor, or by independent labourers, would be altogether unjustifiable." The inspectors of the poor were also at the same time directed to call the attention of the parochial boards to the recent Act 9*th and* 10*th Vict., cap.* 96, for the removal of nuisances, and to the duties required from them under its provisions for preventing the spread of fever and other contagious diseases.

Medical relief.

The parliament had granted 10,000*l.* in aid of the medical relief of the poor in Scotland, and it was important to make this grant as conducive as possible to the improvement and extension of the existing system of relief for the sick, which was admitted on all hands to be faulty and insufficient. The commissioners accordingly prepared a scheme for apportioning the grant, governed in some measure by the area and population of the several parishes, but at the same

---

[y] Ante, p. 205.

time providing that no parish should participate which had not expended in medical relief in the past year, a sum at least equal to double the amount apportioned to it from the grant; and if any parish declined to participate on these terms, its share of the grant was to be distributed among the other parishes in proportion to their actual expenditure. Another condition was, that legally qualified medical officers, at fixed salaries, should be appointed to attend the sick poor, and to vaccinate children, the board of supervision retaining the power of dismissal in case of neglect or incompetency. It appears that 494 parishes complied with these conditions, and thus became entitled to receive their shares of the grant respectively apportioned to them. From 240 parishes no intimation had been received, and 146 parishes declined to comply with the conditions. The commissioners had expected that some of the parishes would so decline, as a participation in the grant would involve an increased expenditure on medical relief in those parishes where the relief was most defective. But the primary object being, they say, to obtain adequate medical relief for the sick poor, "it appeared just and reasonable that each parish should be required to expend from its own funds, a sum at least equal to the share of the grant apportioned to it." Meantime however, medical relief was, as appears by the returns, rapidly extending—the amount expended on it for the year ending February 1846, was 4,055*l.* 17*s.*—for the year ending 14th May 1847, it was 12,879*l.* 9*s.*, and in the present year ending 14th May 1848, the expenditure on medical relief amounted to 30,339*l.* 12*s.* It is probable, the commissioners observe, that nutritious diet and other things not strictly chargeable as medical relief, may be included in this last amount; but after making every allowance, there can, it is thought, be no doubt that the supply of medical relief has been greatly improved.

Lunatic and fatuous paupers.

The commissioners say that they have "completed their inquiries into the condition and circumstances of all the lunatic paupers in Scotland who were not in an asylum, and whose cases had been reported, up to the 1st of July last." The number of these cases is 2,003, in 1960 of which removal to an asylum was dispensed with, and in 38 cases such removal was enforced. The commissioners declare that they have not dispensed with removal to an asylum in any case, in which it was not certified by a competent medical authority that the lunatic was harmless, that his disease was not likely to be aggravated thereby, that the accommodation was suitable, and the attendance sufficient; and in all cases where lunatics were not residing with relations, the allowance by the parish was required to be sufficient for their subsistence, and for securing proper treatment from the persons in whose charge they were. It is then remarked, with a feeling that may well be envied, that "they have thus endeavoured, not unsuccessfully, to improve the condition of this the most helpless class of paupers, and hitherto in many cases the most neglected." The deficiency of accommodation in asylums and licensed houses, still however made it necessary to sanction the continuance of very many lunatics in private residences, whose removal to an asylum would on many accounts be preferable.

Complaints of inadequate relief.

The number of complaints of inadequate relief made to the board of supervision during the year, is stated to have been 793; of these 297 were dismissed on the information contained in the schedules, and 112 after reference. In 305 cases remitted to the parochial boards, the ground of complaint is said to have been removed, and in 8 cases, the ground of complaint not being removed, a minute was issued declaring that the applicants had a just cause of action against their parishes in the court of session. Fifteen cases of complaint remained undisposed of.

Applications to the sheriffs on refusal of relief.

The number of applications to the sheriffs by persons refused relief, during the year ending 30th June 1848 was 1,334, being 291 in excess of the previous year. In 1,039 cases interim relief was ordered to be given, and in only 582 of these did the parish authorities lodge answers in contravention of the statements made by the applicants. On this the commissioners remark—"We cannot but fear there is too frequently on the part of inspectors of the poor, a delay or refusal of relief which is not justified by the circumstances of the cases, and that applicants are thus driven to seek the assistance of the sheriff, in order to enforce their legal rights." It further appears that in 261 cases in which the right to be admitted on the roll was disputed, decisions had been pronounced in favour of the applicants, while in 372 cases the right had not been affirmed. But in many cases, it is observed, in consequence of arrangements between the parties, no further proceedings are taken after the first or second stage, and the final result of many of the applications is not therefore made known. During the year, there had been 275 prosecutions, and 173 convictions, under the *79th and 80th sections* of the Act, and the commissioners continue of opinion that these enactments are salutary, and their operation generally satisfactory, notwithstanding the difficulties frequently experienced by parochial boards in convicting and punishing offenders under them.

Relief of the poor in Shetland and Orkney.

The condition of the poor in the Shetland Islands caused the commissioners much anxiety, and they deemed it necessary to send one of their officers to inquire into the manner in which the duties of inspection and relief were there conducted. A summary of his journal is given in the appendix of the present Report, and exhibits a state of things which, although not altogether satisfactory, "yet leaves no reason to fear that the distress presses more severely upon the paupers, than upon the labouring population." It appears that the relief of the poor in Shetland, is chiefly derived from a system which is there known by the name of '*quartering*.' A parish is divided into a certain number of quarters or portions, and the poor persons disabled by old age or infirmity are severally appointed to each quarter, and authorised to beg from the inhabitants, obtaining in this way a supply of meal, wool, potatoes, fish, and other necessaries. Such contributions in kind are less felt than money payments would be, the inhabitants being generally occupiers of small portions of land, as well as fishermen and owners of cattle. The town of Lerwick however differs from the other parishes in Shetland, the poor being there relieved with money. One class is paid 1*s.* to 2*s.* per week, another class is paid 1*s.* 4*d.* to 2*s.* 8*d.* per month, and the third class is paid 2*s.* 6*d.* to 5*s.* quarterly, but begging in the street is very common. The mode of relief in the Orkney Islands does not differ materially from that practised in Shetland, and the commissioners were assured "that the poor are there well provided and cared for."

The persons thus "well provided and cared for" in Orkney, are the aged and infirm poor. There is no care or provision for the poor who are not aged and infirm, however urgent their necessities may be. This was always, we have seen, the governing principle of the Scottish Poor Law, and by way of making it more clear and certain, the 68*th section* of the late statute expressly declares "that nothing herein contained shall be held to confer a right to demand relief on able-bodied persons out of employment."[z] The prevalence of distress through

[z] See ante, p. 179.

the failure of the potato, and from other causes, seems now however to have raised doubts as to the possibility of maintaining this principle in unmitigated strictness; and the commissioners, while holding the opinion that able-bodied persons out of employment had no right to demand relief, appeared to consider that the entire wording of the 68*th section* "removed the doubts which had hitherto been entertained, as to the legality of applying the funds raised by assessment to the relief of the occasional as well as the permanent poor; and that able-bodied persons out of employment might, if destitute, come under the denomination of 'occasional poor,' and might be relieved out of the funds raised by assessment." This would, if it were established, be an important advance in the way of amelioration; and the commissioners consulted the lord advocate and the dean of faculty on the subject, who were of opinion "that the late Act 8*th and* 9*th Vict., cap.* 83, does not confer on or recognise in able-bodied persons out of employment any right to demand relief, and that such persons are not within the scope of the provisions for enforcing and rendering effectual claims for parochial relief." But on the other hand, they were of opinion—"that the statute removes all doubt as to the legality of affording relief to occasional poor from the funds raised by assessment, as well as from the collections at the church door;" and they were further of opinion—"that able-bodied persons accidently or unavoidably thrown out of employment, and thereby reduced to immediate want, may be regarded as occasional poor to whom temporary relief may lawfully be given out of the funds raised by assessment, but that such persons cannot be admitted on the roll of poor entitled to parochial relief."

Relief of the able-bodied or casual poor.

Fortified with this opinion, the commissioners now declared their understanding of the law "as regards the relief of able-bodied persons to be, that while they have not in any circumstances a right to demand relief, and cannot therefore by any legal proceeding enforce that demand—parochial boards may legally, when they think it advisable, apply the funds raised by assessment to the temporary relief of destitute able-bodied persons who are out of employment, and that half the collections at the church door are applicable to the same purpose." And they further add, by way of commentary—" to this unrestricted discretionary power conferred by statute on the parochial boards, and to the voluntary contributions of the public in extraordinary emergencies, is entrusted the relief of such cases of destitution as may occur among the classes not by law entitled to demand relief."

In connexion with the relief of the casual poor, the question as to the consequences of relief when afforded to unemancipated children was now also raised. It has been hitherto held that relief to a child was equivalent to relief to the parent, who was thereupon bound by all the conditions legally imposed upon recipients of relief, the same as if the relief had been granted to himself. The obligation to support his children naturally devolves upon the parent, and if his children were relieved by the parish, the relief was held to be given to him for the purpose of enabling him to fulfil this obligation. He was considered chargeable to the parish, because he required aid from the parish for enabling him to do that which he was legally and morally bound himself to do. A decision however recently pronounced by the sheriff of Lanarkshire, and which was supported on appeal before the lord ordinary, went to enforce the legal right of children to be relieved independently of the parents, " on the ground that being unable to do anything for their own support because of their tender years, and being destitute by reason of their father's destitution and inability to find employment, they fell under the class of persons entitled by law to parochial aid." The effect of this decision, it is said, would be, that children living with their father might become chargeable, whilst their father himself is neither chargeable nor subjected to the conditions imposed on the recipients of relief; and as it is doubtful whether the children could be separated from their father without his consent, the parish might also, it is said, "be required to relieve the children in their father's house."

Relief of the children of the able-bodied poor.

The decision pronounced by the sheriff of Lanarkshire was carried before the court of session, and pending any final adjudication thereon, and as similar cases might arise, the commissioners deemed it right to address a circular to the parochial boards informing them of the circumstances, and recommending, in the event of their being so called upon to relieve an able-bodied man, or the children of an able-bodied man on the ground that he cannot find employment, that the ground of the claim should be removed by providing employment for the parties. "The poorhouse," it is said, "probably affords the only safe test in such cases," but as it is not certain that a parochial board could require an able-bodied man who thus obtained relief for his children to enter a poorhouse, and as moreover many parishes are not provided with poorhouses, "the board of supervision is of opinion, that for the present it would be advisable to have recourse to a labour test, giving in return relief in food sufficient for his and their subsistence, and where the necessary arrangements can be made, cooked food ought to be preferred."

We here find indications of a nearer approach to the principle of the English Poor Law, than has before appeared in the administration of that of Scotland. It is true the *right* of the able-bodied to relief when destitute, is still denied; but a

Approximation of the English and Scottish laws.

claim to relief on the ground of destitution is practically recognised, and the necessity of some test for proving the existence of the destitution, is also admitted. These constitute in fact the foundations of the amended law in England, and if adopted in Scotland, and acted upon with good faith and efficiency, there will be little to complain of, even although the question of an absolute *right* to relief be left as at present.

1848. Amount of relief.

The sum *expended* on the relief and management of the poor for the year ending 14th May 1848, including 10,971*l.* for erecting poorhouses and fever-hospitals, was 544,333*l.* 15*s.* 6*d.*—being an increase of 110,419*l.* as compared with the expenditure of the previous year, and averaging 4*s.* 1¾*d.* per head on the population at the period of the census in 1841, and equal to 5*l.* 14*s.* 4¾*d.* per cent. on the annual value of real property in Scotland, according to the returns laid before parliament in 1843. The number of *regular poor* on the roll on the 14th of May 1848, was 77,732, equal to 1 in 33·7 of the population. The number of *casual poor* relieved in the year, was 126,684. The *casual poor* relieved last year amounted to 60,399; and they have therefore more than doubled in the present year. In Lanarkshire alone 81,938 persons were casually relieved. This increase of the "casual poor" is attributed to three causes—first the influx of destitute persons from Ireland, next the want of employment through the general depression of trade, and lastly the suspension of railway operations. The new law is therefore, we see, exposed to a continuance of pressure and difficulty, which must be largely felt by its administrators, as well as by the poor and the labouring classes generally.

Numbers relieved.

## CHAPTER V.

Fourth Report of the board of supervision — Occurrence of cholera — Fifth and sixth Reports — Distress in the Highlands and Islands; Sir John McNeill's Report — "Crofters," "Tacksmen," "Tenants," and "Cottars" — Kelp manufacture — Results of the Croft and Cottar system — Emigration the only remedy — Administration of relief in the western districts — Seventh and eighth Reports — Sir John McNeill's Reports on Caithness, and on the free and pauper colonies in Holland — Divergence between the English and Scottish systems of relief — Present practice in Scotland — Approximation of the Scottish and English systems — Conclusion.

1849. Fourth Report of the board of supervision.

THE fourth Report, like those preceding, is dated in August, and is arranged in similar order. The elections are said to have been everywhere conducted satisfactorily, and "to have terminated without litigation, except in the city parish of Glasgow, where the contest was unusually keen." The commissioners had deputed two of their officers to inquire into the proceedings of the inspectors, and the condition and management of the poor in certain urban, suburban, and other parishes; and the Reports of these officers, although for the most part favourable, yet brought to light some defects and abuses which are said to have been corrected, and which it is hoped would not again occur.

Parishes assessed.

Since the last Report, 23 parishes which had raised the funds for relief of the poor by voluntary contributions, resolved to raise these funds by assessment. The number of parishes now assessed was therefore 625, and the number unassessed 255. Twenty-four parishes resolved to change the mode of assessment or the classification previously adopted, and in 20 the proposed change was sanctioned, but in 4 the sanction was withheld. In two parishes,[a] the commissioners say, the discussions which arose about changing the

[a] Inverness and the city parish of Glasgow.

mode of assessment between persons interested in real property on one side, and the rest of the ratepayers on the other, have led to dissensions in the parochial boards. Differences of opinion, it is remarked "are natural and perhaps inevitable, when questions affecting different interests are discussed by popular bodies representing those interests;" but regret is expressed that the discussions in these two parochial boards should have been conducted in a manner not calculated to promote harmony amongst the ratepayers, or to facilitate the administration of the law.

Poorhouses.

Plans and specifications for the erection of three new poorhouses had been approved. The number of inmates which these houses were calculated to accommodate was 1,974, and the population of the six parishes for which they were intended was 141,082, so that there would be poorhouse accommodation in these parishes for 1 in 71 of their population. A table is appended showing that the available poorhouse accommodation in Scotland, either permanent or temporary, was adapted for 4,360 persons at the date of the Report; and that when the plans which had been sanctioned were all completed, there would be room for 2,728 more, making altogether poorhouse accommodation for 7,088 inmates, out of a population of 693,558, which is equal to 1 in 97·82 of the inhabitants.

Medical relief.

The parliamentary grant (10,000*l.*) in aid of medical relief in Scotland, was distributed in conformity with the plan described in the preceding Report.[b] 535 parishes resolved to comply with the prescribed conditions, but of these only 438 established their claim to participate in the grant by proving the required expenditure from their own funds. The commissioners remark, that the medical relief of the poor which was formerly hardly recognised as a duty, had since the new law came into operation continued to increase in efficiency, and

---

[b] Ante, p. 214.

with the aid of the parliamentary grant may now, they hope, be placed on a satisfactory footing. The expenditure for this purpose in the present year amounted to 33,010*l.* 12*s.* 11½*d.*, or 2,671*l.* above what it was returned as being last year; but as nutritious diet and other matters are supposed to have been included in that year's expenditure, and as everything not strictly appertaining to medical relief has been carefully excluded in the present, the increase has probably been far greater than the above figures indicate. Five years ago this description of relief was provided in a few parishes only, and it must therefore be admitted that considerable progress has been now made towards remedying the deficiency. There are still however many parishes in which medical relief is said to be very imperfectly administered, and few in which it is administered with the regularity that it ought to be, and that it might be without entailing additional cost; and the commissioners express a confident expectation that "they shall have the ready co-operation of a great majority of the parochial boards, in carrying out the rules by which it has been endeavoured to give more uniformity and regularity to the system, and to place its administration under such checks as may afford the parochial authorities and the public a reasonable security that the duty is adequately performed."

In connexion with medical relief, it is necessary to state that cases of malignant cholera occurred in Edinburgh early in October 1848, and the commissioners thereupon made application to the general board of health for the directions which that board was empowered by the 11*th and* 12*th Vict., cap.* 123,[c] to issue, "for the prevention as far as possible or mitigation of epidemic, endemic, or contagious diseases." But without waiting for the receipt of such directions,

The occurrence of cholera.

[c] Usually called 'The Nuisances Removal Act.'

a circular was addressed to the several parochial boards calling their attention to the 69*th section* of the Amendment Act, by which they are required out of the funds raised for the relief of the poor, to provide medicines medical attendance, nutritious diet and cordials for the sick, and pointing out the necessity of their providing for the proper medical treatment "of all poor persons suffering from symptoms indicating the probable approach or presence of cholera." If their ordinary means were not sufficient, they are recommended to increase them forthwith, the necessity for immediate relief in cases of cholera being too urgent to admit of delay. The relief necessary to preserve life must, it is said, be promptly given—the inquiries as to the right to demand it, may be made afterwards.

As soon as the directions of the board of health were received, copies of these directions were forwarded to all the parochial boards, together with suggestions in reference to the duties required from them. A great responsibility they were told devolved upon the parochial boards, "who are bound if other parties fail in performing their duties, to see that none of the directions issued by the board of health are left unperformed." The formidable scourge appeared first in Edinburgh, but it soon spread to the neighbouring towns, and early in November it reached Glasgow, and the manufacturing towns and villages in the south and west of Scotland. In Dumfries the disease burst forth with great violence, 269 deaths from cholera having occurred there within a month after its first appearance. At Glasgow the deaths from cholera in one week amounted to 829. "During the height of the epidemic indeed, all Glasgow appears to have been affected."[d] Edinburgh suffered less severely, although it was first visited, the deaths from cholera recorded there (including Leith and Newhaven)

---

[d] See Dr. Sutherland's Report, p. 81.

from the commencement to the 18th of June following, amounted to 554. The disease appears to have subsided in the spring, but during the summer and autumn of 1849, it again assumed its former virulence, attacking most of the principal towns, as well as certain other localities both in England and Scotland.

Progress of the cholera.

The first great outburst of cholera occurred in India in 1817, and after raging there with fearful virulence for some time, it extended its ravages over nearly all the rest of the world. In each of its subsequent visitations, in that of 1831-2 as well as in the present 1848-9, the cholera also appears to have commenced or had its origin in India, whence it travelled westward by successive and well-ascertained stages. On this latter occasion it made its appearance first at Caubul in 1845. Bombay, Kurrachee and Scinde were attacked in 1846. Afterwards the epidemic extended over Persia and Syria, reaching Astrakhan at the mouth of the Volga in June, and Moscow in September 1847, Petersburgh and Berlin in June 1848, Hamburgh in September, and Edinburgh in the beginning of October. On this last occasion the epidemic travelled at the same rate, and by almost precisely the same route as in 1831-2. Its effects in the two instances of Glasgow and Dumfries are noticed above, but there are no means of ascertaining the number of deaths from cholera in the whole of Scotland. This can however be done with respect to England through the Registrar-General's Reports, by which it appears that in London above 14,137 persons died of cholera in 1849, and that the deaths from cholera throughout England and Wales in that year amounted to 53,293,—"The decline of the epidemic was more rapid than its increase. While it was fatal to 20,379 in September, 4,654 died of it in October, 844 in November, and 163 in December."[e] The pestilence

[e] See 'Report on the Mortality of Cholera in England, 1848-9.'

has been far more fatal on this than it was on the former occasion, the deaths in 1831-2 amounting to 30,924, whilst in 1848-9 the deaths amounted to 54,398.[f]

This notice of the effects of the cholera in England, may assist in estimating the effects of the epidemic in Scotland. In both countries these effects are closely connected with the condition of the people, and have an important bearing on Poor Law administration, not only as regards the relief of the poor, but likewise with regard to the sanitary measures, for the due execution of which the Poor Law functionaries are under the Nuisances Removal Act made responsible.

The season under consideration was one of great pressure and difficulty. The high price of food, a near approach to actual famine in some districts through the failure of the potato, the stagnation of trade, the dearth of employment, and the spread of pestilence—all pressing at one time, seem enough to have embarrassed the resources and paralysed the energies of the country. But happily the several parts of our social fabric hang so well together, its gradations are so harmoniously adjusted, and afford such mutual support, each upholding and assisting the other, that events which would almost cause the disruption of society under other circumstances, are here sustained with comparatively little difficulty; and as soon as the season of trial or privation has passed, the efforts and the sacrifices which it exacted are no longer thought of, and the marks of the visitation melt away and disappear before the combined exertions of a free and united people.

Complaints of inadequate relief.

The Report states that the number of applications complaining of inadequate relief during the year amounted to 863, of which complaints, 447 were dismissed on the information contained in the schedules, and 111 after being referred to parochial

---

[f] See 'Report on the Mortality of Cholera in England 1848-9.'

boards. In 256 cases remitted to the parochial boards, the grounds of complaint were removed; and in 4 cases, the ground of complaint not having been removed, the commissioners issued minutes declaring that the complainants had just ground of action against their respective parishes in the court of session. Of the 863 cases submitted to the commissioners, there remained only one, they say, undisposed of, a circumstance highly creditable to their zeal and industry.

The applications in the sheriffs' courts during the year ending 30th June 1849, under the 73*rd*, 79*th and* 80*th sections* of the Amendment Act, amounted to 1,198. Of the whole number of cases in which the claims of persons applying for relief were resisted, a final order in the applicant's favour was made in 251, while out of 572 cases in which answers were lodged, 426 were either dismissed on the merits, or abandoned by the applicants themselves. As poor-houses increase in the different districts, they will, it is observed, "furnish parochial boards with a simple method of testing all cases in which there is reason to doubt the disability or the destitution of applicants for relief," and a confident hope is then expressed "that much of the expense of litigation will thus be saved to the parochial boards, and that the sheriffs will at the same time be relieved to a great extent of what is to them at present a most troublesome and anxious duty."

Applications to sheriffs.

The amount expended on the relief and management of the poor for the year ending 14th May 1849, including 14,775*l*. expended on poorhouse buildings, was 577,044*l*.—being an increase of 32,710*l*. as compared with the preceding year, and averaging 4*s*. 4¾*d*. per head on the population of 1841, and equal to 6*l*. 3*s*. 9*d*. per cent. on the annual value of real property in Scotland, according to the returns laid before parliament in 1843. The number of *regular* poor on the roll on the 14th May 1849 was 82,357—being 1 in 31·8 of the population; and the number of *casual*

Amount of relief and numbers relieved.

poor relieved in the year, was 95,686. While the number of regular poor has thus increased, the casual poor have we see sensibly diminished in the present year, as compared with the last; but this diminution has chiefly arisen from there having been a smaller number of immigrants from Ireland.

1850. Fifth Report of the board of supervision.

The fifth Report makes no mention of the elections, and they may therefore be presumed to have been properly conducted, as was for the most part the case in preceding years. The commissioners considered it necessary to send one of their officers to inquire into the condition and management of the poor in the county of Galloway, and the result was they say, on the whole satisfactory, although abuses requiring to be redressed were discovered in some of the parishes.

Parishes assessed.

Of the parishes which previously raised their funds for relief of the poor by voluntary contributions, 19 had, since the date of the last Report, resolved to raise those funds by assessment. The parishes assessed therefore, now amounted to 644, and the number that raised the funds by voluntary contributions to 236. In 21 parishes the parochial boards resolved to change the mode of assessment or classification formerly adopted, 13 of which changes were sanctioned by the commissioners, but in 7 the sanction was refused, and one was still undecided.

The progressive change from voluntary contributions to assessment, during the five years since the amended law came into operation, has been as follows—

| | | | | |
|---|---|---|---|---|
| In 1845 | parishes assessed | 230—parishes voluntary contributing | | 650 |
| 1846 | ,, | 448 | ,, | 432 |
| 1847 | ,, | 558 | ,, | 322 |
| 1848 | ,, | 600 | ,, | 280 |
| 1849 | ,, | 625 | ,, | 255 |
| 1850 | ,, | 644 | ,, | 236 |

The funds for the relief of the poor in the several parishes were raised in the following manner—

| | | Parishes. |
|---|---|---|
| By the 1st mode specified in the Act, with classification | .. | 96 |
| Ditto do. without classification | .. | 428 |
| By the 2nd mode do. | .. .. .. .. .. .. | 30 |
| By the 3rd mode do. | .. .. .. .. .. .. | 40 |
| According to established usage | .. .. .. .. .. .. | 50 |
| Number of assessed parishes | .. .. .. .. | 644 |
| Parishes which raise the funds by voluntary contributions | .. | 236 |
| Total parishes in Scotland | .. .. .. .. | 880 |

The plans and specification for one additional poorhouse only had been approved in the present year, but it was for a combination of ten parishes, with an aggregate population of 23,133, and was calculated for 362 inmates, so there would be poorhouse accommodation for one in 64 of the population. The several parochial boards had been called upon to frame regulations for the management of their respective poorhouses, in conformity with the 64*th section* of the Act; but these were found to be for the most part so defective, that the commissioners determined to frame such a complete set of rules and regulations for adoption by the parochial boards, as would secure uniformity and efficiency in this highly important part of parochial management. These regulations had, it is said, with slight adaptations to local peculiarities in a few instances, been generally adopted, and were then in force. They conform very closely to the English workhouse regulations, and in transmitting them to the parishes having poorhouses, the commissioners addressed a letter to the parochial boards, pointing out the objects and the importance of these institutions under the new law, and the altered circumstances of the times in which they were to be applied. So long, it is said, as relief to the poor was looked upon as the fulfilment of a charitable rather than a legal obligation, poorhouses were naturally regarded in the light of almshouses for the reception of the infirm or friend-

Poorhouses.

Poorhouse regulations.

less poor. The inmates were generally persons of whose destitution and disability there could be no doubt, and by whom admission to the poorhouse was regarded as a boon. They had their liberty days once a week, "and it was not uncommon to find some of them begging in the streets and highways." Once a week also persons were freely admitted to visit them in the poorhouse. Such of the inmates as were able, or could be induced to engage in any industrial occupation, received a weekly payment for their work, which they spent as they liked on their liberty days; "and one of the first petitions presented to the board of supervision was from the male inmates of a poorhouse, complaining that the weekly sum allowed them as pocket-money was unreasonably small."

Under such circumstances it was, the commissioners observe, unnecessary to establish strict regulations in the poorhouses, as any misconduct might be punished by expulsion. But poorhouses must now, it is said, be prepared to receive a new and wholly different class of inmates—"The altered feelings of the poor in regard to parochial relief, their more perfect knowledge of their rights, and the facilities which the law now affords for enforcing them, have caused a strong pressure upon parochial boards from a class whose claims it would be unsafe to admit, without testing the truth of the allegations on which they are founded." For this purpose a well-regulated poorhouse is declared to be the best of all tests—"while it furnishes sufficient, and even ample relief to the really necessitous, it affords the only available security that the funds raised for the relief of the poor are not perverted to the maintenance of idleness and vice." But a poorhouse will, it is added, "be wholly useless as a test, or rather it will not be a test at all, unless it is conducted under rules and regulations as to discipline and restraint, so as to render it more irksome than labour to those who

The poorhouse a test of destitution.

are not truly fit objects of parochial relief." This is so complete an exposition of the workhouse principle, as recognised and practised in England, that I give it in the commissioners' own words, in order to show more clearly the advance founded on experience, the surest of all guides, which had been made in poor-law administration in Scotland during the preceding five or six years.

The proper objects for admission to the poor-house.

The proper objects for admission to a poorhouse are described as being of two classes—*First* all destitute persons incapacitated by youth or old age or by disease, whether mental or physical, from contributing in any way to their own support; and who from being friendless, or weak in mind, or from requiring more than ordinary attendance, cannot be adequately maintained and cared for by means of out-door relief, except at a cost exceeding that for which they can be maintained in the poorhouse. *Secondly*, all persons applying for or receiving relief whose claims are doubtful, such as persons suspected of concealing or misrepresenting their means and resources, or persons who although not able-bodied, are yet not so disabled as to be incapable of maintaining themselves; but more especially all persons of idle immoral or dissipated habits, who if allowed out-door relief would squander it in drunkenness and debauchery, or otherwise misapply it—For all such, the poorhouse is held to afford the fittest means of relief. Poor persons, it is added, "may not be allowed to starve, because they or their parents are vicious; but the law leaves to the bodies to whom its administration is entrusted, a choice as to the manner of affording relief; and if parochial boards desire to discourage indolence, to detect imposture, to check extravagance, and to reform or control vice, they must make *work*, *confinement*, and *discipline*, the conditions upon which paupers of this class are relieved."

For persons not comprised in one or the other of the

above two classes, the commissioners are of opinion that it will be more to the advantage both of such persons and of the parish, that they should be furnished with out-door relief; "for any systematic attempt to refuse all relief except to such as may be relieved within the walls of a poorhouse would, they say, excite a baneful spirit of discontent amongst the poor and that part of the population with which they are most closely connected, without effecting any saving to the funds of the parish; and far from being countenanced, would scarcely be tolerated by public opinion in this country." The commissioners are probably right as to the state of feeling in Scotland on this point, and it might not have been then expedient to press the subject further; but it seems clear that the principle which they have with so much force and truth laid down in their instructional letter, must eventually, and perhaps at no distant day, lead to the unrestricted use of the poorhouse, without specific preference or exception of any particular class, although poorhouse relief may not be applied in every case, nor its acceptance be universally made a condition on which any relief whatever should be afforded.

Persons to be furnished with outdoor relief.

The arrangements for distributing the parliamentary grant in aid of medical relief, are said to have worked satisfactorily. 569 parishes had resolved to comply with the required conditions, but of these only 498 established their claims to participate in the grant by furnishing the necessary amount of expenditure from their own resources. The sum returned as being expended on medical relief in the current year, was 26,574*l.* 7*s.*

Medical relief.

With respect to insane and fatuous paupers, returns had been received, accompanied by medical certificates, of all those whose removal to an asylum had been dispensed with; and all the new cases reported, as well as those in which the medical

The insane and fatuous poor.

certificates annexed to subsequent returns did not appear satisfactory, had been investigated. In 141 new cases the commissioners dispensed with removal, and in two cases they required that the lunatics should be placed in an asylum. A considerable number of pauper lunatics, mostly fatuous and harmless, were now, it appears, kept in the different poorhouses, and the commissioners are of opinion that for such persons a well-regulated poorhouse is the best place of refuge. Not only, they say, is the cost of maintaining such persons in a poorhouse less than half what it would be in an asylum, but if all the pauper lunatics were to be placed in asylums, the whole of the accommodation it would be practicable to provide, would be occupied by a continually accumulating number of incurables, and the difficulty of obtaining admission for recent and curable cases would be greater even than it is at present. There are, the commissioners observe, certain legal objections to placing harmless pauper lunatics in poorhouses, which might however be overcome by obtaining licences for these establishments; but if this were done, it may be feared that some of the parochial boards would, on the score of convenience and economy, be induced to place in the poorhouses lunatics susceptible of cure, and who ought to be sent to an asylum. The commissioners have they say no authority in the matter; "but the sheriffs of counties, without whose licence no lunatic can legally be detained, are vested with power to determine this question in each case, and can require that any lunatic for whom a licence is granted, shall be placed in an asylum and not in a licensed house."

Complaints of inadequate relief.

The number of complaints of inadequate relief made to the board of supervision in the year amounted to 788, of which 439 were dismissed on the information appended to the schedules of complaint, and 97 after reference to parochial boards. In 114 cases the parochial boards removed the ground of complaint, but in two cases, the ground of complaint not being so removed, the commissioners issued minutes in the terms of the Act, declaring that the applicants had just cause of action against their parish in the court of session. No case, it is said, remains undisposed of; and upon the whole, with reference to these applications and complaints, the commissioners regard the results of the past year "as exhibiting a marked improvement, not only as showing a decrease in the number of applications, but as evincing a juster exercise of discretion on the part of relieving officers, in dealing with those demands upon the parochial funds which seemed either groundless or unreasonable."

Applications to sheriffs.

The returns of the applications made in the sheriffs' courts in the present year by persons refused relief, show that they amounted to 739. In 389 of these cases, answers in resistance of the claims were lodged on the part of the parochial boards. The number of cases in which the applications were either dismissed by the court on the merits, or abandoned by the parties themselves, is stated to have been 332; so that the resistance made to the claims for relief appears to have been successful in 314 out of 389 cases, and to have been unsuccessful in 75.

Amount of expenditure and numbers relieved.

The amount expended on the relief and management of the poor in the year ended 14th May 1850, was 538,738*l.* 5*s.* 0½*d.*; to which must be added for expenditure on poorhouse buildings 42,814*l.* 19*s.* 3*d.*, making a total expenditure of 581,553*l.* 4*s.* 3½*d.* The number of regular poor on the roll on the 14th of May 1850, was 79,031—being 1 in 33·15 of the population; and the number of casual poor relieved in the year, was 53,070. Many of the casual poor are however said to be relieved more than once in the same parish, and sometimes repeatedly in several different parishes. Persons moreover who are subsequently relieved by order of the parochial board, are in the first instance relieved temporarily by the inspector, without such order; so that the numbers of the casual poor given in the returns, represent the number of successful applications to the inspector for temporary aid, rather than the number effectually relieved. The total number of casual poor and vagrants relieved on the 1st of July 1850, was 4,267, of whom 1,542 were males, and 2,725 were females. By adding these to the regular poor on the roll on the 14th of May, it will appear that the number of persons receiving relief at one time in one of the summer months was 83,298, or 1 in 31·40 of the population, according to the census of 1841.

It appears from the foregoing statements, that there was a continual increase in the expenditure, as well as in the numbers relieved, until towards the end of the present year, when a decrease took place in both, especially in the number of casual poor.[g] This result the commissioners consider to be highly satisfactory, not only as indicating improvement in the condition of the working classes, but also as being calculated to allay the apprehensions excited by a continual increase of expenditure, and in the number of the poor seeking relief, during several preceding years. It likewise, the commissioners consider, affords ground for believing, that while the late Act was designed and has tended to increase the amount of relief, and to facilitate the means of obtaining it, the administration established by that Act has been able to regulate such tendency, and to adjust the expenditure to the actual necessities of the poor. The establishment of well-conducted poorhouses will, the commissioners add, contribute materially to confirm this power of regulating expenditure, without injustice to the poor; and they express a hope "that experience and observation of the many advantages

---

[g] See also the Tables of Expenditure and Numbers relieved, pp. 269 and 270.

derived from possessing the means of affording relief in this form, not only in urban but also in rural parishes, will lead to the erection of a greater number of such houses, notwithstanding the present reduction in the expenditure."

The sixth Report of the board of supervision is dated August 1851. Since the last Report, 9 parishes which had previously raised the funds for relief of the poor by voluntary contributions, have resorted to assessment. The number of assessed parishes was now therefore 653, and the number unassessed 228, the total number of parishes having been increased to 881, instead of 880, by Firth and Stennis in Orkney which were formerly considered one parish, being declared separate parishes for poor-law purposes. Of the 653 parishes at this time assessed, there were only 79 which assess "means and substance."

1851. Sixth Report of the board of supervision.

Assessments.

Plans for the erection of two poorhouses, and for the enlargement of others, were approved. Six parishes, containing a population of 8,814, have agreed to combine for the purpose of providing a poorhouse with accommodation for 80 inmates; and two other parishes, having together a population of 7,798, also agreed to combine for a like purpose; but after the arrangements were nearly completed, and the plans prepared, one of them withdrew, and the measure was therefore abandoned, at least for the present. In addition to the parishes which had provided or resolved to provide poorhouses for themselves, there were 48 other parishes, with a population of 289,048, which had made arrangements for placing their paupers in neighbouring poorhouses, under the 65*th section* of the Amendment Act; and the commissioners remark, that "the total population to which poorhouse accommodation for paupers is now more or less available, amounts to 1,062,993, or nearly 2–5ths of the entire population of Scotland."

Poorhouses.

In the current year, 508 parishes appear to have established their claim to participate in the parliamentary grant in aid of medical relief. The entire sum expended in this species of relief was 20,311*l.* 1*s.* 9¾*d.* The population of the parishes which complied with the conditions entitling them to participate in the grant was 2,071,478, and of the parishes that had not so complied 548,706. The expenditure on medical relief by the former was 17,257*l.* 16*s.* 1¼*d.*, being about 2*d.* per head on the population, and by the latter it was 3,053*l.* 5*s.* 8½*d.*, equal to about 1¼*d.* per head on the population. The parliamentary grant seems therefore, in accordance with the benevolent intentions of the legislature, to have led to a more liberal administration of medical relief.

Medical relief.

The number of applications to the board of supervision in the present year complaining of inadequate relief was 764, of which number 472 were dismissed on the information contained in the schedules, and 72 were dismissed after being remitted to the parochial boards for explanation; in 184 the ground of complaint was removed, and in 3 cases minutes were issued declaring that the complainants had just cause of action against their parishes.

Complaints of inadequate relief.

The returns of applications on account of the refusal of relief, continued to exhibit a progressive decrease in the number of those cases to which the jurisdiction of the sheriffs extends, as compared with the returns of former years. After pointing out certain discrepancies in preceding returns, the commissioners observe—"When we look at the number of cases in which an order was made by the sheriff for interim relief, which we consider to be an index of the cases calling for the sheriff's intervention, far more to be relied on than the number of applications made, the real decrease is apparent. We find a reduction from 739 to 539, being somewhat more than one-fourth of

Applications to sheriffs.

the whole number." There is a like diminution under all the other heads of the return, and the general result is considered to be very favourable, as affording indications of the satisfactory working of the law.

Amount of expenditure and numbers relieved.

The decrease of expenditure on account of the relief of the poor, which for the first time the commissioners had last year the satisfaction of reporting, still continued, the entire amount expended in the present year, including 21,576*l.* 1*s.* 8*d.* for poorhouse buildings, being 535,943*l.* 13*s.* 6*d.*, whilst the number of regular poor on the roll on the 14th of May was 76,906 and the number of casual poor relieved in the year was 42,093. The number of casual poor and vagrants relieved on the 1st of January and 1st of July respectively in the present year (1851), has been 5,148 and 6,366. On the 1st of July in the preceding year the number of such persons relieved was 4,267. While the number of casual poor relieved throughout the year has thus been considerably less than in the last, the numbers relieved on each of the two days for which the returns were made, have we see considerably increased. The increase is said "to be chiefly attributable to the distress prevailing in some districts of the Highlands and Islands, and to the temporary relief there afforded to destitute able-bodied persons who are classed as casual poor."

Distress in the Highlands and Islands.

In consequence of the distress in the Highlands and Islands above noticed, and which had prevailed with greater or less intensity since 1846,[h] the board of supervision were directed by government to cause an examination to be made into the state of those districts, and to report on "the means of rendering the local resources available for the relief of the inhabitants." The chairman of the board undertook

---

[h] See 'History of the English Poor Law,' vol. ii. pp. 392-3, and ante, pp. 199, 205, and 217.

the investigation, on which he was engaged from the beginning of February to the middle of April; and the results of his inquiry were embodied in a comprehensive Report, to the most prominent portions of which we will now advert.

The first step taken on all occasions throughout the inquiry, Sir John McNeill observes, was to call a meeting of the parochial boards, which consisted everywhere of the most intelligent persons of the district, and to explain to them that the object sought for was the application of local resources, and not the providing of extraneous aid. Their attention was "directed to the obligation imposed upon them by the statute, to give adequate relief to all disabled and destitute persons who apply for it, and to the necessary consequence, that destitute persons who, from want of sufficient food, ceased to be able-bodied, had a right to relief." They were told, that although the recent Act did not give able-bodied persons out of employment a right to relief, it gave to parochial boards a discretionary power to afford temporary relief to casual poor, including able-bodied persons in absolute want; and that viewed merely as a question of economy, it was well for them to consider whether it might not be more advantageous to give temporary aid to such able-bodied persons, than to withhold it until disablement arises through the pressure of absolute want. The discretion with which they are invested would, they were told, afford the means in any emergency of applying their local resources to the temporary relief of destitution, however arising; "but it was for them to determine in what manner they would use that power, the exercise of which was left entirely to their own discretion."

**Report thereon by Sir John McNeill.**

The inquiry included a portion of the mainland, and extended to the islands of Mull, Skye, Lewis, Uist, Harris, Long Island, Barra, Tyree, and Coll. Sir John McNeill bears testimony to the uniform civility and good conduct of the working classes in all the places he visited, and this under circumstances calculated to excite feelings of disappointment; for they appear, he says, to have formed exaggerated notions as to their right, under the new Poor Law, of being provided with employment and the means of subsistence at home, without being compelled to seek for either elsewhere. They believed that they were legally entitled to the aid they had been annually receiving from the destitution fund and other sources since 1846, and its continuance was confidently reckoned on in the present year. If all else failed, they thought the government, which had hitherto they said done nothing for the Highlanders, "could not refuse to provide the comparatively small amount of assistance they required, when so vast an amount had been given to Ireland." Everything he had to state on these points, was calculated to disappoint the expectations of the people, yet he remarks —"I did not anywhere observe a tone, a look, or a gesture, that indicated resentment or irritation. They frequently argued freely, sometimes with considerable ability and subtlety, never with rudeness, and often with a politeness and delicacy of deportment that would have been graceful in any society, and such as perhaps no men of their class, in any other country I am acquainted with, could have maintained in similar circumstances. Many went away dejected, but none without some parting expressions of personal kindness and obligation."

The first point to be ascertained was, whether any distress existed or was likely to arise, so urgent and extreme as to require assistance beyond what the local resources could supply. The alarm of famine appeared to be general, and a belief everywhere prevailed that many persons had perished from want of food, and that the relief which had been derived from the destitution fund during the four preceding years continued to be still necessary. But on the other hand, the condition of the inhabitants in regard to health was seen to be generally good, and not to indicate suffering from want, although such relief had now been delayed considerably beyond the usual period. This seemed an important fact, and was deemed to be satisfactory as regards the present state of the population; and with respect to the future, it was ascertained that all the parochial boards had authorised the inspectors "to afford temporary relief in urgent cases to persons not entitled by law to demand it"—in fact the parochial boards in the islands had, it is said, "begun to exercise their discretionary power to give temporary relief to able-bodied persons in absolute want, from the commencement of the distress in 1846; had suspended that description of relief while the destitution fund was in operation; and had spontaneously resumed it, on a limited scale, when the fund was understood to be exhausted." The authority which was thus given to the inspectors, made them responsible for the due administration of relief in every case. They were liable to be proceeded against criminally, if from failing to afford "needful sustentation," they allowed any fit object of parochial relief to perish for want of food; and this liability would, in the ordinary course of law, operate as a protection to the poor, and prevent the occurrence of such a painful contingency, although instances of severe distress might not be altogether prevented.

With the advance of the season and the exhaustion of the last year's crop, the number of persons requiring relief would be certain to increase; but it was by no means certain that many of these persons might not maintain themselves by employment elsewhere, and which employment they would probably have sought after, but for the expectation of finding relief of some kind or in some way at home. The means of employment in the western districts, is generally insufficient for the maintenance of the inhabitants throughout the year, and distress in some part of it must therefore be regarded as the natural condition of the people, to be remedied only by a decrease in their number, or by an increase in the means of employment; but both the remedies are attended with difficulty. The population of these districts chiefly consists of three classes, each holding land directly from the proprietor. The '*Crofters*' are persons occupying lands at a rental not exceeding 20*l.* a year, and are by far the most numerous class. The '*Tacksmen*' have leases or 'tacks' generally paying a rent exceeding 50*l.* a year, and in point of circumstances are the most considerable of all the classes. Intermediate between these is another class paying rent of from 20*l.* to 50*l.*, and who not having leases are not 'Tacksmen,' and not liking to be classed with the 'Crofters,' are called '*Tenants.*' Besides these three classes, who hold land directly from the proprietor, there is another called '*Cottars,*' who are numerous in some districts, and who either do not hold land at all, or hold it only from year to year as sub-tenants. There are no manufactures except a little knitting, and the 'Crofters' and 'Cottars' constitute the great bulk of the population.

'Crofters,' 'Tacksmen,' 'Tenants,' and 'Cottars.'

At one time, nearly all the land in the western districts appears to have been held by 'Tacksmen' (generally kinsmen or dependants of the proprietor) with sub-tenants under them. But many of the lands formerly held by tacksmen, came afterwards to be held directly of the proprietor by joint tenants, who grazed their stock in common, and cultivated the arable land in alternate ridges or 'rigs,' hence called 'run rig.' Each person thus got a portion of the better, and a portion of the worse land; but no one held two contiguous ridges, or the same ridge for two successive years. Since the early part of the present century however, the arable land has mostly been divided into fixed portions among the joint tenants, who thus became

'Crofters,' the grazing remaining in common as before. This division of the arable land into separate crofts, no doubt led to improved cultivation; but it also led to other consequences, to which it is necessary to advert.

Whilst the land was held by joint tenants, no one could appropriate to himself any particular share or portion, his co-tenants having a concurrent right over the whole; but on the division and absolute appropriation of the arable land, the crofters generally established themselves each on his own separate allotment. Their houses were and still are of the simplest construction, erected by themselves of stone earth or clay, with a covering of turf and thatch. The furniture consists of a bed, a table, a few stools, a chest, and some cooking utensils. At one end of the house is the byre for the cattle, at the other end the barn for the crop. The peat which the crofter cuts from the neighbouring moss, gives him fuel. His capital consists of his cattle, his sheep, and perhaps a horse or two; of his crop that is to support him till next harvest, and provide seed and winter provender for his animals; of his furniture, his implements, the wood-work and rafters of his house, and sometimes a boat or share of a boat, nets and other fishing gear; with barrels of salt herrings, or bundles of dried cod or ling for winter use. His croft supplies him with food and most of his clothing. The sales of cattle pay his rent, and he lives or rather did live in a rude kind of abundance, comparatively idle, and knowing little of the daily toil by which labourers elsewhere obtain a livelihood. Once established on his small farm, the crofter does not expect to be removed so long as his rent is paid, and the occupation of the croft becomes in fact hereditary, the son succeeding the father as a matter of course.

The crofts appear to have been originally apportioned with a view to the maintenance of a single family. "But when kelp was largely and profitably manufactured, when potatoes were extensively and successfully cultivated, when the fishings were good, and the price of cattle high, the crofter found his croft more than sufficient for his wants, and when a son or a daughter married, he divided it with the young couple, who built themselves another house upon it, lived on the produce, and paid a part of the rent;" and thus many crofts which still stand in the rent-roll in the name of one tenant, became occupied by two three or four families, the population continually increasing, and a large part of the increase having in this way accumulated on the crofts.

The kelp manufacture.

The kelp manufacture, which at one time gave employment in the western districts to great numbers of the inhabitants, contributed to a like result. The process lasted for no more than six weeks or two months, but it was necessary to provide the people employed on it with the means of living throughout the year; and small crofts were assigned to them for this purpose, on the produce of which, with their other earnings, they were enabled to live and increase. But this entailed another serious evil, for when the manufacture of kelp was put an end to by the substitution of a cheaper commodity, the people engaged in it were thrown out of employment; and as they differed in habits and language, and had little intercourse with other parts of the country, they were not disposed to go in search of employment elsewhere, and clung to their wretched homesteads with a tenacity found only among the very poor. It is true that emigration to some extent did take place, and was promoted by the proprietors, who became justly alarmed at the excess of population beyond the means of employment. But those who emigrated were for the most part the better description of tenants and crofters, whose lands were then in most cases let for sheep-farming, by which higher rents were obtained—yet adding at the same time to the disproportion between population and employment, and by consequence tending to depress the condition of the bulk of the people; and thus to render them less capable of bearing up against extraordinary privation, whether arising from failure of the crops, the inclemency of the seasons, or any other cause.

The foregoing explanations may be regarded as applying to the islands and western districts generally, and are probably sufficient for enabling the reader to form a pretty accurate notion of the state of things existing there. There would of course be shades of difference between different parts of these districts; but on the whole, the description above given of the social condition of the people, as well generally as with particular reference to the proceedings under the Poor Law, will with little exception be found applicable to all. As however Sir John McNeill in the course of his investigation examined the principal islands, as well as portions of the main land, and reported separately on each, it may be well to give the substance of a few of these Reports by way of further illustration.

The Isle of Skye.

The population of Skye and the adjacent islands of Raasay Rona and others parochially connected with it, according to the census of the present year (1851) is 22,532.[1] The number of families is 4,335 which gives about five and one-fifth to a family. The annual value of real property returned to parliament in 1843 was 22,109*l.* 15*s.* 5*d.*, thus giving an average of about 20*s.* per head on the population. Besides the higher-rented 'tacksmen' and 'tenants,' there are about 1,900 'crofters' at rents not exceeding 10*l.*, the aggregate of whose rents amounts to about 8,000*l.*, and the average of each taken singly to 4*l.* 4*s.* 1*d.* The produce of a croft of this description will not

[1] In 1755 the population of Skye was 11,252, so that it had just doubled in the intervening century.

provide a family with food for more than half the year, so that the crofter must provide for the remaining half by other means. In addition to these 1,900 families of crofters, there are 1,531 families of 'cottars' making together 3,431 families, or 17,842 individuals, depending either wholly as in the latter case, or during half the year as in the former, on employment other than the cultivation of their holdings for the means of subsistence. With the exception of a little knitting introduced by the committee for the relief of destitution, there is no manufacture of any kind in Skye, and the only employment is such as prevails in pastoral and agricultural districts, with occasional fishing. The rents have nevertheless been generally well paid, and without the necessity of distraining, as have likewise the poor-rates. A large quantity of meal has been purchased by the inhabitants annually, since the potato failure in 1846; and in the year ending 10th October 1850, according to the returns of the excise, the whisky duty paid by retailers amounted to 10,855*l.*, which is "considerably more than double the amount expended on relief by the destitution fund during the same year, and more than double the consumption of whisky returned for the same district in 1845, the year before the distress commenced."

With these facts before us, it is, as Sir John McNeill remarks, impossible to resist the inference that the destitution fund could have done little towards supplying the deficiency of local means; and even when to the relief derived from the fund, is added the expenditure under the Drainage Act, together with the produce of the crofts and whatever else could be earned in the district, the amount would still be insufficient to account for the people being able to pay rent and poor-rates, to purchase large quantities of meal, to keep themselves well clothed and the men well shod, and likewise to pay 10,855*l.* for whisky and probably half as much for tobacco. The fact is, the labourers of Skye, like the harvesters of Ireland, paid their rents and provided what extra articles they wanted or wished for, by the earnings which they occasionally obtained elsewhere. "From the Pentland Firth to the Tweed, from the Lewis to the Isle of Man, the Skye men sought the employment they could not find at home." Previous to 1846, the young men only went, but since then the older men have found it necessary to go. Both old and young however, whether crofters or cottars, return for the winter, and remain at home mostly in idleness, consuming their earnings and the produce of their croft, "till the return of summer and the failure of their supplies warn them that it is time to set out again." Those whose means are insufficient to maintain them through the winter, are necessarily exposed to much privation, and to these the relief from the destitution fund has been chiefly afforded; but although this relief is said to have been "administered with remarkable ability and caution," it is universally considered to have had a prejudicial effect on the character and habits of the people, by inducing them to misrepresent their circumstances with a view to participating in the relief, and causing them to relax their exertions for their own maintenance. Indeed with reference to the whole of these districts, but more particularly to Skye, where the working classes depend more upon what may be called foreign employment than in any other, it is said to be the general opinion, "that the effect of the continued relief after the unforeseen calamity of the first year had been provided for, was on the whole to diminish rather than to increase the means of subsistence in succeeding years." That the population became less frugal, is proved by the greatly increased consumption of whisky.

The Isle of Mull.

The aggregate population of Mull with the smaller islands of Iona, Ulva, Inchkenneth, and others parochially connected with it, was, 8,294 according to the census of 1851. In 1821 the population amounted to 10,612, but it has since then been reduced by successive emigrations. The annual value of real property returned to parliament in 1843 was 17,576*l.* 16*s.* 2*d.* The ownership of property is more than usually divided in Mull, the three parishes of which it consists belonging to no less than twenty-one proprietors, the majority of whom are non-resident, and all with the exception of four or five have acquired their property within the last forty years. On all the recently acquired properties the population has decreased considerably, owing to improvements in agriculture, the formation of large farms, and the conversion of the land into pasturage. But on the old hereditary properties there is still a numerous population of crofters and cottars, and there as well as in the village of Tobermory much distress has prevailed. The chief produce has always been cattle and sheep, but previous to 1846 large quantities of potatoes and barley or bere were annually exported. In 1845 from the port of Tobermory alone, 15,410 barrels of potatoes were exported, at an average price of 4*s.* 6*d.* per barrel. There is no information of the quantities sent from other parts of the island, "but it is probable that the total export of potatoes in that year from the three parishes of Mull exceeded 30,000 barrels, and brought to the producers at least 6,750*l.*"—Since 1846 no potatoes or bere have been exported, but a large quantity of meal, probably not less than 15,000 or 20,000 bolls of 140lbs. has been annually imported, which at 18*s.* per boll would amount to between 14,000*l.* and 18,000*l.*; and if to this be added the value of the former exports, which have ceased since the failure of the potato crop, there will appear to be a loss arising out of that failure of some 20,000*l.* or 25,000*l.* annually. Yet the consumption of whisky has increased since 1845, the quantity of undiluted spirit sold in that year, according to the excise returns, having been 8,701 gallons, whilst in 1850 the quantity sold has been 10,212 gallons. The expenditure on ardent spirits in 1848 was estimated by the minister of Tobermory to have amounted to 6,100*l.*; and as the value of the meal distributed by the destitution committee in that year was 3,202*l.*, it follows "that there was expended on ardent spirits by the inhabitants of Mull in 1848, a sum equal to double the amount of extraneous aid furnished to relieve destitution in that year."

Parish of Kilfinichin and Kilvickeson.

The united parish of Kilfinichin and Kilvickeson in the south-western part of Mull, includes the islands of Iona and Inchkenneth. In 1755 the population was 1,685. In 1841 the population had increased to 4,113. Since which year, and in consequence of the abandonment of the kelp trade, it had been decreased by successive emigrations, partly voluntary and independent, partly with the aid of the proprietors; and according to the census of the present year (1851), the population of the united parish amounts only to 2,999, or one-fourth less than it was in 1841. The number of crofters is now 160, and the number of cottars about 250; so that there are 410 families or 2,132 individuals in the parish depending on wages for the whole or the greater part of their living, the only employment being agricultural, with occasional fishing for cod, ling, and lobsters. These employments are ordinarily inadequate to affording subsistence for the labouring population, and in the four years since 1846, the duke of Argyle appears to have expended in gratuities and wages 1,790*l.* 11*s.* 4*d.* in addition to the revenue derivable from his property in this parish—"Yet all classes concur in stating that the condition of the people has progressively declined since 1846; and in 1850, after the emigration, there were at one time of the inhabitants of this property, not fewer than 1,000 individuals receiving relief from the destitution fund."

Parish of Kilninian and Kilmore.

The united parish of Kilninian and Kilmore, comprising the northern part of Mull, includes the islands of Ulva and Gometra as well as some smaller islands. The land in this parish is divided among nine proprietors, most of whom have acquired their property within the last twenty years. The population in 1755 was 2,590, and it went on increasing till 1831, when it was 4,830; since which it has continued to decrease, and by the census of the present year (1851), it is 3,952. On all the recently acquired properties except the village of Tobermory, the population has decreased. In Ulva it has been reduced from 500 to 150, the proprietor having, as he states, "no alternative but either to surrender his property to the crofters, or to remove them." Nearly the whole of their rents were paid from the wages they earned in manufacturing kelp, and when that failed they were neither able to pay rent, nor to maintain themselves. In four years there had been expended in wages labour and gratuities, with a view to giving employment, not only all the revenue derived from the property, but 367*l.* in addition. In short, it is declared that wherever the crofters have remained undisturbed, there distress prevails, or is only averted by the interposition of the proprietor, often at a cost exceeding the rental of the property. Many of the labourers of Mull, like those of Skye, go to the south for employment in summer, and the number that do so is said to be increasing. The amount of imports, and the expenditure on whisky, while the home produce has so materially decreased, show that their gains must be considerable. They all however, like the other islanders, return home for the winter, their attachment to their native soil and repugnance to mingling with strangers, keeping them from settling among their southern neighbours, notwithstanding the frequent intercourse which has of late years been maintained with them.

Gairloch.

On the Gairloch property, situated on the mainland nearly opposite to Skye, an attempt was made five years ago to enable the crofters to maintain themselves, by introducing improved modes of cultivation. The Gairloch tenantry appear to have occupied the grazing land in common, and to have cultivated the arable land in "run rig," down to 1845 or 1846, when separate crofts were allotted to each. Their number was then about six hundred, but as the land previously in cultivation would not furnish each crofter with a sufficient quantity, waste land was reclaimed for the purpose by the proprietor, the principle proceeded upon being, that a croft of four or five acres properly cultivated, with hill grazing for cattle and sheep, was sufficient for the maintenance of a family and the payment of rent. The land was successively trenched and drained, the crofters meanwhile subsisting on the wages they received for performing the work. In about four years the operation was completed, at an outlay of 6,000*l.* in improving the crofts, and 7,000*l.* more in road-making draining and trenching on other portions of the estate, making together 13,000*l.* expended in payment for labour on this property in course of four years. Of this amount 3,000*l.* was, we are told, furnished by the destitution fund. The crofters were required to adhere to a four-shift rotation of crops, the house-feeding of cattle, and the preservation of liquid and other manures, and an intelligent overseer was appointed to superintend and direct their proceedings. The result however has fallen far short of what was expected, for although the Gairloch crofters have undoubtedly benefited by the money expended among them in wages, and their crofts yield a greater produce, and their mode of management is generally improved, they are yet unable to maintain themselves by their crofts for more than half the year, and for the other half are still dependent on other sources. The improvements made in the crofting system at Gairloch, at so large an outlay, have therefore failed in producing results materially differing from those which have attended the system wherever else it has prevailed.

The state of things exhibited in the foregoing details, which apply generally to the whole of the western districts and islands, is unknown in other parts of Scotland. There must therefore be something peculiar in the circumstances which caused so great an amount of distress in those districts on the failure of the potato crop, while a similar failure was comparatively little felt in other parts of the country. The potato no doubt constituted a larger portion of the food of the inhabitants of those districts than was the case elsewhere, but this alone will not account for the continuance of distress, after other crops might have been and actually were substituted for it; neither will it account for the failure of the efforts which were made to enable the crofters cottars and labouring classes generally, to produce enough for their own maintenance—" efforts (it is remarked) so great and persevering, and involving so large a sacrifice of personal interest on the part of the proprietors, that they reflect credit not only on those who made them, but even on the country in which they were made." One of the reasons usually assigned for this failure is the small size of the crofts, the land which was sufficient to produce food for a family while the potato flourished, being insufficient to supply corn enough for the purpose; and this is doubtless true, but it is not the whole truth. A man must have the means of living whilst he is cultivating his croft, and he must have sufficient seed, implements, and cattle to make the land productive, so as to enable him to pay rent. If he has not the means of providing these things, or the skill to

Results of the croft and cottar system.

apply them, he will not be able to obtain a subsistence from his croft, and the larger it is the more of these things will he require.

But independently of capital and skill, which are always necessary to success whether the quantity of land occupied be large or small, the quality of the soil and the nature of the climate are also important considerations. Some land is so poor that with the best management it will yield but a very scanty return, and there are districts where the climate is so precarious and ungenial that the ripening of corn crops is far from certain. Both these unfavourable circumstances of soil and climate prevail to such an extent in the western districts of Scotland, that oatmeal produced on the eastern coast at the same or a higher latitude, can be supplied to the inhabitants of the west at a fourth less cost than it can be produced at there. The nature of the soil and the uncertainty of the climate are therefore circumstances which materially add to the difficulties of the crofter's position in the western districts, and these difficulties are still further increased by the tendency to an excess of population which the crofting system necessarily gives rise to. The distress existing wherever that system prevails cannot be attributed to the failure of the potato alone, since no such severe and continued distress has been produced where there were no crofters; and it must therefore be regarded as a consequence of the potato failure taking place, concurrently with the prevàlence of a system by which men are led to depend for subsistence on the food produced by their own labour, on land occupied by themselves.

If the occupancy of land were to be made the sole means of subsistence for the population, as the crofting system implies, and if it were possible to furnish every crofter with the necessary capital for this purpose, the plan advocated by some persons of giving to each family land sufficient to maintain them and pay rent, would still be found impracticable. For instance, in the case of Skye, with its 3,431 families—To provide each of these with even as much land as is now let in Skye for 10*l.*, would require more land than both the islands of Skye and Lewis could furnish, and would require every one paying a rent above 10*l.* to be removed; so that even if the requisite capital could be procured for establishing each family on its own croft, the division of land into crofts of a size sufficient to supply the families with food throughout the year, would necessitate the removal of the larger part of the present population, including all those who employ labour, or who possess the means of giving employment. This shows the great disproportion existing between the population and the ordinary means of subsistence, not only in Skye but in the western districts generally, the inhabitants of which are said to "have neither capital enough to cultivate the extent of land necessary to maintain them if it could be provided, nor have they land enough were the capital supplied them."

Emigration the only remedy.

Under these circumstances, the only remedy seems to be emigration. The question is not new, nor the emergency altogether unforeseen. Distress prevailed in the same districts in 1837, and again in 1841, and on both those occasions the necessity for emigration was strongly advocated, as a means of averting the evils that were otherwise certain to ensue. The recommendation was partially acted upon, but not to a sufficient extent, as the present state of these districts abundantly proves.

In commenting on the circumstances of these western districts, Sir John McNeill remarks—"It is curious, and perhaps mortifying to observe, how little the difference of management and the efforts of individuals appear to have influenced the progress of the population, and how uniformly that progress corresponds to the amount of intercourse with the more advanced parts of the country, and the length of time during which it has been established." The proprietor no doubt has it in his power to promote or retard advancement, "but the circumstances (it is observed) that determine the progress of such a people as the inhabitants of these districts, in the vicinity and forming a part of a great nation far advanced in knowledge and in wealth, appear to be chiefly those which determine the amount of intercourse between them. Where the intercourse is easy and constant, the process of assimilation proceeds rapidly, and the result is as certain as that of opening the sluices in the ascending lock of a canal. Where the intercourse is impeded or has not been established, it may perhaps be possible to institute a separate local civilization, an isolated social progress; but an instance of its successful accomplishment is not to be found in these districts."

This proposition is exemplified by a reference to the Highland parishes on the borders of the Lowlands, which, although still inhabited by the original race, are said to be "hardly distinguishable by their aspect or the condition of their inhabitants from those which bound them to the south or east. Proceeding northward and westward, the change is gradual and uninterrupted, till the utmost limits are reached in the outer Hebrides, where it is complete." The extent and urgency of the distress, it is added, increase in like manner with the distance from the centre of civilization and industry, and are greatest where the intercourse is least. "The state of the population is most advanced where the intercourse has been longest established, and there too the distress is less severe, and the prospect of extrication more hopeful." It follows therefore, that whatever tends to facilitate and promote intercourse between these districts and the more advanced parts of the country, ought to be encouraged, as being the most certain if not the only way of bringing about a state of things similar to that which exists in other parts, where less than a century ago the people were as badly situated, but are now self-sustaining and prosperous. Every attempt at improvement that is opposed to or inconsistent with this progress of assimilation, will not only be unsuccessful, but will, it is observed, tend eventually "to subject the people involved in it to another process of painful transition." Of the correctness of this opinion there can be no reasonable doubt, and it behoves the proprietary and influential classes to keep it constantly in view, in whatever efforts may be made for ameliorating the condition of these districts.

Administration of relief in the western districts.

With respect to the administration of the Poor Law in the western districts, it is said to be "on the whole creditable to the local boards, when the difficulties they have had to contend with almost since their foundation are taken into account." The composition of the boards is said to be generally good, and the election of a certain number of the members by the ratepayers has here as elsewhere given confidence to their proceedings, and increased their efficiency. The defects are such as almost necessarily arise from the great extent of the parishes, the difficulty of communication, and the limited choice of efficient officers. The funds now raised, are far greater than were raised in 1845, and seem sufficient for meeting the ordinary calls for relief under the statute. They appear moreover to be fairly assessed, and are collected with less difficulty and fewer arrears than was to be expected, considering the number of small ratepayers and the distress that has prevailed. The parochial boards in the distressed districts, are now, it is said, relieving all able-bodied persons who are in a state of destitution, and Sir John McNeill concludes his Report by declaring, that "there is good reason to hope that this season (1851) will pass away, not certainly without painful suffering, but without the loss of any life in consequence of the cessation of eleemosynary aid." If hereafter however, the population should be left entirely dependent on their own resources, "some fearful calamity" will, it is added, probably occur, unless a portion of the inhabitants remove to where the means of subsistence are obtainable in greater abundance, and with greater certainty, than where they now are.

The foregoing description of the distressed districts of the west, chiefly abstracted from Sir John McNeill's comprehensive Report, will it is hoped not be deemed irrelevant or unimportant. The circumstances of these districts are in no small degree exceptional, and as the Poor Law applies to them in common with the rest of Scotland, some account of their actual state appeared to be necessary for judging of the operation and applicability of the law; and from no other source could such an account be so appropriately drawn.

We will now turn to the Report of the board of supervision, the seventh of the series being the next in order.

1852. Seventh Report of the board of supervision.

It appears that several of the parochial inspectors had either failed to perform their duties, or been negligent and irregular in the execution of them, and the board of supervision had found it incumbent upon them to dismiss six, and to accept the resignation of others whose conduct it would otherwise have been necessary to bring under investigation. Several of the inspectors likewise were admonished on account of their failing to observe the regulations, more especially that which prohibits their deriving any profit or emolument directly or indirectly from dealings with paupers. Indeed it would seem that the members of the parochial boards were not themselves altogether faultless in this respect, there being, it is said, reason to fear that in some cases the prospect of a preference in executing work, or in furnishing supplies, had served as an inducement for seeking

The parochial inspectors.

a seat at the board. This is obviously and perhaps unavoidably a weak point in the system of parochial management, and it requires a vigilant watchfulness on the part of the superintending authority. Experience showed that a frequent examination into the proceedings of the parochial boards was necessary for securing efficiency and preventing malversation, and a visiting officer was accordingly appointed, whose duty it was to visit the different parishes, and report upon the manner in which the law was administered in each. For this purpose the country was divided into districts, to be visited in succession, somewhat in the way that the inspectors' districts are attended to in England.

Assessments.

Since the last Report, 18 parishes which had before raised the funds for relieving the poor by voluntary contributions, resolved to raise them by assessment. The number of parishes now assessed was 671, and the number still adhering to the voluntary system was 211, the total number having been increased to 882 by the parishes of Stronsay and Eday in Orkney, previously conjoined, being now declared separate parishes. The parishes assessed on "means and substance" were 5 less than last year, although the number of parishes assessed is we see considerably greater.

Poorhouses.

Four parishes in the Isle of Skye, containing a population of 13,569, had combined for the purpose of erecting a poorhouse, the plans of which have also been approved, as have likewise the plans for improving and enlarging several others. The number of permanent poorhouses in operation was 24. The number of parishes that have poorhouses either singly or in combination with others, was 44; and besides these, there were 119 parishes with a population of 529,761 which take advantage of the existing accommodation by boarding their paupers in the poorhouses of other parishes. The whole of the population to which poorhouse accommodation is thus in some way available, amounted to 1,283,805, or nearly half the entire population of Scotland.

In reference to a communication from Lord Selkirk, describing the successful operation of the Kirkcudbright poorhouse, and which is given in the appendix to the present Report, the commissioners observe, that "the result has been not only a considerable pecuniary saving to the combined parishes, but a great diminution of labour to the persons engaged in the management of the poor; and what is even more important, a great diminution of the demoralizing effects produced on certain classes by the temptations of out-door relief, in the absence of sufficient means of checking abuse by applying an adequate test." The opinion thus expressed by the commissioners, will not cause surprise to those who have attended to the progress of the Poor Law in England; but that the conclusion should have been drawn from the experience acquired in administering the law in Scotland, is peculiarly gratifying, and is calculated to give increased confidence in the soundness of the principle on which the English workhouse system is founded.

**Medical relief.**

With respect to medical relief, it appears that 599 parishes have complied with the conditions entitling them to participate in the parliamentary grant, being 41 more than last year. The whole amount expended on medical relief in the present year has been 21,436*l.* 6*s.* 9*d.*; last year it was 20,311*l.* 1*s.* 9*d.* Some of the parochial boards are said to be in the practice of electing their medical officer annually, which so far as the commissioners have had opportunity of observing appears, they say, "to have been prejudicial both to the harmony of the board and the interests of the poor." The annual election, they observe, "is apt to degenerate into an annual contest between rural practitioners, in which the most respectable and worthy are unwilling to engage. Each candidate is supported by partisans, in whose estimation professional skill or fitness for the office is not always the primary consideration; and the fact that the election is only for one year, apparently tends to produce recklessness in the choice."—It seems impossible to deny the truth of these observations, or to doubt the inexpediency of such annual elections. The right mode of procedure, as proved by all English, and now likewise by Scottish experience, is to make the appointment permanent, subject only to good behaviour and efficiency on the part of the medical officer.

Complaints of inadequate relief.

The number of applications to the board of supervision complaining of inadequate relief, during the year ending 30th June 1852, was 684, of which 415 were dismissed on information contained in the schedules, 66 were dismissed after reference, 32 for other causes; and in 164 cases the ground of complaint was removed by the parochial boards. The increase and decrease in the numbers complaining of inadequate relief, are said to follow the increase and decrease of the registered poor; although as the Poor Law functionaries gained experience, and were able to meet such complaints by an offer of relief in the poorhouse, the proportion of cases in which the commissioners considered the complaint well founded, has they say, progressively diminished.

Applications to sheriffs.

The applications in the sheriffs' courts of persons refused relief by the parochial boards, and claiming a right to be relieved, have likewise continued to decrease. The number of interim orders issued in the present year has been 503, of which 267 were afterwards disputed by the parish authorities; and of these, the applicants in 137 instances were ultimately ordered to be admitted on the roll.

Amount of expenditure and numbers relieved.

The amount expended on the relief and management of the poor during the year ending 14th May 1852, including 21,186*l.* expended on poorhouse buildings, was 535,868*l.* 9*s.* 10*d.*, being

75*l.* 3*s.* 8*d.* in excess of the expenditure the year preceding. The number of regular poor on the roll or registered on the 14th of May 1852, was 75,111, being a decrease of 1795 since the same date last year. The number of casual poor relieved in the year was 46,031, being an increase as compared with the last year of 3,938. The casual poor and vagrants relieved on the 1st of January 1852, amounted to 5,294, or 146 more than on the 1st of January 1851. On the 1st of July 1852, the number was 5,070, or 1,296 less than on the 1st of July 1851. The registered poor thus appear to be decreasing, while the casual poor rather show a tendency to increase.

With regard to the expenditure and the numbers relieved, the commissioners remark—" When the statute of 1845 came into operation, the relief afforded in many of the parishes was merely nominal, and in the great majority inadequate. The more efficient administration of the law which was then established, led to an immediate increase in the expenditure, which was accelerated and augmented by the dearth of food in the succeeding years, and by want of experience in the parochial management. In the year ending May 1849, that expenditure had reached the highest point it has attained, and since that time has annually decreased; but for the last year the diminution has been so inconsiderable, that the expenditure may be regarded as stationary, and may perhaps have arrived at its ordinary amount. The average for the last seven years has been about 500,000*l.*—for the last two years, exclusive of the outlay on poorhouse buildings, it has little exceeded that sum; and it is probable, if nothing should occur materially to affect the condition of the working classes, that it will for some years fluctuate but little above or below that amount."

The eighth Report like those preceding it is dated in August, and commences by declaring that the representations of the visiting officer who was appointed last

1853. Eighth Report of the board of supervision.

year, and who had been actively engaged in investigating the manner in which the law was administered, had satisfied the commissioners that the poor were generally well provided for. A special inquiry regarding the administration of the law in Caithness had been made by the chairman of the board, whose Report thereon will hereafter be noticed.

Assessments.

Since the last Report, nine parishes which had previously raised the funds for relief of the poor by voluntary contributions, have resolved to do so by assessment. The number of parishes now assessed was therefore 680, and the number voluntarily contributing was 202. The progress of the change from voluntary contributions to assessment, in the eight years since the amended law came into operation, has been as follows :—

| | Assessed. | Voluntary contributions. |
|---|---|---|
| 1845 | 230 | 650 |
| 1846 | 448 | 432 |
| 1847 | 558 | 322 |
| 1848 | 600 | 280 |
| 1849 | 625 | 255 |
| 1850 | 644 | 236 |
| 1851 | 653 | 228 |
| 1852 | 671 | 211 |
| 1853 | 680 | 202 |

The funds for relief of the poor in the several parishes are now raised in the following manner—

| | | | Parishes. |
|---|---|---|---|
| By the first mode specified in the Act, | | with classification | 110 |
| Ditto | do. | without classification | 457 |
| By the second mode | do. | | 29 |
| By the third mode | do. | | 35 |
| According to established usage | | | 49 |
| | | | 680 |
| By voluntary contributions | | | 202 |
| | | Total parishes in Scotland | 882 |

The parishes assessed on "means and substance," are three less than they were last year, although the total number of parishes assessed is greater by nine. This particular mode of assessment, in favour of which little can be said, is obviously on the decline, and will probably ere long be altogether abandoned.

Poorhouses.

In course of the present year resolutions had been adopted, and the plans have been approved, for erecting poorhouses in the parishes of Inveresk, Latheron, Dundee, and Kelso, and in the combination consisting of nine parishes in Upper Nithsdale, and in the Linlithgow combination of eight parishes—making together twenty-one parishes, with a population of 129,319. The number of parishes which now have poorhouses, either singly or in combination with others, is 62; and when the buildings at present in progress are completed, the number will be 88. There are also 120 parishes which, under the 65*th section* of the Amendment Act, have arranged to board their paupers in the poorhouses of other parishes. The population to which poorhouse accommodation is now available amounts to 1,442,735, or one-half the entire population of Scotland, which at the census in 1851 was found to be 2,888,742.

Religious instruction of children in the poorhouses.

Complaints having been made respecting the religious instruction of the orphan and deserted children maintained in the poorhouses, it became necessary for the commissioners again to interfere with this delicate question. They had on a previous occasion given it as their opinion "that all children ought to be registered as belonging to the religious persuasion of their parents or surviving parent, when that is known or can be ascertained; unless in cases of desertion by their parents or surviving parent, who in that case appeared to have voluntarily abandoned the natural right to conduct the religious instruction of their offspring." To this opinion the commissioners now deemed it right to add—"that when the religious persuasion of a child, even though deserted, has once been inserted in the register, the parochial board has not the power to alter the register for the purpose of describing that child as of another religious persuasion, without the child's consent; and that with reference to religious instruction, effect must be given to the original registration in the manner described by the statute, and the rules and regulations for the management of poorhouses."[k]

Medical relief.

The conditions on which a participation in the parliamentary grant in aid of medical relief was conceded, were complied with by 560 parishes, being eleven more than in the last year. The whole amount expended on the medical relief of the poor in the present year is 21,737*l.* 6*s.* 8*d.*, equal to 1*d.* and 8-10ths per head on the entire population. The amount expended in the 560 parishes entitled to participate in the grant, is 19,577*l.* 5*s.* 6*d.*, which is equal to about 2*d.* per head of the population of those parishes; and the amount expended in the 322 parishes not so entitled, is 2,160*l.* 1*s.* 2*d.*, which is equal to less than 1*d.* per head on their population—thus showing that the medical relief of the poor in the parishes participating in the parliamentary grant is, rateably on the population, double the amount of that which is afforded in the parishes not so participating; and consequently, it may be presumed, doubly as effective.

Lunatic and fatuous paupers.

During the present year, application had been made to dispense with the removal to an asylum of 169 lunatic paupers. In 165 of these cases the commissioners dispensed with the removal, and in four cases they enforced it. In the preceding year there were 194 of such applications, of which 191 were conceded, and three were refused. Although the instances

[k] See the 64*th section* of the Amendment Act, and the 23rd, 49th, 50th, 51st, and 52nd sections of the 'Rules and Regulations for the Management of Poorhouses,' in which provision appears to be made for every case of this nature that can arise.

of refusal are here so few, there can be no doubt that the requiring applications to be made and reasons assigned for dispensing with the removal of pauper lunatics to asylums, has secured for these unfortunates greater care and better treatment than they would else have received, and their condition under the new system is altogether a great improvement upon what it was under the old.

Complaints of inadequate relief.

The applications to the board of supervision complaining of inadequate relief, amounted this year to 705—of these 430 were dismissed on information contained in the schedules of complaint, 101 were dismissed after being remitted for explanation, 34 for incompetency and other causes, and in 140 cases the ground of complaint was removed by the parochial boards.

Applications to sheriffs.

The returns which were obtained of proceedings in the sheriffs' courts, show that the number of interim orders for relief issued in course of the present year, amounted to 426, with respect to 202 of which the parish authorities lodged answers objecting to the order, and of these 92 were ultimately directed to be admitted on the roll. These numbers are all less than in the previous year, when also they were less than they had been in years preceding. This may be taken as a proof of progressive improvement, and of a better knowledge of their duties by the local administrators.

1853. Amount of expenditure.

The expenditure for the relief and management of the poor in the present year ending 14th May 1853, including 22,176*l.* 15*s.* expended on poorhouse buildings and for sanitary purposes, has amounted to 544,552*l.* 19*s.* 9*d.*, being an increase of 8,684*l.* 9*s.* 10*d.* over what had been expended for like objects in the previous year. The commissioners then considered, that the expenditure had reached what was likely to be about its average in succeeding years; but the amount of relief is liable to be affected by so many circumstances general and particular, by revulsions in trade, unfavourable seasons, a change in prices, the prevalence of disease, and other causes, independent of the more or less efficient administration of the law, that it is impossible to reckon with confidence upon a steady or equable action in this respect. In England all these causes had been more or less in operation, and produced corresponding fluctuations. Thus we see that between 1818 and 1853, the rate of expenditure for relief of the English poor had varied from 13*s.* 3*d.* per head on the population in the former year, to 5*s.* 6*d.* per head in the latter; and there were very considerable variations during the thirty-five intermediate years.[m] In Scotland also, as was to be expected, having regard to the recent operation of the amended law, the variations had been considerable, from 2*s.* 3*d.* to 4*s.* 5*d.*, and in the present year 1852–3 to 3*s.* 9*d.* per head on the population. This last amount contrasts favourably with the rate per head in the same year in England, which was two-thirds more; and the Scotch people have so far an advantage over their neighbours in the south, on whom a remnant of previous malpractice still heavily pressed.

It may be convenient for the purpose of comparison, to exhibit a statement of the expenditure during the eight years since the passing of the Scotch Amendment Act. This is shown in the following table, arranged under appropriate headings, together with the rate per head on the population, and the rate per cent. on the annual value of real property as returned to parliament in 1843—

---

[m] See 'History of the English Poor Law,' vol. ii. p. 466.

TABLE OF EXPENDITURE.

| The year. | Relief of poor on the roll or registered. | Relief of casual poor. | Medical relief. | Management. | Law expenses. | Poorhouse buildings. | Sanitary purposes. | TOTAL. | Rate per head on population.† | Rate per cent. on real property according to returns in 1843. |
|---|---|---|---|---|---|---|---|---|---|---|
| | £. s. d. | £. s. d. | £. s. d. | £. s. d. | £. s. d. | £. s. d. | £. s. d. | £. s. d. | s. d. | £. s. d. |
| 1846* | 246,542 17 1 | 24,633 9 3 | 4,055 17 7 | 17,454 13 1 | 2,545 10 11 | . . | . . | 295,232 8 1 | 2 3 | 3 3 4 |
| 1847 | 336,515 7 9 | 36,340 0 1 | 12,879 9 6 | 43,158 0 9 | 5,022 11 3 | . . | . . | 433,915 9 6 | 3 3½ | 4 13 1 |
| 1848 | 401,885 15 2 | 53,384 7 7 | 30,339 12 5 | 42,033 13 4 | 5,719 6 11 | 10,971 12 0 | . . | 544,334 7 6 | 4 1¾ | 5 16 9 |
| 1849 | 417,462 16 4 | 51,470 5 10 | 33,010 12 11 | 51,804 18 6 | 8,519 11 11 | 14,775 16 7 | . . | 577,044 2 4 | 4 4¾ | 6 3 9 |
| 1850 | 414,680 9 11 | 31,556 18 9 | 26,574 7 1 | 50,881 8 9 | 10,660 2 8 | 42,814 19 3 | 4,384 17 9 | 581,553 4 3 | 4 5 | 6 4 9¼ |
| 1851 | 404,218 14 3 | 25,917 13 5 | 20,311 1 9 | 52,009 4 1 | 10,872 12 5 | 21,576 1 8 | 1,038 5 7 | 535,943 13 6 | 3 8½ | 5 14 11¾ |
| 1852 | 401,954 3 11 | 25,986 16 7 | 21,436 6 9 | 51,644 18 10 | 13,266 8 4 | 21,186 8 10 | 393 6 5 | 535,868 9 10 | 3 8½ | 5 14 11¾ |
| 1853 | 411,135 8 11 | 24,114 5 8 | 21,737 6 8 | 52,352 6 11 | 13,036 16 5 | 21,644 10 0 | 532 4 11 | 544,552 19 9 | 3 9 | 5 16 10 |

* This year ended on the 1st of February, all the others on the 14th of May.

† Calculated for the first five years on the census of 1841, and for the last three years on the census of 1851.

The number of the poor on the roll or registered on the 14th of May 1853 was 75,437, which is 326 more than on the same day in the previous year. The number of casual poor relieved on the 1st of January 1853 was 4,951 and on the 1st of July 1853 the number was 4,706 being respectively 343 and 364 less than on the corresponding days of 1852. It will be convenient by way of illustrating the table of expenditure just given, to insert here a corresponding table showing the number and class of persons annually relieved during the same period—

TABLE SHOWING THE NUMBERS RELIEVED.

| The Year ending | Population. | Number of poor on register at this date. | Number of casual poor relieved during the year. | Number of casual poor relieved on | | Number of poor persons removed to England Ireland or other parishes. | Number of insane or fatuous poor. | Number of orphans or deserted children. |
|---|---|---|---|---|---|---|---|---|
| | | | | 1st January. | 1st July. | | | |
| 1st Feb. 1846 . | 2,620,184 | 69,432 | 26,894 | .. | .. | .. | .. | .. |
| 14th May 1847 . | .. | 74,161 | 60,399 | .. | .. | 8,453 | 2,945 | 4,794 |
| Do. 1848 . | .. | 77,730 | 126,684 | .. | .. | 13,733 | 3,480 | 6,121 |
| Do. 1849 . | . | 82,357 | 95,686 | .. | .. | 9,396 | 3,574 | 7,459 |
| Do. 1850 . | .. | 79,031 | 53,070 | .. | 4,267 | 6,306 | 3,421 | 7,969 |
| Do. 1851 . | 2,888,742 | 76,906 | 42,093 | 5,148 | 6,366 | 5,102 | 3,520 | 7,542 |
| Do. 1852 . | .. | 75,111 | 46,031 | 5,294 | 5,070 | 5,253 | 3,634 | 7,681 |
| Do. 1853 . | .. | 75,437 | 49,658 | 4,951 | 4,706 | 2,415 | 3,787 | 8,338 |

The only points in the above tables calling for remark are—the decrease in the number of the casual poor—the decrease in the number of removals to England Ireland or to other parishes—and the increase in the number of orphan or deserted children under charge of the parochial boards. The two first must be regarded as indications of improvement in the general condition of the people, perhaps also of improvement in the administration of the law; and although the same cannot be predicated of the latter circumstance, it may still be looked upon as manifesting increased care for the preservation of infant life, which is usually characteristic of improved civilization.

The Report on Caithness by the president of the board which has been before referred to,[n] is a very interesting document. Sir John McNeill's visit to Caithness appears to have been undertaken, partly with the view of giving the parochial authorities there the benefit of his advice in regard to their administration of the Poor Law, and partly also for the purpose of ascertaining how far the conclusions at which he had arrived with respect to the Islands and districts of the west, and which are stated in his previous Report,[o] were borne out by the state of things existing in the neighbouring county of Caithness.

Report on Caithness.

The inhabitants of Caithness are it appears divided into two portions, the Highland and the Lowland, the origin language and habits of the two being markedly different. The Highland population occupy the hill country bordering on Sutherland, and are in language and modes of life similar to their neighbours further west. Their occupations are almost exclusively agricultural and pastoral. They are very poor, their dwellings are far from the coast, and few of them engage in fishing. They seldom work in the quarries, and they are not good agricultural labourers. The Lowland population occupy the more fertile part of the country, extending from the hills to the sea. They are of Scandinavian origin, do not speak Gaelic, and are hardly distinguishable from the more southern inhabitants of the east coast. They are active and laborious, and are occupied in fishing, in agriculture, and in quarrying. At the end of the last century, the value of the cured fish annually exported from Caithness did not exceed 13,000*l*. The cured herring cod and ling exported in the last

---

[n] Ante, p. 264. [o] Ante, p. 257.

ten years, give an annual average of not less than 130,000*l*., whilst the whole land of the county is only valued at 66,000*l*. in the parliamentary returns of 1843. The quarries of Caithness also afford considerable employment, and conduce to the well-being of the population, which at the census in 1841 amounted to 36,343. Agricultural improvements appeared to be everywhere in progress, and the condition of many of the farms would be deemed creditable in any part of the kingdom. The small "crofter" has almost disappeared, and has been replaced by the farmer and the labourer for wages. A limited number of small farms of from 30*l*. to 60*l*. rental, have however been retained, which industrious and frugal labourers may hope to acquire the means of occupying. These small farms are, it is said, so many prizes for industry frugality and good character, and form a ladder by which the agricultural labourers may ascend to the level of the class above them.

Inquiries were made in Caithness, similar to those which had been made in the west Highlands, as to the extent of land on which a Lowland Caithness man could maintain a family, and pay rent from the produce of his farm or croft. The difference in climate, in the facilities of intercourse with the more advanced districts, and in the greater length of time these facilities have been enjoyed, all led to the expectation of a considerable difference of result in the two cases; but it was found that the answers given in Caithness on these points, were almost identical with the answers given in Skye and other places on the west coast. Without the addition of a considerable range of hill pasture, a man in Caithness was unable to maintain a family and pay the customary rent, from the produce of ten acres of arable land of average quality. To enable him to do so without hill pasture, would require twenty acres; and whenever persons holding less land are able to maintain themselves, it is "because agriculture is not their principal occupation, or the main source of their subsistence."

With respect to the proceedings under the Poor Law, it was impressed upon the several parochial boards, that the successful administration of the law depended upon the careful examination of each case by themselves and their officers, not only in the first instance, but upon the occurrence of every change of circumstance subsequently. If those upon whom the legislature had imposed the duty of administering the law, and whose interests as ratepayers were involved in its operation, evaded the performance of that duty, and found that their interests suffered, they were told not to attribute to the law a result which was the consequence of their own neglect. One of the most efficient means of protection against abuse, they were told, would be the erection of poorhouses, which they had not yet provided; and they were cautioned against the thriftless practice to which many parochial boards, not in Caithness only but throughout Scotland had resorted, of appointing inefficient officers at inadequate salaries.—In conclusion, Sir John McNeill expresses a hope that his visit to Caithness will have tended to remedy some defects, and to the introduction of some improvements in what had been the previous system of management. We have seen that it led to the determination of erecting a poorhouse in the parish of Latheron.[p]

Report on the free and pauper colonies in Holland.

There is another Report by Sir John McNeill which on account of its importance requires to be noticed. It appears that a considerable number of the parochial boards had latterly become desirous of devising some plan for the employment of the partially disabled poor, and by many it was thought that the labour of such persons in agriculture, would be more profitable than it could be made in a poorhouse.

---

[p] Ante, p. 265.

Repeated applications were made to the board of supervision on this subject, and the pauper colonies of Holland were referred to as showing the advantages of such a system. In the spring of this year therefore, the president of the board of supervision resolved to visit the colonies in the north of Holland, with a view to satisfy himself by personal observation and inquiry whether such a system might be adopted with advantage in Scotland.

The free colonies.

After describing the origin and management of the free colonies, the average number of persons located in which during the last ten years was 2,640, consisting of about 425 families, Sir John McNeill observes, that "regarded as an attempt to make these families maintain themselves by agricultural labour, the free colonies after an experience of thirty years are not only a complete failure, but there is no reason to believe that the scheme could possibly have succeeded." The most intelligent of the officers were of opinion, that even if the colonists had been selected from the class of agricultural peasants, the colonies could not have been made self-sustaining, so long as maintenance was secured to the colonists irrespective of what was produced by themselves. The persons employed in manufactures, and in some of the handicrafts, whose labour is said to be profitable, are exclusively women and children, or persons who have not strength for agricultural labour. The persons employed in agriculture, are the able-bodied men and women, whose labour is found to be so unprofitable, that besides swallowing up the assumed profits of the others, it entails a large amount of annual loss on the institution.—"The failure of an experiment conducted with so much care, by men of the highest intelligence, with means so large, supported by the government and the nation, established on a scale so extensive, and persevered in for so many years among a people remarkable for business habits, agricultural skill, and industry—is (it is justly observed) a valuable lesson."

Having, as it was at the time supposed, provided for the indigent persons of good character by the establishment of the free colonies, it was determined to establish other colonies for the reception of paupers and mendicants who were not of good character. By the law of Holland, begging is an offence punishable by imprisonment; and it was resolved that persons found guilty of mendicancy vagrancy or similar petty offences, instead of being imprisoned, should be sent for a certain number of years to one of the penal or pauper colonies. Ere long however, it was found that many persons resorted to begging for the purpose of being sent to these colonies; and to prevent this mendicants were subjected to a certain term of imprisonment, before being sent thither. On admission, the person's name, description, cause of committal, and the commune chargeable, are entered in the register. His hair is then cut close, next comes a bath, after which the dress of the colony is put on, quarters are assigned, and work is commenced. The sexes occupy separate apartments. They all rise at a quarter past 5 in summer, and an hour later in winter, and are allowed three-quarters of an hour for dressing, washing and breakfast. They have dinner at half-past 11, with rest till 1, supper at 6, at 7 roll-call, and to bed at half-past 8.—The grounds are surrounded by guards to prevent the escape of the inmates, and there are veteran pensioners attached to each colony, ready to repress any disturbance. The punishments consist of imprisonment, solitary confinement with or without irons, not exceeding fourteen days, beating with a stick not exceeding forty blows, and finally flogging.

The pauper colonies.

The object proposed in establishing these pauper colonies, was to train the persons sent thither to habits of industry and economy, by subjecting them for a time to rigid discipline, by holding out inducements to exertion in a maximum and minimum rate of wages according to the work executed, and by enabling the pauper to obtain his discharge when he had saved a certain sum, with a view to which part of his wages are set aside for his support until he could find employment. It must be admitted that these arrangements are all good in themselves, and seem calculated to attain the desired object; but they were nevertheless found to be practically ineffective. It was estimated on apparently sufficient data, that it required fifteen of these pauper colonists to perform the field-work of one good day-labourer; so that if the paupers in a colony amount to 1,500, the labour performed by them will not exceed what would be performed by 100 good day-labourers, the whole of whose wages at the usual rate in Holland of 1*s.* 3*d.* per day, or 7*s.* 6*d.* per week, would not maintain three of these pauper colonists on the average of their annual cost to the country. It may therefore well be questioned whether habits of industry and economy are promoted by a residence in these colonies. The moral effect can perhaps be best estimated by observing the number who are again sent back, after having been discharged from the colonies. Now with respect to this point, it appears that on the 31st of December 1851 the number of pauper colonists in Omerschans and Veenhuisen was 4,250. Of these, 1,923 were there for the first time, 1,163 for the second time, 721 for the third time, 458 for the fourth time, 190 for the fifth, 42 for the sixth, 14 for the seventh, 3 for the ninth, and one for the tenth time. It is plain therefore, as stated in the Report, that a part of the population is here fluctuating between mendicancy and the colonies, as elsewhere between vagrancy and the workhouse; and that the training in the former has failed to reclaim this class, which despite of every effort for their improvement appears destined to subsist on the labour of others.

In the pauper colonies of Holland, each colonist is

said to cost the country on an average more than 6*l.* 13*s.* 4*d.* annually, in addition to the produce of his labour. The average cost of paupers on the roll or registered in Scotland, during the seven years for which there are official returns, is about 4*l.*, and in England does not amount to nearly so much as in the Dutch colonies. On the other hand, the scale of living among the labouring classes in Holland is said to be considerably lower than in Scotland. "The wages of a good agricultural labourer in the Netherlands during the summer months, do not exceed 1*s.* 3*d.* per day, or 7*s.* 6*d.* per week; the same man would receive in most parts of Scotland 10*s.* per week. The proportion is therefore as 3 to 4, and would raise the proportional cost of paupers maintained on the Dutch colonial system in this country, to 8*l.* 17*s.* 8*d.*" Neither the lodging nor the food in those pauper colonies is such as would be tolerated in Scotland, and the means of coercion are such as could not be here lawfully resorted to.

The foregoing summary of facts in connexion with the Dutch pauper colonies, shows how totally unsuited the system is for being introduced into Scotland; and Sir John McNeill's Report could hardly fail to set the public mind at rest on the subject, and to remove whatever desire may have been felt for entering upon the experiment of extracting profit from pauper labour. The information conveyed in that Report, perfectly accords with what was obtained by the author, when he visited Holland in 1838, as do likewise the views expressed with regard to the free and pauper colonies. An examination of these colonies was not the immediate object of my visiting Holland at that time, but being there, it was natural that I should make inquiries respecting them; and such inquiries could only lead to conclusions similar to those stated by Sir John McNeill.

Having now brought the account of the Scottish Poor Law down to the period at which my 'History of the English Poor Law' terminates, I here close this portion of my labours, which although I have found not to be without difficulty in the execution, has yet been on the whole more interesting and more instructive than I had ventured to expect. The interest and the instruction have in great measure arisen from tracing the almost identity of origin in the Poor Laws of England and Scotland, as well as the almost identity of their progress, down to the passing of the Act of *James 6th*[q] in 1579. The power of assessment for relief of the poor conferred by that statute, was not however, we find, generally acted upon, if acted upon at all; and in time got to be considered as supplemental only to the voluntary contributions, as a kind of last resort in absolute necessity, and on the failure of all other means. Whilst in England, on the contrary, after the 14*th Elizabeth* in 1572, assessments in some form were frequent, and after *the* 43*rd Elizabeth* they became a regularly organised means of relief in every parish throughout the country, and have so continued to the present day. The voluntary contributions relied upon in Scotland, were chiefly collected at the church doors, and were dispensed by the kirk session, less according to the actual wants of the poor, than to the amount of the collections received. To contribute to the relief of the poor was not a legal obligation, as in the case of assessment, but was urged by the clergy upon their respective congregations as a religious duty; and the dispensing of the contributions thus obtained, naturally devolved in a great measure if not entirely, upon the clergy themselves.

Identity of origin of the English and Scotch systems.

The systems established and relied upon for relieving the poor in the two countries, thus markedly diverged from 1579 downwards. In the one

Divergence between the systems.

---

[q] *Cap.* 74. Ante, p. 16.

it was imperative, in the other voluntary; in one it was a duty imposed upon all and enforced by law; in the other it depended on the depth of religious feeling in the people, and on the zeal character and influence of their pastors. It is impossible to deny that the people and clergy of Scotland fulfilled their duty in these respects for a series of years, and that too in a manner that has perhaps never been surpassed in any country. Yet it is equally impossible to deny, that the reliance solely upon voluntary contributions for the relief of destitution, has latterly, under the altered circumstances of the country, been the cause of great suffering and privation, which might be and which ought to have been prevented.

The rigid economy observed in everything connected with the relief of the poor in Scotland, was no doubt a means of preventing many of the evils which occurred in England from practices directly the reverse. But either extreme is to be deprecated, and the pertinacity with which the able-bodied poor had been excluded from relief, however urgent their necessities, has now been so far modified, that able-bodied persons in immediate want may be relieved as occasional poor, and the board of supervision have felt warranted, under the provisions of the Amendment Act of 1845, in suggesting to the distressed parishes in the Highlands, that as a question of economy it was well for them to consider, whether it might not be more advantageous to give temporary aid to able-bodied persons, than to withhold it until disablement arises through the pressure of absolute want. It appears moreover that the parochial boards in these districts did afford relief to all able-bodied persons who were in a state of destitution.[r] Not only therefore do we find that assessment has become the rule instead of the exception, as was

Present practice.

[r] See opinion of the lord advocate and the dean of faculty on a case submitted to them by the board of supervision, ante page 219. See also Sir John McNeill's Report on the Highland Districts, ante page 241.

formerly the case in Scotland, but we also find the policy of relieving the able-bodied poor under certain circumstances admitted, and the practice adopted.

Approximation of the Scottish and English systems.

The divergence which took place between the theory of the Poor Laws in England and in Scotland, as well as in their practical application, appears now therefore to have been in a great degree corrected, and the systems of relief in the two countries are again approximated, although still far from being identical. The able-bodied poor continue to be formally, and for the most part actually excluded from relief in Scotland; but as poorhouses are increased in number, and placed under proper management, we may expect that the approximation in the two countries will become closer, and that in Scotland as in England destitution will be held to constitute a claim for relief, and that the actual necessity of the claimant will be tested, at least in all doubtful cases, by the offer of Indoor Relief.

# INDEX.